To Paul.
h all good wishes for a
ppy birthday and many
ppy returns. July. 1994.
Guyette Doricott.

£5
GR

# *Coarse and Game*
# FISHING

*Coarse and Game*

# FISHING

*Edited by Michael Prichard*

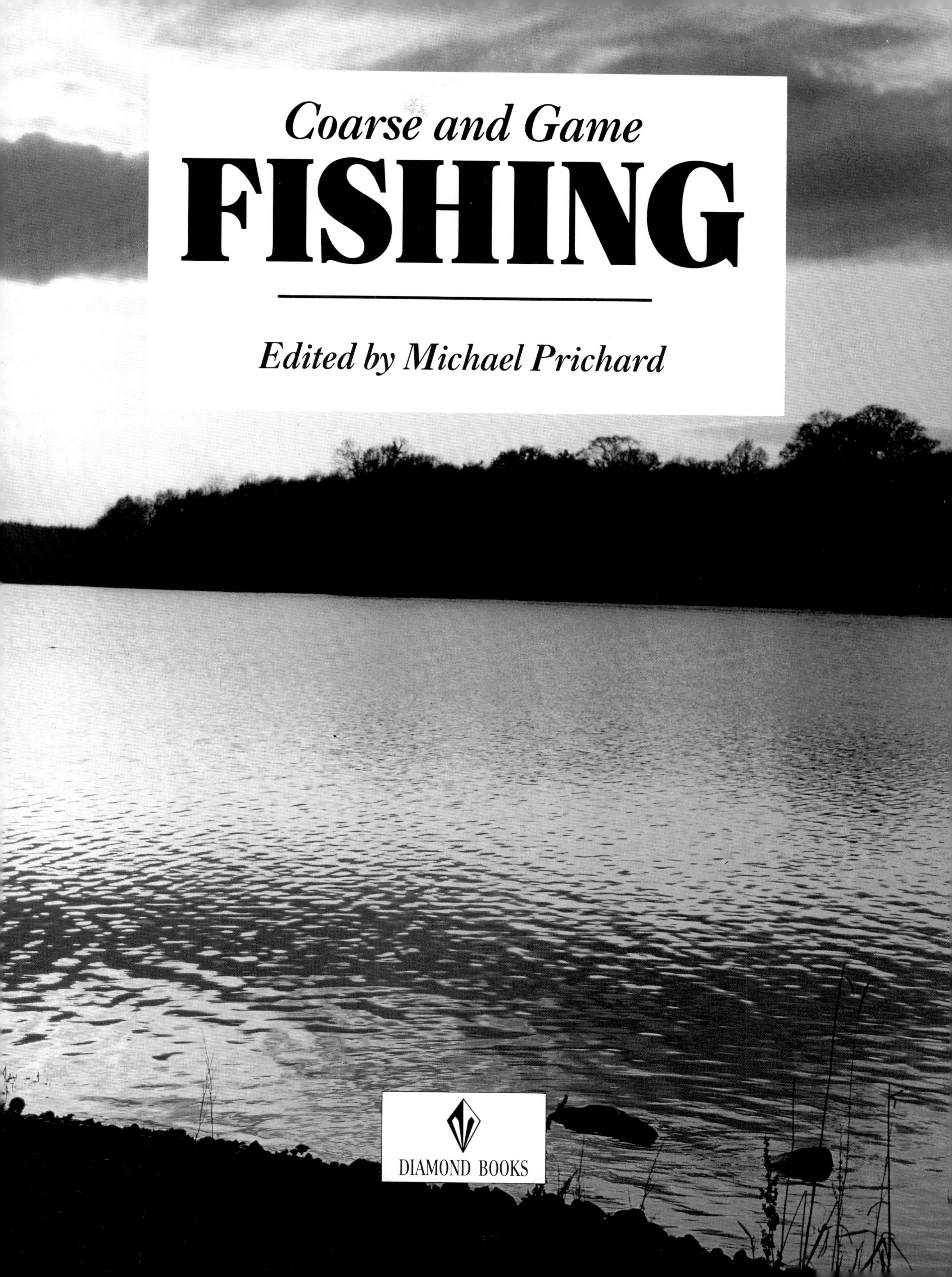

DIAMOND BOOKS

# Credits

**Photographs** (other than those listed below) *by Michael Prichard ARPS*
**Design and Illustration** *by Peter Burt and Rod Sutterby*
**Fish Species Illustrations** *by Dietrich Burkel*

Page 5. photograph *by Malcolm Greenhalgh*
Page 8. photograph *by Roy Stevenson*
Page 49. Pic. A *by Bob Baldock*
Page 79. Pic. B *by Bob Carnill*
Page 93. Pic. B *by Simon Farrell*
Page 96. Pic. A *by Malcolm Greenhalgh*
Page 97. Pic. C *by Malcolm Greenhalgh*
Page 102. Pic. A *by Malcolm Greenhalgh*
Page 103. Pic. B *by David Winterbottom*
Page 104. Pic. A *by David Winterbottom*
Page 105. Pic. B *by Simon Farrell*
Page 109. Pic. A *by Rod Sutterby*
Page 111. Pic. D *by Malcolm Greenhalgh*
Page 112. Pic. B *by Malcolm Greenhalgh*
Page 113. Pic. C *by David Winterbottom*

The text and illustrations in this book were previously published in the *Collins New Encyclopedia of Fishing in Britain and Ireland.* This edition published 1993 for Bookmart by Diamond Books, 77–85 Fulham Palace Road, Hammersmith, London W6 8JB.



The fish illustrations by Dr. Dietrich Burkel and some of the diagrams and photographs appeared in the *Encyclopedia of Fishing in the British Isles*, first published in 1977 and reprinted, with revisions in 1982, eleven times, and in *Collins New Encyclopedia of Fishing in Britain and Ireland*, published in 1990.



A CIP catalogue record for this book is available from the British Library.

Printed and bound by
HarperCollins Manufacturing, Glasgow

# Introduction

The real angler is one for whom the state of perfect happiness is achieved only when he (or she, for some of the best anglers are women) holds a fishing rod in the hands or is sorting out fishing tackle and planning the next trip to the water. If you are thinking of taking up the sport of angling, beware! Angling is a wonderful disease that creeps over you slowly and usually lasts for life.

Compared with almost every other sport, angling offers the greatest diversity of action. In cricket it is simply a matter of which side gets the most runs and loses fewest wickets; in soccer how many times 22 players knock a spherical object into a big landing-net using only their toes or heads. In freshwater angling the result might be a brace of fine tench caught at dawn from a reed-fringed mere, a catch of big winter roach from a clearing river, some lurking chub taken on free-lined floating crust from a sun-drenched stream, a beautifully speckled wild trout caught on the most delicate of dry flies, a brace of silver sea trout taken on a big fly in the dead of night, a fresh-run salmon, and so on *ad infinitum*.

There is also something unpredictable about angling, for no one can be sure what will take the bait, spinner or fly. The whole mackerel bait might be taken by a tiny jack or a 20 lb-plus pike. A Size 16 grayling wet fly might at any time be grabbed by a huge salmon. Two maggots on a Size 16 hook meant for a 1 lb roach could easily be sucked down by a 10 lb carp. This sort of thing happens – often, judging by reports in the angling press.

Of course, most anglers become specialists in just one or two aspects of the sport. This is usually a consequence of where they live as well as personal preferences. It is not surprising, for example, that only a tiny proportion (indeed if any!) of anglers in the Outer Hebrides go match fishing or that few anglers from London fish frequently for salmon. However, I would advise any who do not fish at present and are thinking seriously of taking up the sport to sample as wide a range of fishing that they can. Try fly fishing. Go piking in the winter. Try to catch some specimen coarse fish. Enter a couple of coarse-fishing matches. When you have sampled, you will find that you are quickly drawn to the kind of fishing that suits you best.

Most of my time is spent fishing with a fly rod for salmon, trout, sea trout and grayling. But I have many happy memories of specimen hunting for coarse fish and match angling. And I still enjoy these kinds of fishing a few days every year. In my opinion this is important, for some anglers can get quite snobbish about their chosen branch of fishing. There is no need to adopt this attitude. We are all brothers and sisters of the angle. As Martin James, that great specimen hunter of coarse fishes and good all-round angler, put it: 'Provided it bends the stick and pulls the string, I am happy!'

This book provides a thorough description of all kinds of angling that are available in the lakes and rivers of the British Isles, written by a team of enthusiastic well-known specialists. Follow their advice and you will not go far wrong.

However, one point must be made at the start. In angling the fish should always come first. If you want to kill a fish to eat then kill it as soon as you have landed it. Never let a fish die slowly. Never kill more than you can eat. Remember that every fish, coarse or game, that you return unharmed to the water alive might provide sport for you in the future.

Handle carefully all fish that you are going to put back. Unhook them in the landing net and release them immediately. The heat of the hand can damage the slime that covers and protects the fish's skin and let in fatal infection. If you have to handle a fish, cool and wet your hands in the water first.

Each year thousands of innocent waterside creatures die because careless anglers discard hooks, shot, monofilament fishing line and litter. Always take everything home with you. Leave only your footprints.

All anglers should be members of the Anglers' Co-operative Association. The ACA is the organisation that fights for anglers against the government, water industry and polluters to try to keep our lakes and rivers clean and pure so that we have more fish and better fishing. Join the ACA. Their address is: 3, Castlegate, Grantham, Lincolnshire, NG31 6SW. You owe it to your sport.

MALCOLM GREENHALGH

# Index to Fish Illustrations

## Coarse Fish



## Game Fish

# Contents

# Contributors

## Michael Prichard
*General Editor*

*Michael Prichard – the editor of this encyclopedia – is an Associate of the Royal Photographic Society and a well known photographer-journalist. He was art editor of the now defunct magazine* Creel, *then edited by Bernard Venables, and is the author of eight books on the sport of fishing and fish identification.*

*Michael Prichard will fish for almost anything, enjoying fresh as well as saltwater sport. Angling has taken him to many parts of the world – halibut fishing in Japan, seatrouting in Norway, swordfishing in Portugal, fishing for shark in the Arabian Gulf, casting a fly to arctic char in the glacial streams of Greenland and carping in the Canadian wilderness – but he earnestly believes that some of the finest fishing is still to be had in and around the British Isles. The author now lives close to the German border in Holland. Angling forays involve lengthy journeys to Ireland and mainland Britain, all undertaken joyfully and with greater selectivity of venue and species than in his earlier fishing days! He is keenly interested in all forms of natural history, believing that the true sportsman is someone that understands both the need to conserve creature habitat and ensure species preservation.*

## Allen Edwards
*Coarse Fishing for Pleasure*

*Born on the opening day of the coarse fishing season in 1930, Allen Edwards took his first roach under the tuition of 'Ginger' Brain from Cannon Hill Park pool and has been fishing for this classic coarse species ever since. Edwards has written for many angling magazines and a newspaper. He is also well known to Nottinghamshire radio listeners as the BBC's angling correspondent. As Director of the Anglers' Cooperative Association, Allen Edwards is angling's fighter against pollution. He is carefully monitoring water privatisation and all that that implies. Describing himself as a 'family-man angler' Allen Edwards dedicates his contribution to this volume to his wife Helen and grandson Ian.*

## Dietrich Burkel
*The Artist*

*Born in 1936 in Wildau, Germany, Dr Dietrich Burkel studied natural history, especially fish. In 1948 the family went to Scotland where he gained a PhD in palaeontology at Glasgow University. Burkel fished for pike on Loch Lomond and tope in Luce Bay. In the early 1970s he caught the first rod-caught Scottish porbeagle, 81.6 kg (179 lb), from a dinghy near the Mull lighthouse. He went to Hamburg University in 1975, joining German ichthyologists on a research voyage to the West Coast of Britain. Once fish recorder for the Scottish Federation of Sea Anglers, he drew accurate identification lecture aids as well as collecting museum specimens. Dr Burkel is now Keeper of the Public Exhibition of the Zoological Museum of the University of Hamburg. The illustrations in this book show him to be a gifted artist.*

## Tom Pickering
*Matchfishing to Win*

*Tom Pickering is deadly with every matchfishing method. His greatest gift, apart from the sheer mastery of methods, is to know exactly what to do in every given situation. While in England's World Championship side he has fished eight times for his country and helped England to their first and long-awaited team title in 1986. He was there when they won for the second time in 1987 and won the World Individual title in Bulgaria in 1989; was Macpherson UK champion in the same year and won the prestigious Swan Vesta crown just before his World Championship triumph. In his early 30s, Tom Pickering is regarded as one of the outstanding talents in British matchfishing. Not a full-time professional, Tom Pickering runs a tackle business in Doncaster and the National Angling Exhibition.*

## Bob Carnill
*Fly Fishing for Trout*

*Nottingham-born Bob Carnill began fishing the Trent and local gravel-pit at the age of four and became a dedicated coarse angler for the next 18 years. At 24, Bob began fly fishing for trout, learning from books, tips given by other fly fishermen, and experience. In the following 26 years he designed new ranges of flies; ran courses in fly fishing and fly tying; contributed to a best-selling book on the same subject; made two videos on fly fishing and fly tying, and wrote over 100 magazine articles. He organises and judges the Benson & Hedges Fly Tying Competition. He has achieved one of two ambitions: on August 29 1980 at Rutland Water, landing a 3.8 kg (8 lb 1 oz) rainbow from the bank. His next target is a brown trout of 4.5 kg (10 lb) or more either on a fly or lure.*

## Crawford Little
*Salmon: Amazing and Marvellous*

*Crawford Little, one of the modern generation of thinking salmon fishermen, is also a champion of traditional techniques and values. He caught his first fish, a roach, at the age of three and the following year was learning to fish for salmon on the River Spey. Little trained in Estate Management, subsequently working for an earl, a duke and a prince, later starting a publishing company and sporting magazine. He now divides his time between writing, casting demonstrations, instructing, and running his own agency for sportsmen seeking shooting or fishing in Scotland. With his wife and sons he lives close to a salmon river in Dumfriesshire. He travels widely in his study and pursuit of the silver leaper.*

## Len Cacutt
*Associate Editor*

*For over 25 years Len Cacutt has been engaged in every form of angling journalism. He was Founder-Editor of a National fishing newspaper, then Editor and compiler of angling books, partworks and magazines, at the same time writing books and articles. He has fished for almost every salt and freshwater species both in home waters and abroad but the competitive side of the sport has never appealed to him. For years he was Chairman, Sea Commodore and finally President of the City of London Piscatorial Society and holds membership of a number of other angling societies. Over the years Len Cacutt has developed a great interest in fish evolution and ichthyology which, added to fishing, keeps him closely in touch with the all-important matter of conservation.*

ALLEN EDWARDS

# COARSE FISHING FOR PLEASURE

Fishing is a pleasure. The satisfaction which the sport engenders is a compound of a love of nature, excitement, competition with the elements and friendly rivalry with angling companions. This recipe is an intensely personal thing. I am among those for whom the pleasure comes with the quiet seeking of each species in turn as the seasons pass. And so for me, late winter is the time to be fishing for pike.

It is a human nature to boast. Some do it so quietly and skilfully that they become known for their modesty. For these piscatorial paragons the pike will furnish ample raw material for their 'one which did *not* get away' story, for the following reasons. In the winter, pike, which gather in loose packs to follow their fodder fish, begin to respond to the urge to reproduce. If water conditions are satisfactory, pike spawn from late February until May or even later at the northern edge of their distribution. Year after year, the species tends to return to the same spawning areas and these gathering points become the angler's 'hot spots' – the places from which big pike may be caught, but locating them can be the pleasure angler's biggest problem.

### WINTER PIKE

The most important factor governing the situation of holding points of big pike is the closeness of cover. This may be in the form of relatively deep water or, in late spawning situations, among weedbeds which are easily visible. For instance, pike spawn on readily recognisable

Fishing is a pleasure . . . even when the angler is alone. Only the wind hissing through the reeds and the occasional curlew fluting over the wetlands breaks his concentration.

*The scientific (Latin) descriptions of freshwater fishes follow Greenwood, Rosen, Weitzman and Myers, Bull. Am. Mus. Nat. Hist 131(4) 339–457. The general classification follows the European Fisheries Advisory Commission publication EIFAC.*

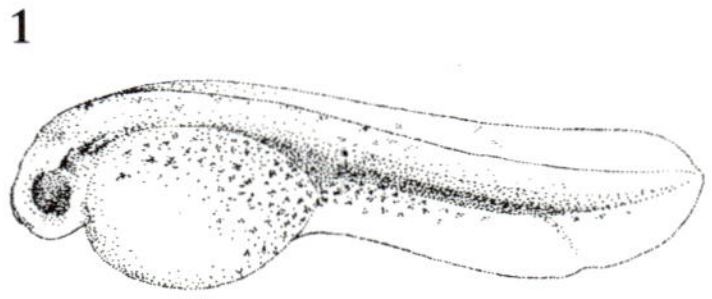


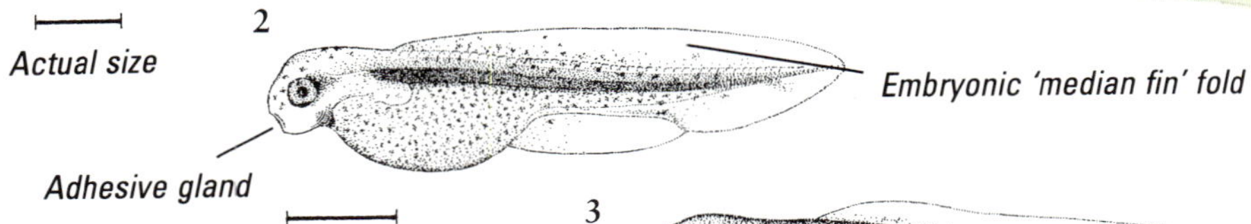


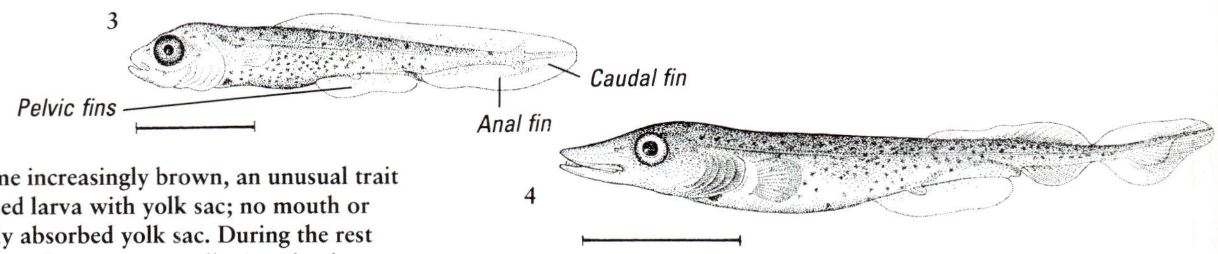


PIKE LARVAE; GROWTH AND DEVELOPMENT

**At all stages pike larvae become increasingly brown, an unusual trait in fish larvae. 1. Newly hatched larva with yolk sac; no mouth or gill openings. 2. With partially absorbed yolk sac. During the rest stage, lasting for eight to 12 days, larvae use an adhesive gland to hang from underwater objects while the body absorbs the yolk sac; the body elongates and mouth and gill openings form. 3. Caudal and anal fins develop from median fin fold. Larvae begin feeding on plankton. 4. Fins are now well differentiated, but the tail is still heterocercal, reflecting the ancestral form where the vertebrae run up into the upper lobe of the caudal fin. Although still but a few inches long, the pike is now a fully developed predator and also cannibalistic if there is no other food source. Growth from stages 3 to 4 takes only a few days.**

flooded and marshy meadow land or in shallow drains and ditches.

Of course, the pike *will* spawn, and if all other factors are borne in mind an intelligent assessment can be made as to where this is likely to be. It is not necessary, nor is it even desirable, that such prospecting should be carried out solely with the eyes. It makes much more sense to use the sporting method of fishing to locate the ideal, but possibly unrecognisable, spawning points, but when found these areas will hold the larger female fish.

Spinning in all its forms must rank as the most attractive method of taking pike and as a tool for pin-pointing concentrations of *Esox* it has no rivals. On most waters a good tackle combination is a 2.4 m (8 ft) medium spinning-rod of carbon, used with a fixed-spool reel holding 3.6 kg (8 lb) breaking strain (b.s.) line. The rig is completed by tying a swivel to the reel line and then attaching a 0.3 m (12 in) wire trace with a link swivel at the end. On to this, a wobbling or a spinning lure is mounted. Some lures are prone to cause kinking of the line unless an anti-kink vane or weight is used, which should be placed on the reel line just above the top swivel.

In all but the strongest of waters a lure of 21–28 g (¾–1 oz) will give a positive fall through the water once a cast has been made. It is possible to find the deeper, holding waters by casting, engaging the pick-up and counting the seconds until the bait reaches the bottom. As soon as the lure touches the lake or river-bed, the rod-top should be lifted and the bait retrieved in as slow and erratic a manner as possible. Three casts into each area are enough, including one to get the depth and to create an interest in the pike. The lure should not be allowed to hit the bottom on casts two or three. Start the retrieve just a second or so before the spoon is due to touch. After the third cast the angler should move to another spot. These actions should be made in a series of fan-shaped casts. (Fig. 3, p. 14)

It is not always necessary to catch a pike to recognise that a holding area has been discovered. A close watch should be kept behind the bait at the moment it is being lifted from the water. Quite often pike will follow the retrieve of a spoon or wobbling bait in an interested but wary manner and the first sign the angler has is the fish's two baleful, forward-looking eyes close behind the lure. For this reason the angler must stand back from the bank so that a carelessly cast shadow does not spook the fish.

Once a gathering point has been located, the angler's problems become much more simple. It comes down to a question of choice: Which method will prove to be the most effective in the prevailing conditions? Which method gives the angler the most pleasure? Some will prefer to carry on using spinning lures; others will decide that a static or moving dead-bait is the way to take their fish. Others will use their spinning gear allied with plugs.

Spinning will account for big pike and it is an active

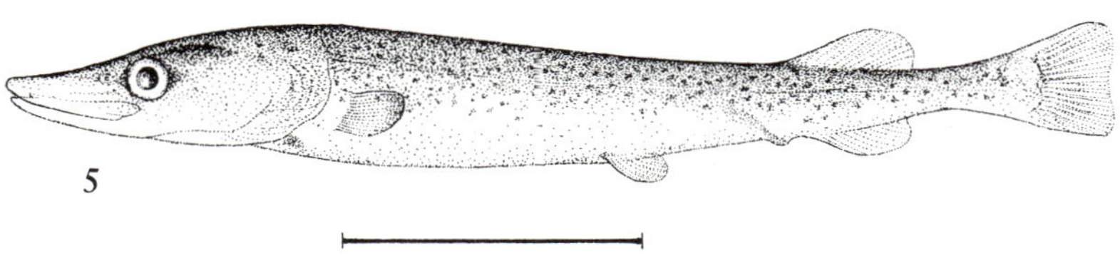

5

5. The fully formed pike, still brown and with an elongated body. Growth now depends on availability of suitable food, including plankton and larvae of fish including its own species.

## PIKE

*Esox lucius*

The pike, widely distributed throughout the British Isles and Republic of Ireland, is found in rivers, lakes, canals, gravel-pits and the smallest of farm ponds. Its principal requirement is a good supply of fodder fish which might be perch in a Scottish loch, bream in a Midland reservoir or trout in a neglected stretch of a Southern chalkstream. In British waters the maximum weight is probably about 22.8 kg (50 lb), but any double-figure pike is considered a good fish on most waters.

Bait: Most freshwater fish are acceptable livebaits; herring, sprat and mackerel are deadbaits, with all spinning lures being very effective.

way in which to fish. But the technique has a disadvantage which is not always apparent. It is repetitive and reduces many anglers to the level of an automaton: the lure is cast, the reel handle turned and the pick-up engaged, the lure retrieved. The movements become automatic and the angler ceases to think. Sheer boredom can impel the angler to move – often away from where the pike are concentrated. Apart from this danger, spinning will take pike of all sizes although many anglers believe that it accounts for mainly smaller fish. Spinners work because they induce a feeding response from the pike by triggering unpremeditated and reflex actions.

Spinning should begin in earnest once pike have been located but a heavy spoon, used to pin-point the fish, may not be the ideal weapon with which to catch them. A lighter lure can often be retrieved more slowly, thus creating more opportunities for the pike to attack on every cast. Spin as close to the bottom as conditions will allow.

Pike need a reasonably steady target on which to focus their binocular vision. Ideal retrieves are those which retrieve the bait through 0.9 m (3 ft) long, level or slightly rising movements. This is because throughout its life a pike instinctively drives into shoals of fodder fish. The natural response of these small fish is to panic and escape as quickly as possible, the action resulting in an upwards and curving movement, a glitter of silver and red and this

*FIG 1* SPINNING FOR PIKE

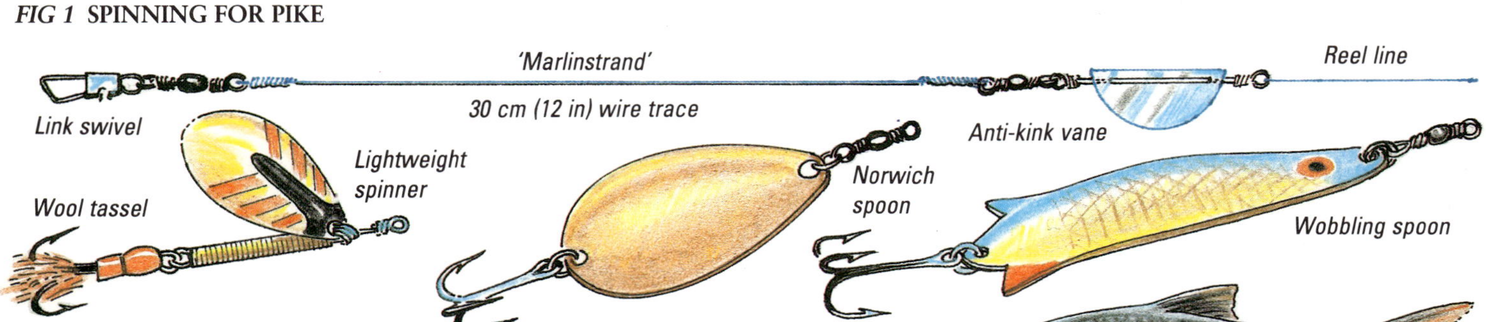


*FIG 2* DEADBAIT WOBBLING RIG

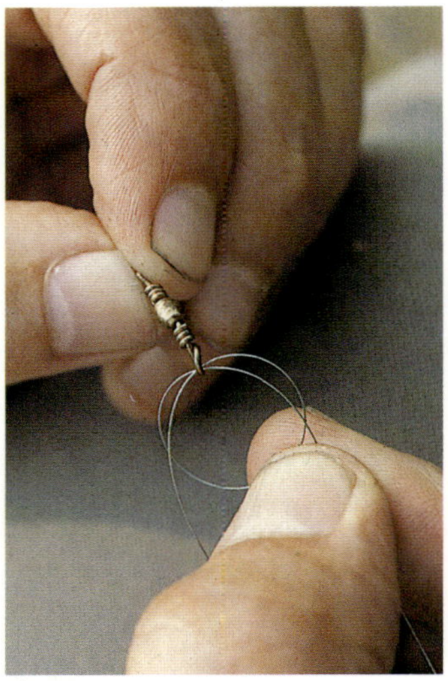

A

B

C

FIG 3 FAN CASTING

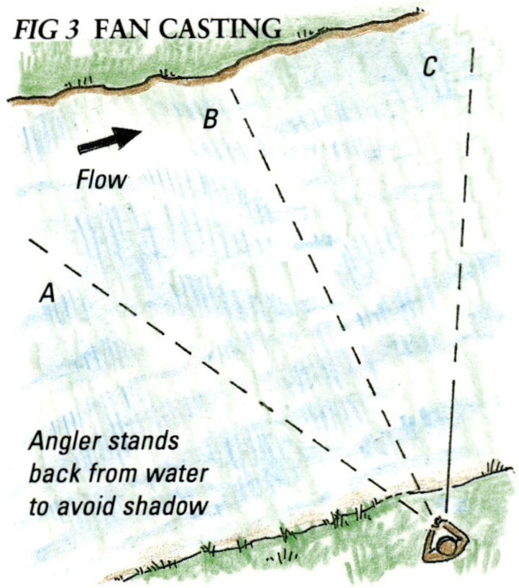


**A** **Making a Marlin Strand pike trace. Pass the wire twice through the eye of the swivel, then clip surgical forceps to the short, loose end.** **B** **Hold the swivel in one hand and the wire in the other, then spin the forceps round the wire to bind the short wire end tightly.**

**C** **The trace wire joined securely to the swivel, the knot tight. Clip off the short wire end.** **D** **Edwards releasing his pike unharmed after the careful removal of all hooks while the fish remained in the keepnet. This ensures the minimum of injury or trauma to the fish.**

flash is the final trigger for the pike's attack. It makes sense for the angler to try to imitate this escaping-prey effect to induce a take from the pike.

To catch pike in any way is a pleasure but I get the most satisfaction from taking them with spinning tackle using deadbaits to imitate that escaping-prey movement. The rod and reel are the same as those used for ordinary spinning but the terminal rig is different. I make a trace of braided wire (Marlin Strand) and find that 6.4 kg (14 lb) b.s. is fine and flexible enough both in knot and twist to enable a swivel to be fixed at one end and a pair of Size 8 treble hooks in tandem at the other. The upper treble is used to close the mouth of the deadbait, the other is nicked through the wrist of the tail of the bait. The little fish, a smelt or sprat, or any freshwater fish, should be kept as straight as possible and wobble *but not spin.* (Figs 1, 2, p. 13)

This rig, which permits an instant strike by the angler, is used to tempt the pike into reacting at once: here is a meal and it must be grabbed quickly before it escapes. If larger baits are used it is important to take into account the pike's method of attack, which is usually a short, savage lunge from ambush. The prey is seized crosswise and gripped in the large canine-like teeth while the pike returns to its holt. There, the baitfish will be turned and swallowed head-first. This attack-and-swallow pattern will appear to be a continuous movement and in clear water I have watched a pike strike, then settle on the bottom to digest its meal and the only visible sign of any action has been a water-borne settling and twinkling of scales dislodged in the first moments of the pike's attack and a hovering cloud of mud disturbed by the powerful sweep of its tail-fin. The holding and pressure work from the pike's powerful jaws is often longer for a large baitfish.

If fish baits heavier than 57–85 g (2–3 oz) are used it is sensible to step up the scale of the tackle. A 3.6 m (12 ft) carbon rod which has a test curve of 1.14 kg (2½ lb) will cast baits of around 142 g (5 oz) well and is an ideal weapon to beat the largest pike. Not that the weight of the bait to be used is the only consideration, it is not, for the greatest problem in pike fishing is that of setting the hooks. Pike have strong, bony jaws and the rod must be capable of transmitting sufficient power to pull the hook-point through the bait and into those jaws.

When striking, put a bend into the rod by winding the reel handle, at the same time lowering the rod tip sideways until it is about 0.6 m (2 ft) from the surface of the water. At this point a firm sweep to either side, and parallel with the surface, should result in the hooking of the pike. The rod tip should then be raised and the fish played out in the usual way. Playing a small pike is usually a short affair. If a larger fish has been hooked this may involve allowing the fish to run against the combined drag of the lightly set slipping clutch of the fixed-spool reel and pressure on the rim of the reel drum from finger or thumb. The fish is brought nearer to the landing net by clamping the finger on the rim of the reel and pumping the fish in with alternate dipping of the rod while leaning back and raising the rod tip so that the fish is drawn steadily nearer. An important point to watch while pumping a fish towards the net is that tension must be maintained, any slack on the line may mean the loss of the fish. A lively fish must be allowed to run against the slipping clutch if it gets a burst of energy on seeing the net, but to avoid putting kinks into the line the handle of the reel should not be turned while line is being pulled off the spool.

Working a deadbait is an efficient and enjoyable method of taking pike but the popularity of static dead-bait fishing increases year upon year. This style, too, is effective and often tempts the larger specimens. The range of deadbaits upon which the pike will feed is tremendous, it includes all of the freshwater fish species including eels, sea and estuarial species such as smelt, sardines, herrings, sprats, sandeels and mackerel.

If the static method of deadbaiting has a disadvantage it is that its use is more likely to lead to the deep-hooking of pike. This happens because the pike is conditioned to swimming round picking up dead or stunned victims from

*D*

*E*

*E* **Allen Edwards keeps his rod at the correct angle while he fights a sizeable pike deep down. The water is the famed Shannon at Tarmonbarry, Co. Longford, Ireland.**

***Fig 3*** **Fan casting allows proper coverage of the water.**

a previous driving attack. There are no sudden moves from the pike, just a stealthy and imperceptible scoop, turn and swallow. For this reason I prefer to use a float when laying-on with a deadbait and to strike immediately there is a movement from it, but other anglers prefer to use electronic bite alarms to signal a run from a pike.

For deadbaiting I keep my rig simple. The terminal tackle consists of a No. 8 treble hook which is whipped to the end of a 0.46 m (18 in) flexible wire trace. One point of this hook is nicked into the bait just behind the head. A No. 2 single carp hook is then slipped down the trace to act as a holding hook through the wrist of the bait's tail. The hook, secured to the trace by a couple of extra turns, is then pulled firmly through the wrist. The trace is run as closely as possible along the flank of the bait which should be kept straight. My rig is completed by joining the trace to the reel line with a swivel.

This tackle is used in conjunction with a slider float set a little over-depth and stopped with a knot, an arrangement which works well on hard-bottomed waters with gravel or clay ledges. It is less effective on waters which have a deep bed of fine silt because the action of wind, wave and under-currents usually pulls the bait through an arc, often burying it in the process. In these conditions I doctor my deadbait by pushing a small piece of polystyrene tile down its throat to give buoyancy. An alternative to this, and one which gives a head-down feeding look to the bait, is to cut a small slit behind the vent of the deadbait and to substitute some of the flesh with polystyrene. It makes sense to prepare these baits at home because they require sewing, using white cotton. On the bankside, I use a hypodermic syringe to carry out buoyancy building and perhaps to inject flavour or pilchard oil into the deadbait.

The deadbaiting style can be boring, so I temper this by using plug baits as well as spoons, fished as close as possible to the ledgered deadbait. This technique tends to draw the pike towards the static bait, which is sometimes taken in preference to the artificial lure.

There comes a time when the pike angler has to admit that spoons, plugs, static or moved deadbaits, allied to skilful presentation, will not tempt pike. Often, the smaller, male, jack pike will fall but the cunning, stony-eyed 'Jill' resists all temptation. Even the female, however, may fall to livebaiting tactics, and there is no doubting the attraction which the method holds for many anglers, those for whom there are no qualms about this form of fishing.

It is sensible to attract fodder fish such as bream or roach into the pike-fishing area, they will home in on the ground bait and loose-fed maggots or casters. The pike, in turn, follow their prey and will often take a tethered livebait.

Standard livebaiting gear in stillwaters includes a 3.3 m (11 ft) carbon rod with a test curve of 1.24 kg (2¾ lb) allied to a fixed-spool reel loaded with 5.5–9.0 kg (12–20 lb) b.s. line and a sliding float stopped at the correct depth setting by a knot made from nylon. Non-toxic weights, prevented from sliding down the line by a swivel, must be used. This rig is completed by a braided-wire trace and the armoury of hooks. I believe that most anglers overload their rigs with too many hooks, most of which are too large as well! In shallow water the old-fashioned Jardine snap tackle works well, permitting an instant strike; in water which is over 3.0 m (10 ft) deep I prefer a single treble hook. One point only is inserted under the dorsal fin of the bait which ensures that the livebait will stay active for a considerable time. It seems to me that pike strike with more confidence at these depths, often being cleanly hooked in the corner of the jaws, the area known as the 'scissors'. (Fig. 4)

For livebaiting in moving waters I use the two-hook rig, an invention by the late Captain Eric Parker for use on the Hampshire Avon. A single No. 2 carp hook is put through the top lip of the bait. The other hook, a treble, is attached to the trace with one point lightly nicked into the underside of the fish to act as a keel. When fishing the livebait it is essential to set it at the correct depth. The pike, unless it is on a feeding rampage, is usually low in the water. The bait should be set to swim 0.6 m (2 ft) above the bottom although it never bothers me if the fish is set over-depth and the bait is hard on the bottom, because it will rise from time to time and flutter in a half-circle, producing attractive vibrations on which the pike can home-in. (Fig. 5a)

In very deep water I dispense with the float and weights other than that of the swivel, trace and hook. Here, the technique of freelining is used. This involves using a short trace, a single treble hook through the dorsal fin of the bait and the patience to await the arrival of the fish in the depths. It also demands the angler's concentration on the rod tip, alert for bite detection to avoid the danger of gorge-fishing results. In known pike-holding areas, the simple static ledgering of the livebaits will often produce results but a float has its fascination and in these circumstances the paternoster allied to a sliding float comes into its own. (Figs 5b, 5c)

Late winter is a time of opportunity for the pleasure angler after pike. Reasonable deductions and sensible fishing are necessary in order to take the large specimens. It is a time when varying conditions dictate the skilful use of sporting methods. Females of most species are recognised as being the most deadly, a fact clearly demonstrated in the case of pike the females of which are not above making a meal of their suitors.

Ledger rigs for pike fishing are prone to tangling but this may be overcome by the judicious use of rig tubing. The trick is to use a swivel to connect the reel line to the

**Pike rigs using either dead or livebaits (a practice which is losing favour) must present the pike with an acceptable food source and simplicity is all-important.
*Fig 4* A livebait float rig using a single Size 8 treble, causing as little injury to the fish as possible, suspended from a slider-float.
*Fig 5A* For running water the bait must sit in the stream in a lifelike manner, attached by a single hook and a treble nicked into the belly. *Fig 5B* When a bait is freelined in deepwater the rig must be as simple as possible. *Fig 5C* The paternoster is very effective with livebaits, but the bait must be able to swim as freely as possible.
*Fig 5D* Ledgered rigs for pike can be very basic, or the hook-link separated by polythene rig tubing.**

***FIG 4*** **LIVEBAIT FLOAT RIG**

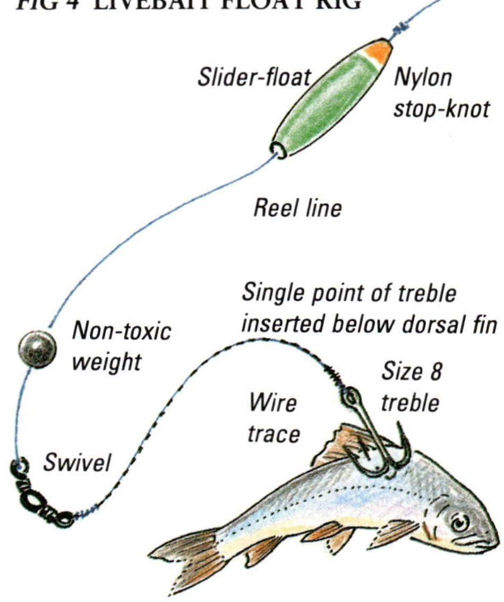


***FIG 5A*** **RUNNING-WATER RIG**

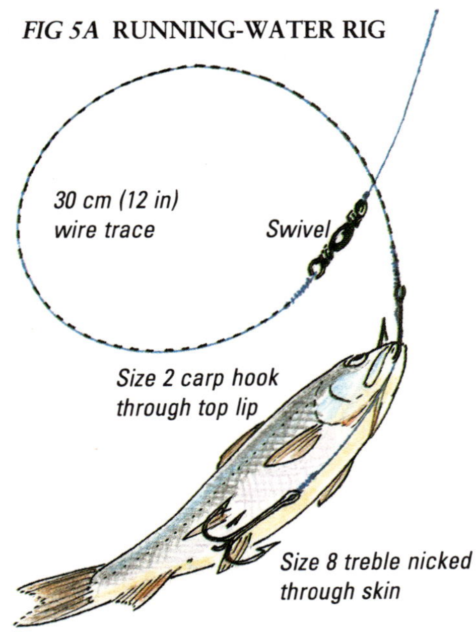


***FIG 5B*** **FREELINE RIG**

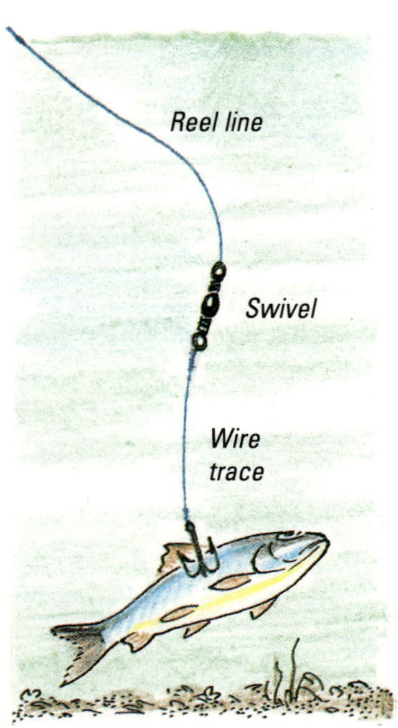


***FIG 5C*** **PATERNOSTER RIG**

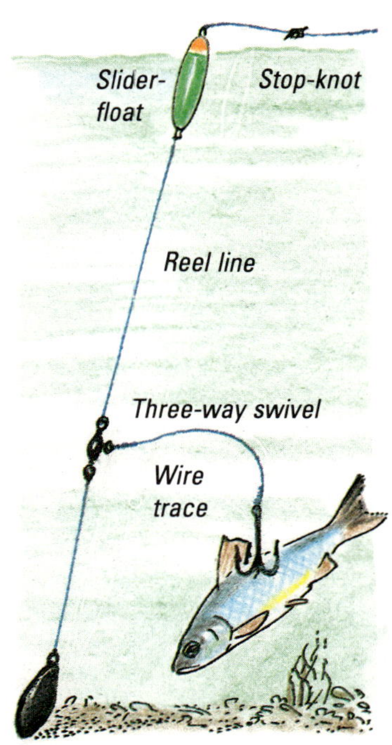


***FIG 5D*** **LEDGER AND FLOAT-LEDGER RIGS**

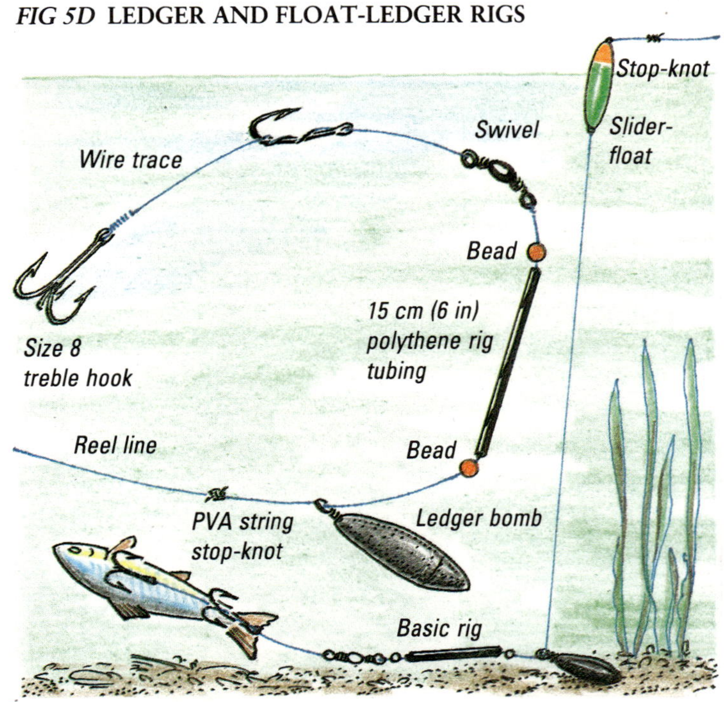

trace but to incorporate a short length of rig tubing between the swivel and the weight. Some anglers place a swivel some way up the line but I prefer to tie a stop-knot as devised by the late Billy Lane so that the rig becomes free-running. To do this, the stop-knot is tied with a piece of water-soluble PVA string, a substance which has a number of very useful applications in fishing. The angler makes the cast and after a few moments the knot dissolves. When the pike scoops up the bait the predator is free to move off without feeling any resistance. (Fig. 5d)

When ledgering it is never a good idea to let the fish run for very long before striking, because the pike will often take and begin to turn a static bait before moving off. A fish lost after a long run means that the pike was probably a small one; a bigger specimen likewise hooked indicates that the fish is deeply hooked, which is not good news for its survival.

A float used in conjunction with the basic ledger rig is a good idea. Once again, rig tubing is used to cut down the number of tangles. The basic benefit, however, comes from the fact that a take from a pike is signalled as the float rises, lies flat, then begins to dive. I find it best to hit the fish with a sweeping strike the moment the float lies flat.

**Plugs come in a fantastic variety of weights, shapes, colours and actions. A plug that has sufficient weight for adequate casting without the addition of further weight up the line is preferable for its better action. Whether used as a surface, mid-water or deep-diving lure, action is vital, it must trigger off an attack response from a feeding, predatory fish.**

## LATE WINTER: THE CHUB

There are those who will tell you that the chub is a fish for all seasons. It is not. True enough, the species may be caught at all seasons, for its greed is legendary. In the summer, chub swarm over the well-oxygenated runs and ripples to recover from spawning and may be taken easily, but at this time the species is not in good condition. Catch the same fish in the winter and it is a different tale. The chub is aggressive, bold, not too bright but with just enough awareness of danger to make its capture far from a foregone conclusion. Chub may be taken by a variety of methods, including fly fishing, but in the winter it usually comes down to a choice of presenting a bait with a float or ledger, perhaps even with a swimfeeder. There is no denying the satisfaction of watching and controlling a float to run a bait downstream to the feeding chub. Time spent in casting, trotting and retrieving a spoon speeds by and this is very therapeutic in itself.

My basic tackle when ledgering for chub consists of a three-section carbon-fibre rod, 3.45 m (11 ft 6 in) long, which has a built-in quivertip, weighs 255 g (9 oz) and was designed to cast a loaded swimfeeder. A fixed-spool reel is used loaded with 1.8–2.7 kg (4–6 lb) b.s. line. The rig is complete with split-ring, weights or swimfeeder and eyed hooks which may be as small as No. 12 or as large as No. 2. (Fig. 6, p. 18)

Ledgering used to be considered as the last resort on an unsuccessful day. In inexperienced hands this method, or series of methods, still qualifies for that denigration of a classic fishing style. There are two aspects which lift the method from the chuck-it-and-chance-it category. One is simply that of recording the bite when it comes, the other lies in making the correct choice of weight. The chub bite is often a smash-and-grab affair which puts a real bend into the quivertip; but there are times, especially in very cold conditions, when the fish will simply mouth the bait. In these circumstances touch ledgering, coupled with watching the quivertip, gives all the indication required to strike and to connect with the fish.

Concerning the choice of weight, the simple rule is to choose just enough to put the bait in front of the fish and to hold it there for as long as you wish it to stay.

Maggots, casters, cheese, bread, luncheon meat, tinned and fresh sausage, worms, shrimps and live and dead fish will all take chub. I have caught many fine River Trent chub on spinners and discovered that a deadly if somewhat expensive bait is a 19 mm (¾ in) cube of stewing steak. For long-range ledgering I prefer lobworms, cheese and little cocktail sausages; I reserve bread-based baits for closer work.

Apart from the catching of fish the real pleasure from ledgering stems from the practised control and the placing of the bait where it should be. Late winter fishing for chub provides the perfect opportunity for indulging in the use of the rolling ledger, perhaps the most enjoyable method of presenting a bait to bottom-feeding chub.

Winter floods have cleared much of the weed growth and scoured the bottom of autumn leaf deposits. Now, the way is clear to roll or shoot the ledger and attendant bait across the front of feeding fish. The terminal tackle is made up of a split-ring which is slipped up the line and stopped from sliding down to the hook by a lead-substitute weight or small swivel. A piece of nylon, of lower breaking strain than the reel line, is tied to the split-ring. To this link, which should be about 25.4 cm (10 in) in length, is tied a non-toxic ledger weight and this may be of any weight from 0.035–57 g (⅛–2 oz) depending upon the strength of the current. An eyed hook is tied direct to the reel line. (Fig. 7)

The cast is made across and slightly downstream but the pick-up of the reel is not engaged at once. This is to allow the bait to move into the fishing area. An immediate engagement of the bale arm means that the bait will be swept round and away too quickly from the shoal-holding area. In the first instance the rod is held at an angle of 45 deg. while the bait is persuaded to move through the swim by gently lifting the rod tip; the pressure of the water on the line then sweeps the ledger downstream. The bait is thus alternately static and rolling and bites may be expected at any time. The take may come as a slight pull or as an honest-to-goodness thump in which the rod tip is slammed over.

Variations on the ledgering theme include upstream ledgering, especially useful in the summer for placing baits at the tail of long strands of water crowsfoot and ranunculus weed. With this style the bite is indicated by a slackening in the line. Snaggy waters may demand the use of the static ledger but the rolling ledger may be stopped in position by maintaining a fixed angle upon the rod.

Float fishing for chub is always a pleasure. Most of my fishing in this category is carried out with a 3.9 m (13 ft) carbon-fibre match-fishing rod and fixed-spool reel, but where the fish are at long range then a 3.6 m (12 ft) Avon rod is brought into play to enable a long, sweeping strike to be made, but the reel may differ. Some anglers maintain that it is not possible to trot a bait successfully while using a fixed-spool reel and prefer to use the traditional, free-running centrepin and there is real pleasure and satisfaction to be gained from the correct use of this kind of reel. The line strength should be the same for both, never below 1.5 kg (3½ lb) and up to 2.7 kg (6 lb) in snaggy and overgrown conditions.

Float selection is the key to successful trotting. It is a mistake to use floats which are too small. They must be visible for a long way and well able to support a lot of weight to get the bait down to the fish. Large balsa floats, or a combination of cane and balsa, are my choice for this style of fishing. (Fig. 8, p. 20)

A typical float-fishing session for chub includes the use of groundbait which incorporates samples of the hook-bait. For sheer convenience, therefore, bread baits, maggots, worms, wasp grub and shrimps are first-rate choices when float fishing. In the case of wasp grub and shrimp

Pharyngeal teeth of the chub

## DACE

*Leuciscus leuciscus*

An active, delicate fish of the fast water, inhabiting shallows and aerated rapids. This silvery shoal-fish is often mistaken for an immature chub, but easy identification can be made between the species by comparing the concave dorsal and anal fins of the dace with the rounded, convex chub dorsal and anal fins. A small fish, the dace averages 226 to 283 g (8 to 10 oz).

**Bait:** Surface-fished bread and the smaller grub baits. The dace can also be caught by fly-fishing using both wet and dry flies in the smaller sizes.

Pharyngeal teeth of the dace

*FIG 6* SWIMFEEDER RIG

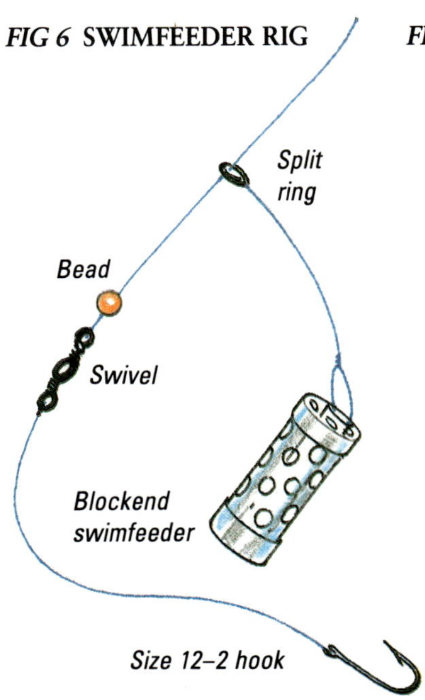


*FIG 7* SLIDING LEDGER RIG

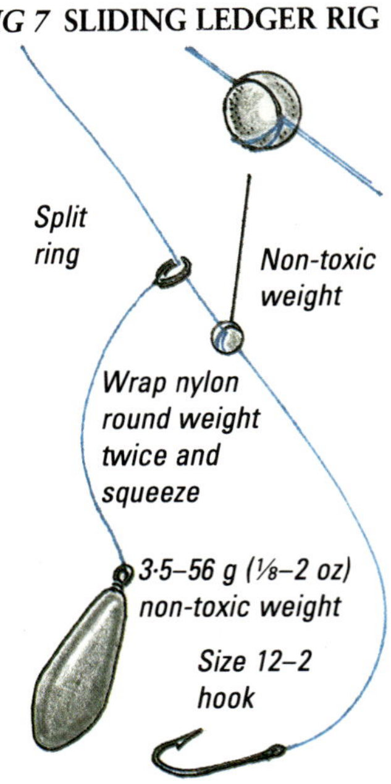

# CHUB

*Leuciscus cephalus*

Widely distributed in England, but absent from Ireland, most of Scotland, the extreme west of Wales and south-west Cornwall, the chub is found naturally in rivers but can adapt to stillwaters such as flooded ox-bow lakes and backwaters. A powerful, large-mouthed fish, the chub is reported to reach weights of 4 or 4.5 kg (9 or 10 lb) but a fish of 1.3 kg (3 lb) is regarded as a good specimen.

At its best at the back-end of the season.

**Bait:** Plugs and spinners, most cereal and grub baits as well as artificial flies and livebaits.

*Fig 6* One of the greatest innovations for the pleasure and matchfisherman was the swimfeeder carrying its own ledger weight.
*Fig 7* Simplicity in terminal tackle is a way of avoiding tangles, and it saves a lot of time in tackling up. This rig is the simplest of sliding ledgers.

An unforgettable moment! Hundreds of mature chub spawning in a few inches of water, over shingle in the River Trent at Newark. The fish were totally oblivious of the photographer's presence, indulging themselves for many hours!

*FIGS 8, 9* AVON TROTTING RIGS AND FLOATS

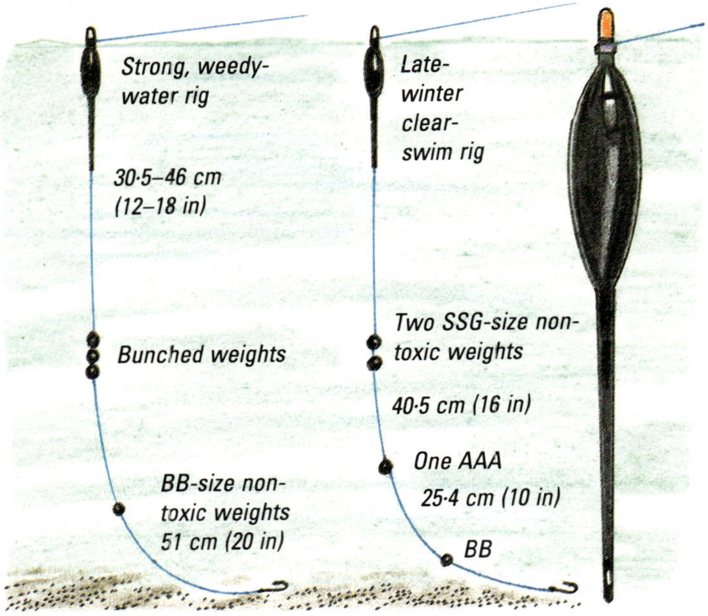


*Figs 8, 9* Weighting patterns will vary when fishing in different water conditions. *Fig 8* More weight is needed in mid-water when the flow is strong and the weed growth is thick. *Fig 9* As the water clears in late winter more weight is required nearer the hook.

*A* Flyfishing for chub with a minnow fly on the River Trent. Fast water running between gravel banks creates an ideal habitat and hunting ground for these marauding, large-mouthed predators.

*A*

baits nothing should be wasted. Every piece of the comb and every last bit of shrimp shell and whisker should be mixed in with the feed.

As always, hook size should be tailored to the hook-bait. A bunch of maggots on a Size 10 hook will take chub. A hook to hold breadflake or crust to be trotted through the same swim might be a Size 6 through to a Size 2 depending upon the size of the bait. I have taken good chub from the Upper Witham on a Size 12 hook baited with two kernels of wheat. The chub has a large mouth, so the criterion becomes the size of the bait to be fished. No hook is too big to use for the chub.

Much more important than hook size is the question of getting the bait down to the fish. Time is wasted if the bait is set too shallow and is swept through the swim well above the heads of the feeding chub. For this reason I usually fish over-depth when trotting and make sure of correct presentation by holding the float back slightly. The exception to this rule comes on those rare instances where a long, clear swim of even depth has been located. In this ideal situation the classic trotting method of setting the float at the exact depth may be enjoyed.

The chub has an almost national distribution, the exceptions being parts of the West Country and Scotland. It may be caught throughout the season, but for the pleasure angler seeking this big, brassy and beautiful fish, the best results come in the late winter.

## LATE WINTER ROACH

The roach is the angler's most popular coarse fish species. Distributed from the approaches to the Scottish Highlands to the South Coast and in Ireland through the Shannon and River Erne systems, for many anglers it is the prime species to be fished for throughout the season. I prefer to fish for roach in the winter when the banks and river beds are clean and the fish are localised.

This classic fish has a mixed diet which includes algae, snails, freshwater shrimps and fly larvae, which means that the angler can use a wide range of baits to tempt the fish. In practice, however, most roach anglers are content to operate with variations of three: bread in diverse forms, seeds such as hemp and wheat and, most important to many anglers, the larval stage of the bluebottle, the maggot. For many the chrysalis stage (known to anglers as the caster) of the bait is more deadly than the wriggling maggot.

To fish the maggot or caster in running water I use a 3.9 m (13 ft) carbon match rod. It is light and has a tippy action enabling me to connect with the sometimes lightning-swift bite from the roach.

For roach fishing, the reel may be a centrepin or a fixed-spool loaded with line from 1.8 kg (4 lb) b.s. down to 0.45 kg (1 lb). A choice is made based upon the strength of current, the length of the swim to be fished and the size of the fish likely to be encountered. Problems with bait presentation or line-shy fish can be solved by adding a much finer hook link. Wind condition and the strength of the current dictate the choice of float but a combination of cane or balsa or cane and wire stem will be used for swimming the stream. A switch will be made to a peacock quill if a downstream wind is making fishing difficult. A Size 20 hook is used to present the caster or single maggot. A Size 12 hook, or larger, may be required to present a bunch of maggots or bread flake. (Fig. 9)

Crushed breadcrumb is best for groundbait now but is used sparingly in winter as in the cold water the roach are inclined to feed less than in the summer. A little groundbait and loose feeding of the hook bait concentrates the shoal and soon the fish begin to take the bait on the drop. In these circumstances a good combination is the stick float with an evenly weighted line below it to a Size 20 hook baited with a single caster. The bait is run through the swim over the groundbait and held back slightly every once in a while. The caster will rise and flutter in the water and often induces a take from the roach.

There are times, however, when the fish prefer a bait which is dragging or is laid on the bottom. Sometimes,

*B*

*C*

*D*

Three reliable lures: *B* Bushy floating fly, fished on a floating line or alternated with a live insect for dapping in overgrown river stretches. *C* Small spinner, a tiny fly spoon fished on a fly or light spinning rod. *D* Freshly killed natural minnow or a quill minnow, fished on a light spinning outfit. *E* Allen's leaded chub minnow fly, dressed on a long-shank hook. Tie on black peacock hurl with black silk, then thread on Mylar tubing. Make fast with a whip finish. Tie the Mylar down at the hookeye and dub on a collar of red, fluorescent wool. Complete the dressing with a black chenille head.

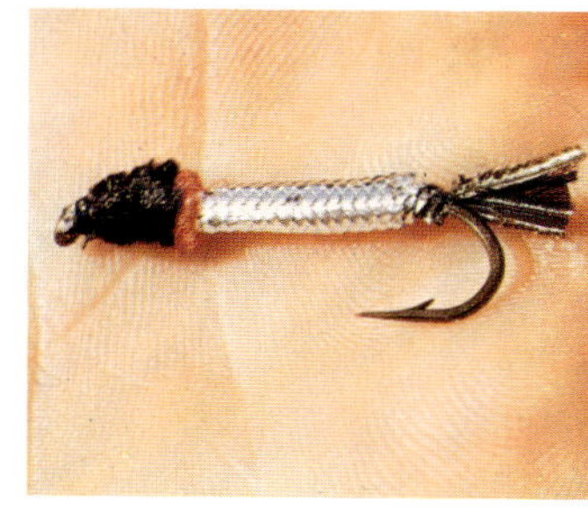

*E*

*FIG10* ROACH FLOATS

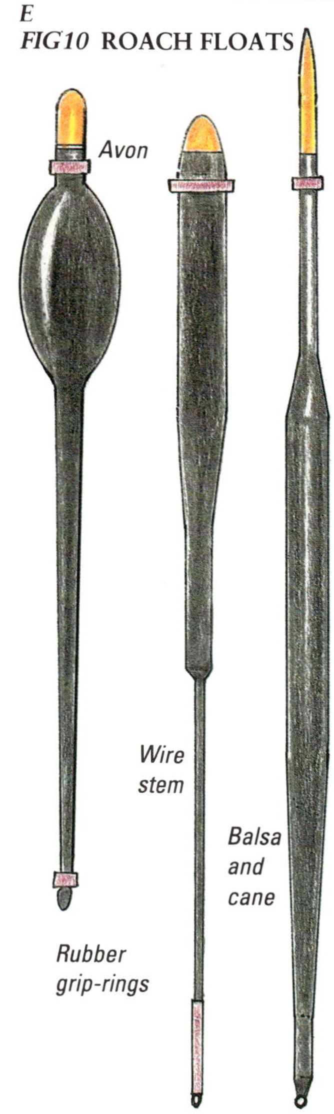

*F*

*F* A superb 0.9 kg (2 lb) roach from Loch Lomond. The vast Scottish trout and salmon water is also home to Lomond's famous pike population.

*Fig 10* Wind and water conditions can dictate what kind of float body is needed.

too, a downstream wind will dictate the use of the dragging-bait technique. For this I use a peacock quill waggler-type float fixed by a non-toxic shot at either side of the base of the float. In extreme conditions it may be necessary to attach a shot some 0.46 m (18 in) above the float and to plunge the rod tip below the water surface so that the line from tip to float is completely submerged. (Fig. 11)

Avon-type floats are my choice when fishing for roach at long range but in heavy water I prefer a balsa which has a wire stem. This combats the ripple and makes for better bait presentation. (Fig. 10, p. 21)

There comes a time when the roach, although present in the swim, are not responding to the trailed, trotted or held-back bait. A switch to straight ledgering tactics may produce results, but, especially in the winter, the roach is a shy biter, which means that intent concentration on the quivertip is critical.

Sometimes the fish cannot be taken on the ledger because it is not possible to be accurate in placing the bait in the groundbaited area. At this time a switch to pole-fishing tactics often proves successful. I use an 8 m (26 ft) carbon pole weighing 879 g (31 oz) or as many sections of it as are required to fish the chosen pitch. Using the pole permits accurate plumbing and pin-point accuracy with groundbaiting by use of a bait-dropper. (Fig. 12)

The pole may be used with ordinary running-through terminal tackle, but I prefer to use it as a specialist laying-on or stret-pegging technique. The baited hook is swung out and gently lowered into position over the groundbait and the float is then held back until a bite is registered. The line between float and rod tip is kept as short as possible but the length of line from hook to rod tip is never longer than the length of the pole.

Good bait preparation is important in all styles of fishing but for the roach it is vital. To prepare wheat, for example, large kernels of either the red or white variety should be washed in a sieve and soaked in a pan overnight. The next step is to bring the pan to the boil and to allow it to simmer until the kernels swell and split, showing the white, fluffy interior. Surplus water should be drained off and the wheat transferred to a cloth bag rather than a plastic one.

These preparations are basic for all seedbaits, including hempseed and tares, but care must be taken with the latter to soak overnight and to carry out the final rinsing with hot water. A dousing of cold water will split the bait, which is wrong for tares. Not that ruined baits should be thrown away, they should always be added to the groundbait. An addition to the boiling process for both hemp and tares is a pinch of bicarbonate of soda. This produces a dark, shining, clean and effective bait.

Wheat may be used on running-through tackle, but the deadliest combination is the pole, peacock quill float and laying-on set-up. There are a couple of problems associated with the use of seedbaits. The first is that it may take some time for the fish to respond to them. This should be overcome by loose feeding sparingly. The second, especially with tares and hemp, is that of false bites caused

**A breadpunch makes neat hookbait the size of a grain of hemp that does not have to be handled and is ideal to present on a Size 20 or smaller hook. Other punch heads can be fitted to alter the bait size.**

*FIG 11* DRAGGING-BAIT

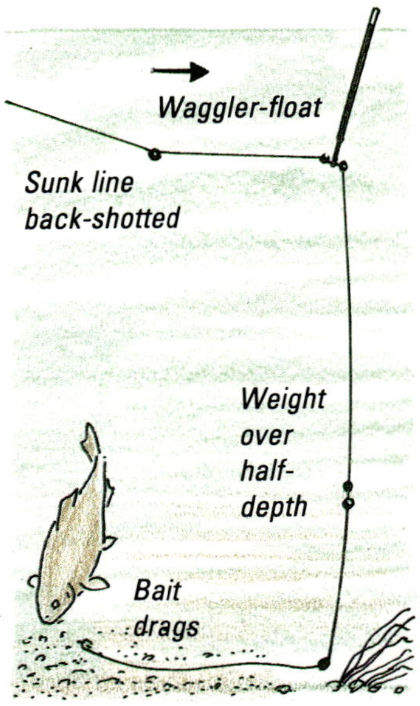


*Fig 11* Sometimes fish can be tempted by a bait dragged along the bottom. To be effective, this rig must have the line sunk and back-shotted. *Fig 12* The pole offers extremely sensitive presentation, especially when laying-on. *Fig 13* Quill floats have long been admired for their delicacy of presentation with the minimum of weight.

*FIG 12* LAYING-ON

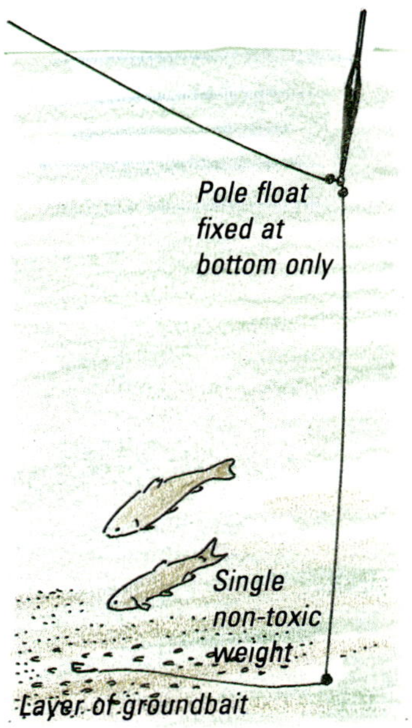


*FIG 13* QUILL RIG

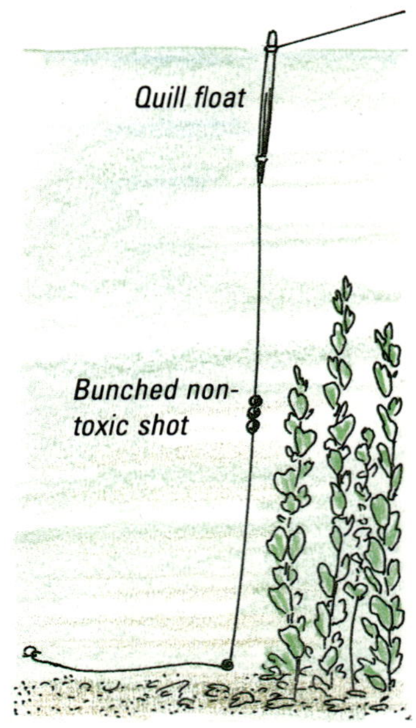

## ROACH

*Rutilus rutilus*

Probably the most important fish for the coarse angler, the roach occurs throughout the British Isles, but is not widely distributed in Ireland. It is a shoal-fish in both still and running water where it feeds on minute aquatic creatures and some plant-life. There can be confusion between the roach and the rudd. The roach has a dorsal fin positioned directly above the pelvics, and both jaws are of equal length. A 0.9 kg (2 lb) roach is considered a specimen.

**Bait:** Bread, grubs, seeds, small berries, cereals, worms.

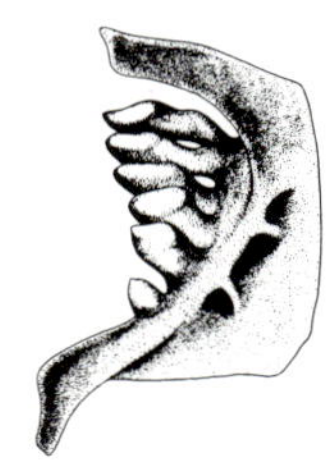

Pharyngeal teeth of the roach

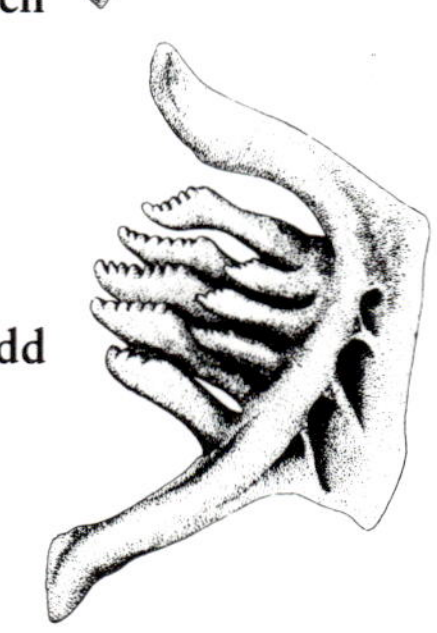

Pharyngeal teeth of the rudd

## RUDD

*Scardinius erythrophthalmus*

A deeper-bodied fish than the roach, with golden scales and bright red fins; the eyes have a brilliant red iris. The rudd's dorsal foredge begins from behind the pelvic fins and the lower jaw is longer than the upper. It is found in England, Wales and in Ireland, where confusingly it is often called the roach. The handsome rudd prefers stillwaters and quiet slacks and eddies of slow-running rivers. A 0.9 to 1.3 kg (2 to 3 lb) rudd is a specimen in any water.

**Bait:** All roach baits as well as a small dry fly.

when the fish mistake the shot for the bait. One way to combat this is to bunch your shot.

Bread, in all its forms, has been tempting roach since fishing began. To make a good, soft paste take the inside of a stale loaf, saving the crust for adding to the groundbait. Place the bread on to a large piece of clean cloth and, by picking up the four corners of the cloth, put the whole lot into a large bowl, cloth underneath and draped over the sides of the bowl. Add a few drops of water to the bread and, keeping the cloth between your hands and the bread, knead it. Keep adding water until a good, soft paste is made. Additives such as sugar, honey and aniseed are added by folding back the cloth but the angler can avoid leaving any hand scent if the cloth method is used.

Two other attractive bread baits are best taken from a new loaf: crust, cut into small squares, and flake from the inside make good, slow-sinking baits. Held back with a float or used on a long trail with a ledger, their fluttering movements often induce a take. I rarely fish bread baits on anything smaller than a Size 12 hook and often find that a Size 8 or 10 is needed to fish the bait properly. The exception to this is when fishing with fine tackle in gin-clear waters such as disused canals. In these circumstances I use a bread-punch to make tiny baits.

Such small waters present the pleasure angler with a challenge. I prefer to tackle them by using small balsa floats which have been fitted with a fine cane tip. In still conditions the floats are fixed top and bottom but if there is a wind or a surface drift the float is fixed at the bottom only. Maggots, casters, bread may all be used on this rig but there are others which are effective. These include woodlice and bloodworms. A fine-wire Size 20 hook is necessary to present these baits.

In coloured-water conditions the worm comes into its own. The tail of a lob or a couple of redworms will often tempt fish. I find that both these baits are the most effective when laid-on. To take the roach, then, requires patience, judgement and skill. A roach, whether it be a 152 mm (6 in) specimen from a polluted canal or a 0.9 kg (2 lb) fish from the Hampshire Avon, will not fall to anything but the finest tackle.

## SUMMER FISHING: THE HANDSOME TENCH

In 1878, the Mundella Act imposed a close season upon freshwater fishing. For the coarse species, twelve weeks were set aside during which the fish might spawn without let or hindrance from anglers. But fish will spawn when the time is right for them and in the case of the tench this is often as late as mid-July. Despite this, the tench is the fish traditionally sought on June 16 when coarse fishing begins again. A handsome fish, strong, and found almost everywhere except the north of Scotland, the tench feeds on the larvae of midges, small pea-mussels and snails and spends much of its time head-down, sifting the silt. In doing this it creates areas of coloured water as from its gills the fish releases streams of tiny bubbles which are often the first indication that tench are in the swim.

It is possible to arrive at the water's edge and trust to luck that the tench will show up. It makes much more sense deliberately to create the disturbance made by feeding tench. This is done by dragging and raking the bed of the swim, freeing in the process myriads of midge larvae and water-hog louse. Tench will move quickly into such areas though the natural attraction is increased by ordinary breadcrumb groundbait laced with chopped-up worms and dried ox-blood. If maggot is to be the hookbait I add blanched maggots to the mix. These are produced by dropping them into boiling water for a few seconds, when they stretch and become white. This is an advantage on a freshly raked, silty bed where they are visible and still.

The choice of baits for tench fishing is large since they will take most of the angler's seed and animal baits. In practice, it usually comes down to a choice between bread, worms and maggots. My preference is for breadflake because its use solves most of the problems created by the feeding habits of the tench. When well and truly on feed they stand on their heads, and with tail-fins waving they pirouette, fanning pectoral fins and emitting streams of bubbles from the gills. All this makes for considerable disturbance of the silt, which buries heavy worms and bunches of maggots. On the other hand, breadflake tends to be wafted up by this movement and will tempt the tench which are moving in towards the baited area.

This is a strong fish which grows satisfyingly large and is rarely far from the cover of lily-pads and reeds. It means that the tackle must be capable of putting real pressure on the fish, and I use a 3.3 m (11 ft) carbon rod with a test curve of 0.56 kg (1¼ lb). With this I use a fixed-spool reel loaded with 1.8 kg (4 lb) b.s. line. Hook size is as always governed by the type of bait to be used. A big piece of breadflake sits well on a Size 8 hook. (Fig. 13, p. 22)

Bite detection is rarely a problem with tench and any of

*A*

*E* Certainly one of the strongest fighting coarse fishes in British freshwater, this specimen tench, hooked and fought in the half-light of dawn, severely tested Edwards and his tackle.

*A* The long stretch to a summer tench, coming to the net from a man-made coarse fishery, Sycamore Lake, at Skegness.
*B* This superbly conditioned and hard-fighting tench was taken on maggot bait.
*C* A positive lift to swing the fish out for the camera. *D* A moment's care with the disgorger ensures that this fine fish is unharmed by its fight, capture and quick release.

*E*

*B*

*C*

*D*

♂

♀

The tench is the only coarse fish in Britain which exhibits sexual dimorphism, an external difference between the male and female. Not at first obvious, the differences are confined to the shape of the pelvic fins, those of the male being more solidly constructed. As shown in the two photographs on the left (top, male; lower, female), when spread sideways the male tench's pelvic fins show a distinct hump in front, an external reflection of differences in skeletal structure between the sexes. Other examples of sexual dimorphism are the kype on the lower jaw of the male salmon and the white tubercles that develop on the heads of male cyprinids during the breeding season.

Pharyngeal teeth of the tench

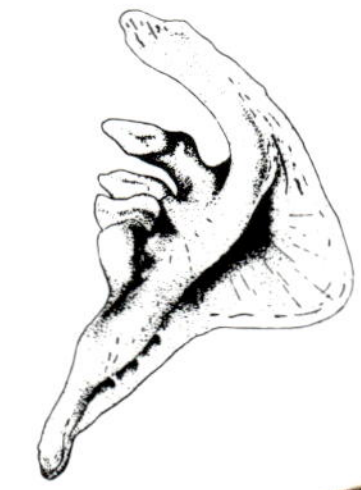

*FIG 14* BITE DETECTION METHODS FOR LEDGER FISHING

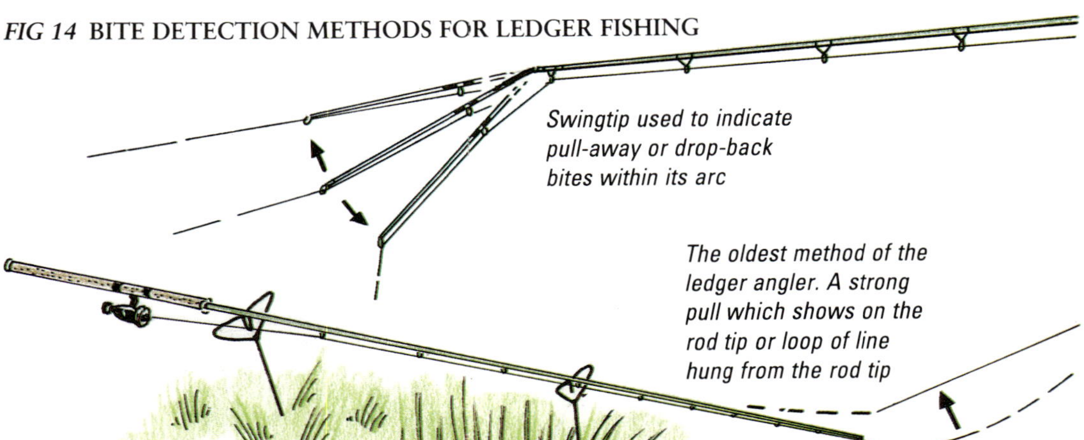


*FIG 15* FLOAT-LEDGERING FOR TENCH

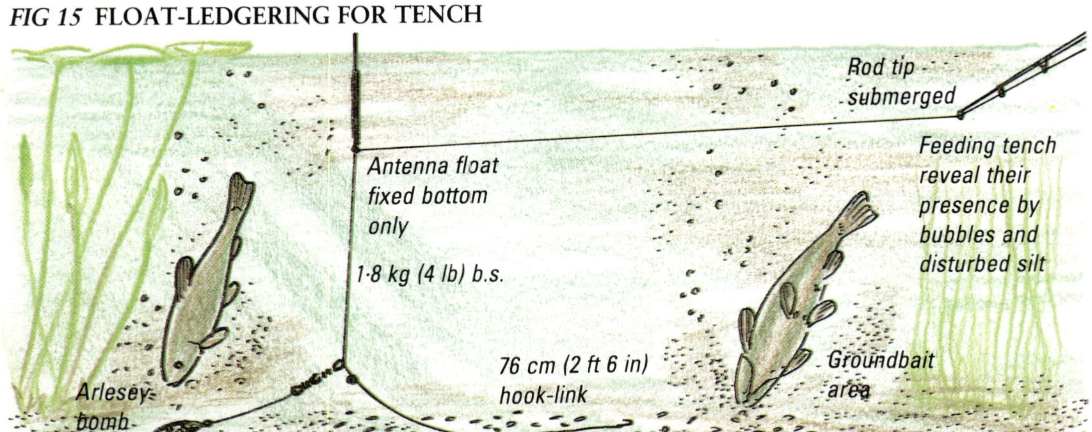


Bite detection comes in many forms from finger-touch to today's highly sophisticated electronic systems with their flashing lights and buzzers. *Fig 14* In ledgering, watching for a pull on a loop of line was once the prime method, but the swingtip now gives a more positive indication as it drops away or makes a sudden movement. *Fig 15* When float-ledgering for tench the weight should be kept away from the baited hook, which avoids the fish nudging the line and producing false bites.

**TENCH**

*Tinca tinca*

The tench is traditionally fished for on the opening day of the season. A handsome, thick-bodied, powerful fighter, found in stillwaters and sluggish rivers, the tench is a bottom-feeder down in the mud where it can find the small worms and insect larvae on which it feeds. The tench's tiny scales, covered in a thick layer of mucus, are embedded in the skin and tend to be overlooked. Two barbules are present at the corners of the mouth. As the first of the winter frosts cools the water the tench move down into the mud and lie dormant until the coming of spring.

**Bait:** Worms, bread baits of all kinds, grubs and other water life.

the tip or butt indicators, or electronic bite-alarms, will be suitable. But tench fishing for me is wrapped up in the beauty of the summer dawn much of which is missed if all one's concentration is centred on a bite indicator, so I prefer to use a float. In still conditions I employ light float and laying-on tactics. If longer casting is required similar tactics come into play but I tackle up with a much larger float, fixed at the bottom-end only. Surface drift or a ripple is catered for by using a float-ledger set-up and here I use the lightest weight practicable. This is linked to the reel line by finer monofilament than the main one and is intended to break away in the event of my terminal tackle becoming snagged. The bomb sinks into the silt or weed but leaves the bait well presented. Again, the float is an antenna fixed at the bottom end only. (Figs 14, 15)

With either the float or float-ledger methods, the swim is over-cast and the tackle drawn back so that the hook-bait is in the raked and groundbaited area. It is rare for the nearest weight to be closer than 0.76 m (2½ ft) to the hookbait. This removes the problem of false bites and hopes as the tench move about the swim, nudging the float in the process. The bite is usually a sail-away affair.

## SUMMER: CARP

Much more than any other fish, the carp can transform a pleasure and leisure activity into an obsession, the reasons for which are not difficult to find. The fish can often be seen shouldering their way through weedbeds as they prospect for food. They are strong and that strength, when apparent in the speed and power of the run of a hooked carp, leaves you in no doubt that you have a battle on your hands. For many anglers the first experience of this power is the catalyst which converts the pleasure angler into a dedicated carp-fishing fanatic. For these *Cyprinus carpio* worshippers the attraction of the carp holds fast throughout the year. I am not one of them, preferring to set aside the period from mid-June until October's end as the time when it is fun to catch a carp.

Thanks to the popularity of carp fishing, and to the efforts of club secretaries to cater for their members' interests, the numbers swell year by year. Except in carp-only waters (and these are few) the problem is to catch the carp while avoiding the tench, bream, roach and eels with which many waters abound. This problem is compounded by the fact that the carp appears to be more intelligent than the other coarse species.

I regularly fish a swim on the River Trent at Muskham, near Newark, Nottinghamshire. It is an unusual swim for that river in that it is relatively still and it is quite possible to groundbait heavily in a small area. My experience is that if a carp is hooked and either lost or landed from that swim then two hours is the average waiting time before another carp may be expected. The chub, bream and

## LEATHER CARP
*Cyprinus carpio*

## MIRROR CARP
*C. carpio*

## WILD CARP
*C. carpio*

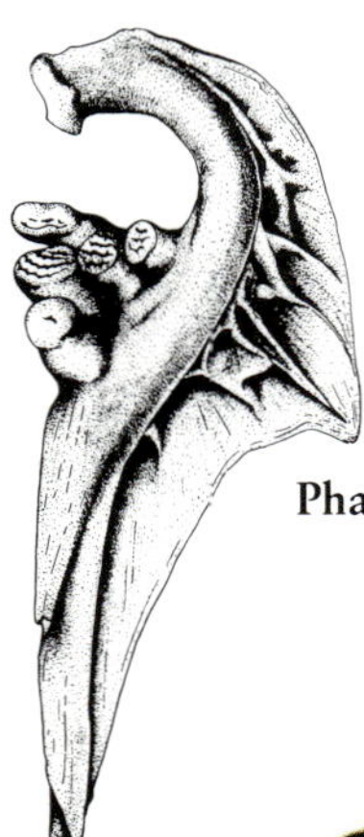

Pharyngeal teeth of the carp

## COMMON CARP
*C. carpio*

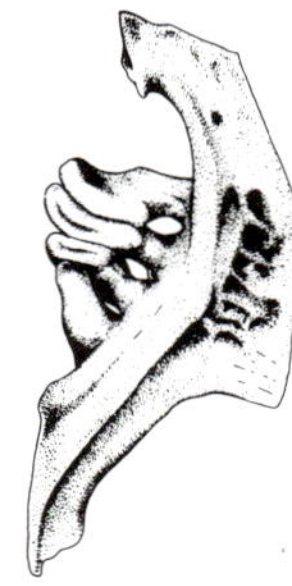

Pharyngeal teeth of the crucian carp

Pharyngeal teeth of the goldfish

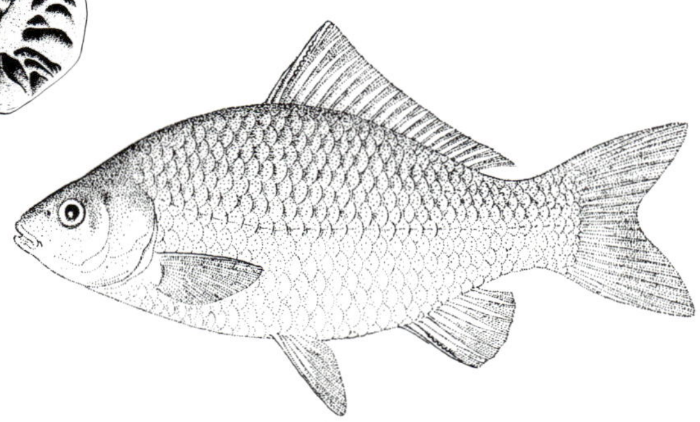

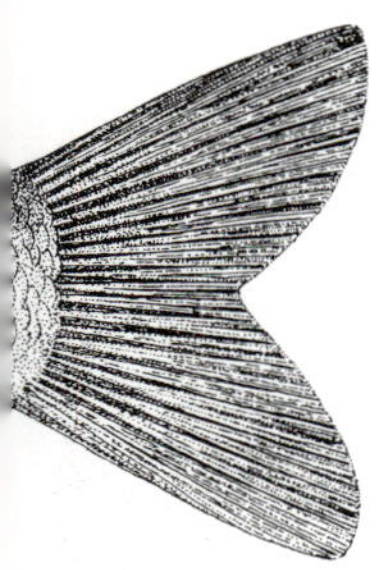

## CRUCIAN CARP

*Carassius carassius*

A small, deep-bodied fish found in a wide variety of waters but generally confined to small ponds. It resembles the larger carp but has no barbules on the mouth, which is small and blunt, with the upper jaw slightly longer than the lower.

**Bait:** Small pellets of bread, tiny worms and single grubs.

## GOLDFISH

*Carassius auratus*

A carp relative that exhibits a fantastic variety of both colour and fins as a result of selective breeding by man. This is not an angler's fish, but in some lakes it can grow to considerable size. When both species are present, the goldfish and crucian carp may spawn together, producing fish with crucian coloration.

## CARP

*Cyprinus carpio*

Carp live in stillwaters of all kinds natural and man-made, and also some slow-running rivers and drains. There are three varieties of the common carp, the fully-scaled, mirror (with large scales along the lateral line), and leather (having a total absence of scales). There are two distinct types of common carp, a huge, deep-bodied type that has been introduced to many stillwaters from a Continental-bred stock, and a slimmer, slightly-built fish known as the 'Wildie' supposedly derived from carp brought to Britain in the Middle Ages. The carp has four barbules, two from above the upper jaws and one at each corner of the mouth. The species prefers soft, muddy bottoms in which they find much of their food of small invertebrates and vegetable matter and into which they sink during the cold winter months. In the summer, carp can be described as surface feeders. Carp reach 22.8 kg (50 lb) or more.

**Bait:** Anglers have conditioned carp to accept most baits, including worms, grubs of many kinds, insects, bread in all its forms, meats, potatoes, fruits including cherry and banana, tinned animal foods.

roach carry on feeding over the groundbait but the more wary carp seem to recognise that this is a place of danger and keep well clear.

The standard gear for tackling the carp includes a carbon rod of 3.3 m (11 ft), with a test curve of 0.56 kg (1¼ lb). There are plenty of adequate carp rods on the market but many anglers, especially those who fish at a distance, prefer to step this tackle up and to use a rod with a test curve of 1.24 kg (2¾ lb). For my favourite Trent carp swim, a fixed-spool reel is used loaded with 1.8 kg (4 lb) b.s. line. This is employed in conjunction with an eyed hook. In unknown waters the line strength should be increased up to 3.6 or 4.5 kg (8 or 10 lb).

For carp, the basic tackle has changed little for many years but baits and terminal tackle-rigs certainly have. Simple baits such as bread are always worth a try but here the problem of attracting unwanted species must be recognised. The same may be said of worm baits for there is nothing more frustrating to the carp angler than to strike into a fish and then feel the sinuous backing-away of an unwelcome, unwanted eel.

The list of baits which will tempt the carp is endless. Cheese-flavoured pastes, banana, honey, sausage, tinned cat and dog foods, dried blood, minced worms, maggots and casters, all have taken carp. Current favourites in the armoury of dedicated carpmen are combination baits which have a high protein content. Known as boilies, they have the advantage of enabling the angler to switch flavours and textures so that the carp are not able to treat them all as a danger signal. (Figs 16, 17)

Most fishing tackle shops now carry a range of commercially made boilies but they are easy to prepare at home. The ingredients include casein (an extract of milk protein), Bemax (a wheatgerm health food), stock cubes of various flavours and a yeast product. These are mixed in a bowl with a couple of eggs and made into a smooth paste. This is rolled into bait-sized portions and dropped into boiling water for a minute or so, which has the effect of putting a shell on the bait, so helping to deter the smaller, unwanted species. Even so, the attentions of bream, tench and even eels must be borne philosophically. Boilie baits freeze well and can be taken to the water in a thermos flask, where a No. 2 hook can be slipped into the bait with the aid of a baiting needle. A long cast is made and after a few minutes in the water the bait will have thawed into a highly tasty, correctly textured bait to tempt the carp.

One does not need to fall into the trap of fanaticism to get pleasure from carp fishing. On many carp-holding waters the optimum feeding time is around dawn and a sensible evening-time pre-baiting session, coupled with the careful approach and tackling-up sequence of an experienced angler, is all that is required to take a fish or two before breakfast.

However, the 'carp bug' does bite many anglers and when that happens the addiction inevitably shows itself in a compulsion to be at the water's edge for 24 hours or more at a stretch. The variations which this produces in fishing techniques are minimal in the case of the angler

*A*

*B*

*FIG 16* BUNCHED WORMS

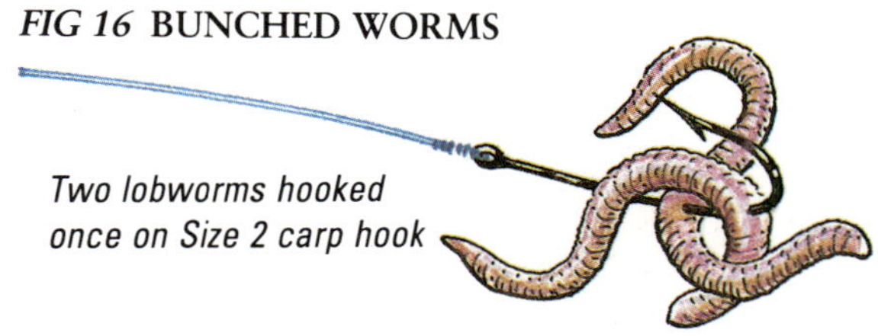


*FIG 17* BOILIE STOPS

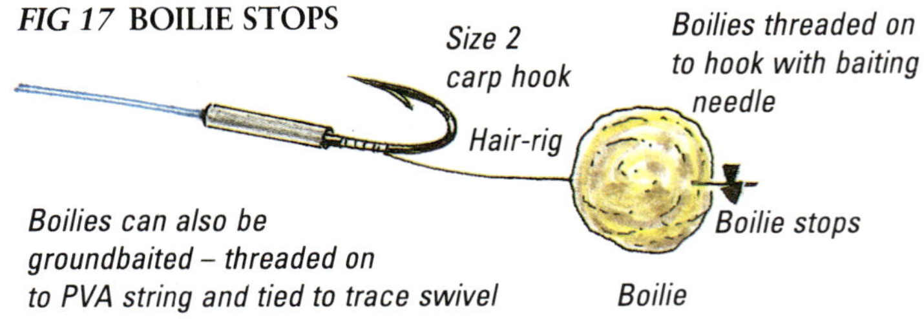

who intends to fish the night through. Groundbaiting with samples of the hookbait is carried out, a couple of rods are set up with two rod rests for each rod. Bite detection is likely to be more of a problem at night so it is best to use an electronic bite-alarm.

On many waters which receive attention from visitors, anglers or just people who feed the ducks, there is a constant supply of half-soaked bread much of which is wind-drifted to the edges. The carp become conditioned to this additional food source and when all is quiet they patrol the margins methodically gulping-in the bread. A good hunk of bread or crust lowered gently into the path of one of these wanderers will often be taken in confidence. It is exciting fishing and it is best to wait for the pull on the line before striking.

But, sadly, there are days when the best of groundbait carpets and the most cleverly presented hookbaits will be ignored while individual fish can be seen feeding and throwing up characteristic clouds of mud. These carp can be stalked and will often fall to a bunch of worms presented on scaled-down tackle. But be warned – landing such powerful, feeding fish is a very different matter indeed.

There is no denying the fascination which carp hold for the pleasure angler. Not the least of these attractions is the fact that the fish are often visible or give clear indications of their whereabouts and at times they are easy to catch. At other periods they can be totally infuriating as they cruise about like inviolate, fat-bodied submarines well

*C*

*D*

*E*

*F*

*A* Allen Edwards' carp-hunting ground, the dark water beneath a road bridge over the River Trent at Muskam. *B* Roy Stevenson hooked his carp in the shadowy stream but the fish immediately ran out into the hard sunlight. *C* After a tough battle Roy's fish nears the reeded bank, Allen is already standing by with the net. *D* Success as another Trent fish slides over the net rim. *E* A quick weigh-in which takes the balance down to a sound 5.5 kg (12 lb). *F* A beautiful, fully-scaled carp from the River Trent's streamy water. The fast-flowing Trent has in recent years become one of Britain's best-known river carp habitats.

aware of the angler's presence and totally ignoring all hookbaits the angler presents.

On reflection, perhaps this is the greatest fascination of carp fishing. The water positively reeks of carp; the angler knows that the fish feed readily in the summer but he also knows that he will have earned every fish that he lands, for carp do not 'volunteer'.

There have been two revolutions in carp fishing in recent years. One has been in the increase in the technology associated with production of the baits used to tempt the fish; the other is in the terminal rigs used to present the ever-increasing range of baits, sometimes at extreme casting range. At great distances it is difficult to pick up line in order to strike into the fish but the bolt rig, designed at first to fool shy-biting carp, will generate runs which solves this problem.

The fish sucks up what is an apparently freely offered hookbait, feels the hook and tries to eject it, but is hooked as the back stop is pulled against the lead. A 57 g (2 oz) lead is used and to prevent snap-offs a shock leader of 6.8 kg (15 lb) b.s. is used. This should be twice the length of the rod and a little more to get a couple of turns of the leader on to the reel. The line is passed through the centre of a bead, through one end of a link swivel, through another bead and is tied to a swivel. The hook link is tied to the other end of the swivel. The stop-knot is tied on with Power Gum, a stretchy product more commonly used as a shock resister when fly fishing for trout on reservoirs.

Sometimes it is necessary to go down to very fine leaders when nymph fishing. The gum works well in cushioning some of the smash-takes from trout. The bead helps to cushion the shock as the lead flies up the line for the short distance between swivel and back-stop. A hook-link, which may be 152 to 203 mm (6 to 8 in) long, is passed through a short piece of silicone tubing to ensure that the bait, which may be anything from a single grain of sweetcorn to a large boilie, sits correctly. Sometimes the hair rig is simply tied to the bend of the hook.

A selection of baits can be dropped close to the hookbait by using water-soluble PVA string and a baiting needle. Some anglers prefer to bait the bolt rig by pushing the hook straight through the bait to leave the point of the hook exposed.

When they are cast into the middle distance many rigs are prone to tangles which can be overcome by using an anti-tangle tube rig. These may be used to produce a bolt rig by fixing the eye of the swivel well into the tube. If a running ledger is required then the tube should be cut flush with the eye of the bead which is on the tube and tangles can be avoided by making the hook link less than half the length of the tube. (Figs 18, 19)

If a water is not more than 1.8 m (6 ft) deep the carp are as likely to be taken on the surface as in the depths. Samples of the hookbait can include breadcrust, fried bread, cat and dog biscuits and air-injected worms, catapulted or drifted into the chosen pitch, which is usually in a reedy corner away from the bankside vibrations or on the edges of dense patches of water lilies. Carp 'feel' safe there, as they do under the over-hanging branches of

*FIG 18* CARP BOLT RIG

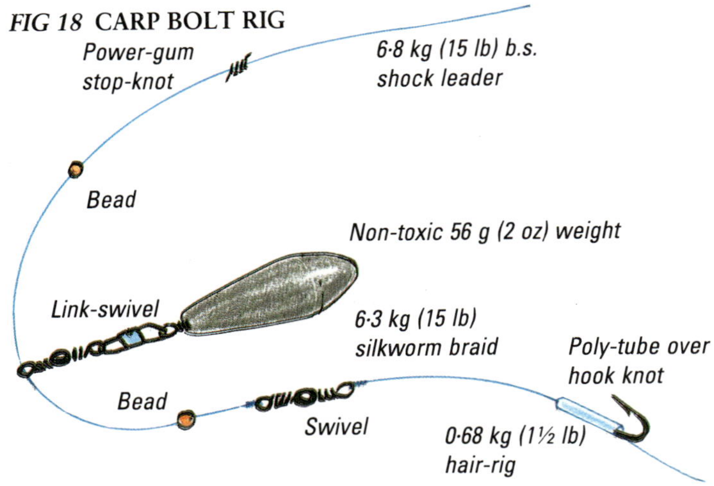


*FIG 19* ANTI-TANGLE TUBE RIG

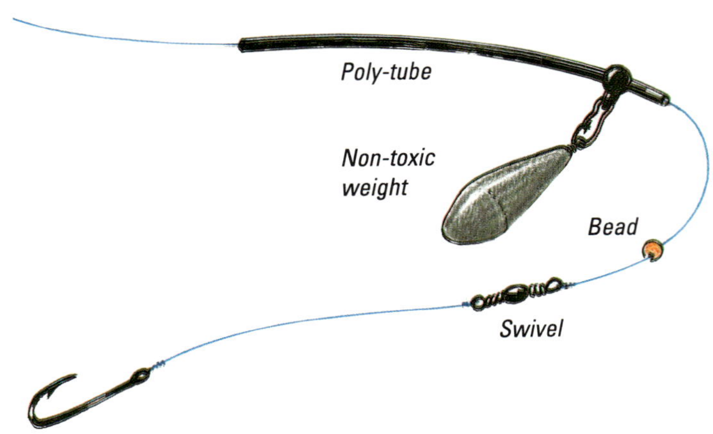


*A* A group of small mirror carp from a tiny but prolific Nottinghamshire fishery. Seen congregating among dense surface weed, these sturdy mirrors were caught on the classic floating-crust bait and on something old-time anglers never knew about – sweetcorn.

*Fig 18* When a strong fish takes the bait and runs, the bolt rig absorbs the initial stress on the tackle. *Fig 19* This is one of the ideas for avoiding rig tangles. *Fig 20* Keeping the bait away from the float is the objective here. Depth adjustment is crucial. *Fig 21* The float prevents the weight sinking into the mud.

*A*

*FIG 20* FLOATING RIG FOR CARP

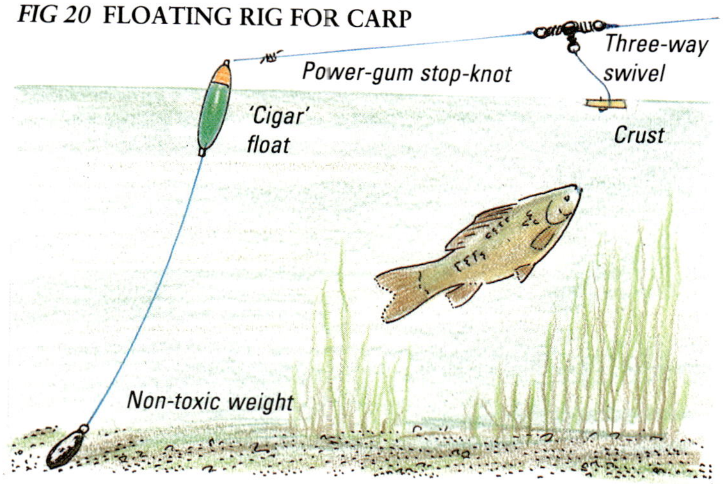


*FIG 21* CRUCIAN CARP RIG

willows and providing they are not spooked by too much casting they will feed well.

One way to tempt carp is to float a bait at them, taking care to grease the reel line first, by using a silicone spray which the modern-day trout fisherman uses to ensure that dry flies stay that way. A more accurate method is carefully to plumb the depth, then to tether a suitable float at the correct depth. The reel line runs from this float up to the rod top and from this line is fixed, by way of a small three-way swivel and hook-link. The bait is lowered or raised from the surface by altering the angle of the rod, but of course, this is not a method for use at extreme distances. Any modern fishing tackle shop will stock commercially made boilies which float but if you prefer to make your own all you do is double the usual quantity of eggs in your boilie recipe and cook the mixture as you would a cake, in the oven for between 1½ and 2 hours. There can be fewer more exciting methods of catching carp than presenting them with a floating bait. It may – but should not – be a hit-or-miss affair. The fun may not be entirely from carp for all ducks will eagerly take a surface bait and tufted duck may become preoccupied with boilies – you have been warned! (Fig. 20)

## SUMMER: CRUCIAN CARP

As we have said, the catching of large carp may so affect the psyche that the game is no longer fun. It becomes more like a religion to be practised with all the will and determination of a zealot. The crucian carp, which never grows very large, tempers this situation and is seen by many as presenting the opportunity for a little light relief. This species has a similar distribution to the larger carps but will exist in conditions which the barbuled carp and many other coarse fish cannot tolerate.

I have caught the crucian carp from the tiniest of farm ponds where they have shared perhaps 0.6 m (2 ft) of water over 0.3 m (1 ft) of silt, with a population of stunted tench and roach. Crucians have also come to the net as part of a mixed bag on the River Trent. A 0.9 kg (2 lb) fish is a good size for the species so it can be fished for with the lightest of tackle. This may pose a problem for the angler since crucian often share a large water with tench, which tend to grow much heavier. It is a mistake, however, to anticipate catching the bigger fish and so step up the strength of the tackle since this affects bait presentation for the crucian. They browse in the most delicate manner so it is better to scale the tackle to suit the crucian and to play a marauding tench with care when it does show up and takes your bait.

My tackle for the crucian consists of a 3.9 m (13 ft) match-rod or in blustery wind conditions the carbon roach-pole. For the match-rod I load a fixed-spool reel with 0.9 kg (2 lb) b.s. line but in very clear water it is not unusual to scale this down even further. In my experience, I find that a loaded canal-style float is satisfactory and the hook may be a No. 18 up to a 12 if breadflake is used as bait. This form of coarse fishing is great fun – fishing in miniature, with one or two anglers sharing the bank of a tiny farm pond. (Fig. 21)

The typical crucian-holding water has a soft, oozy bottom and worms and maggot quickly bury themselves. It is best to loose-feed such baits sparingly. Great care should be taken in plumbing the water before fishing, taking special note of the likely depth of the ooze. Your float tackle should be rigged so that any weight does not rest on the very soft bottom, the only variation to this rule being where the fish has been found in waters having a harder clay or gravel bed. In circumstances like these the lift method, which involves placing one shot on the bottom, will be effective.

Care is also required when groundbaiting for crucians. It should be done lightly on the little-and-often principle. Breadcrumb is satisfactory but I have found that crucians respond better when a little sugar is added to the mix or it has been possible to groundbait with biscuit-crumb. Samples of the hookbait should always be included and these include maggot or caster, tiny redworms or small pieces of breadflake. A breadpunch is useful in this respect since it produces standard-sized baits; the punch also makes it possible to nick the hook into the bait so that it is not touched by the hands.

While the angler is in action with ordinary float-fishing gear, a crucian will often mouth the bait without it registering a bite. For this reason I prefer to bait up a pitch which is close to broad-leaved pondweed if it is present. With a breeze and consequent drift it is possible to lay the line across the top of a strand of the weed and in this way to hold the bait in position. The pole is also useful in these conditions since the bait can be held in the baited area against the drift.

Fishing for crucians, then, is the essence of pleasure fishing. No one should have heart-failure from excitement when fishing for crucians, just a lot of fun.

## SUMMER: THE GREGARIOUS RUDD

If asked to name the most handsome species on the British coarse-fish list I would nominate the rudd. It is true that the perch has its devotees but a big rudd, in good condition, has it beat. Short and deep-bodied, with vermilion fins, brassy flanks and a back topped off with dark green to black shading, the rudd makes a pretty picture. The fish is widespread in Ireland but has a patchy distribution in England and Wales.

Swarming as it does, the rudd is a relatively easy fish to catch in large numbers. It takes much of its food from the surface layer and in and around reedy margins, often betraying its presence by jostling competitively for emerging insects. Rudd will feed on the hottest of July or August dog-days and, in this respect, is very much a bonus fish. Specimens of 0.9 kg (2 lb) are quite common but there is always the chance of a larger fish turning up. I recommend an Avon-style rod and 1.3 kg (3 lb) b.s. line on a fixed-spool reel as the ideal tackle with which to fish. This tackle will set the hook in response to a sweeping strike. The rudd is shy and if approached in a clumsy manner it moves on to other reedbeds. Long casting is often necessary.

I prefer to fish for rudd from an old-fashioned, two-man punt. These craft make stable platforms and are not likely to set up rudd-scaring waves as can ordinary dinghies. The punt and long casting are just part of the equation in fishing for rudd. The third and probably most important need is to attract the fish into a comfortable fishing area. Rudd, and this applies particularly to the larger fish, spend a lot of time in the reedbeds where they browse away on the stems taking insects and little snails. They will also feed on the odd terrestrial casualty which is blown on to the water.

## NECESSITY OF GROUNDBAITING

Groundbaiting is the answer to the problem; first to get the fish feeding on the intended hookbait and secondly to draw the fish to the front of the reedbed and into open water. Bread, maggots and casters are all good baits for rudd and it makes sense to use them as groundbait. The bread may be skimmed out or just drifted to the edge of the reeds where the rudd soon find it and, in feeding on it, break it into even smaller pieces. The angler can easily imitate these by pinching a piece of breadflake around the shank of a hook. Maggots and casters are most accurately delivered to the place where they will do the most good with the aid of a throwing-stick or catapult.

The rudd is not hook-shy unless it is spooked by clumsy casting and heavy movement from the boat. It will take a bunch of maggots on a Size 12 gilt crystal hook with

*FIG 22* 'ON-THE-DROP' RIG

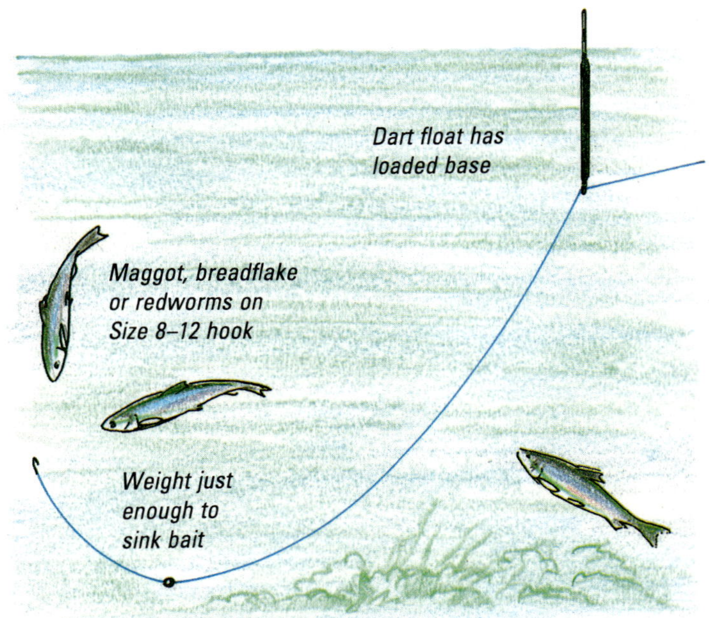


confidence. A Size 8 or 10 will not be too large if breadflake is being used. Small redworms will also take rudd but whatever the bait it should be presented so that it sinks through the water as slowly as possible, which means that the weight must be bunched beneath the float or that a loaded float should be used. Rudd make a considerable disturbance at the surface when feeding which, I suppose, is the reason that they do not seem to object when a large float comes splashing down among them. It would scare off most species. (Fig. 22)

I get a deal of pleasure from angling for rudd with fly-fishing tackle, for it produces the slow-falling bait to perfection. Maggots are the best bait for this operation since a bunch on a hook will stand up to the false casting which is required. Not that it is necessary to use any bait other than an artificial fly, for the rudd will take both dry or wet patterns as used in trout fishing, but natural bait or artificial, the rule is to fish as close to the surface as possible. When using the wet fly allow it to sink a little, then impart movement with a steady pull on the line between the rod handle and the first rod ring, at the same time lifting the rod tip. This often induces a take. Flies that glitter are the most effective; silver- or gold-bodied offerings such as the Butcher, Wickham's Fancy, Cinnamon and Gold are favourites. For dry fly fishing, tiny Black Gnats work well with a finely tipped leader which is sprayed with silicone to ensure that both fly and the line float well on the surface.

Shoaling, gregarious fish, rudd are in competition with each other so the rise to the fly is often a nudging, scrambling affair. Whatever the method used to take them, a hooked rudd should be steered away from the shoal as quickly as possible. A fish which is allowed by a clumsy angler to thrash around on the surface will soon put the others down.

This small fish can trigger off a life-long addiction to fishing, for it is often found in small farm ponds, just the places where small boys can learn the ropes.

Much under-appreciated, the rudd is a deep-keeled, beautiful plump species with majestic coloration. It is a fish which provides for a wide variety of angling methods on both lakes and riverbeds in the cooler months of the season. As the weather improves and the water warms the rudd rises to the surface in search of natural insects.

Three important ways of fishing for the fast-moving dace: *Fig 23* The line controller assists fishing at a distance where a float's action is impeded by the current. *Fig 24* A laying-on rig with maggot bait is a favourite style of dace fishing; while *(Fig 25)* fly fishing has always been popular.

The rudd is a fish of great beauty. It is found in the most beautiful of environments. To catch one – and of course return it unharmed – is always a pleasure.

## SUMMER: DACE

The old English name for the dace is the *dart*, a title which paints an accurate picture of this little fish for which a specimen weight is 0.45 kg (1 lb). It is common, being found in the streamy runs of most unpolluted rivers in England and Wales. Often it rivals in numbers and, in the water, competes for habitats with the roach. It thrives too in small tributaries where differing techniques are required from those which take fish from the main stream.

I catch dace by using similar methods to those used for roach fishing in streamy waters. The range of baits is the same, with any preference given to casters, maggots, redworms and wasp grub, but both bread and hempseed are also effective. I have enjoyed splendid fishing for the dace on the white-water runs of the River Teme, which rises in Wales and meets the Severn in Worcestershire. The Teme and the Upper Severn push with white-fronted energy from side to side of the channels and the result of each succeeding run is a hollowed-out pool where the river regains its breath and the chub reign supreme. On many of these white-water runs there are dace-holding pockets of water looking like old stains on a freshly laundered baby's bib and the dace in these are superb, fine sporting fish of half the specimen size.

A method which I have used with success in these conditions has involved the use of an ordinary roach-action rod, a fixed-spool reel and 1.14 or 1.8 kg (2½ or 4 lb) b.s. line. A float will not register bites because of the press of the water. A 76 mm (3 in) length of cigar-shaped balsa, painted to make it water-proof, is used as a controller to present the bait. My controller is fitted with an eyelet at each end through which the reel line is passed. A stop-shot is pinched on to the line to ensure that the controller does not pass down to the hook. Fishing is done by wading into the edge of the current, holding the rod-tip high and allowing the controller to run down-stream until the slightly darker water is reached. Here, the cigar is manoeuvred and held, for as long as possible, in the slightly slacker water. Ideal terminal tackle is a No. 12 hook baited with wasp grub. A steady trickle of bait is fed into the stream and each possible holding spot is tested. Bite detection is not a problem as the line is held between finger and thumb and the take is felt as a distinct pluck, but this is trout water and the attentions of unwanted browns have to be borne philosophically. (Fig. 23)

On broader shallows of large rivers such as the Trent the dace provides great fun on fly-fishing tackle. I use a 1.8 m (6 ft) old split-cane rod which casts a No. 5 floating line very well. The trick with this is to cast a fixed length of line while slowly wading up the shallows. Runs between islands are productive. Floating patterns, tied to No. 16 hooks, are Black Gnat and Red Tag. The cast is made up

*FIG 23* LINE CONTROLLER RIG FOR DACE

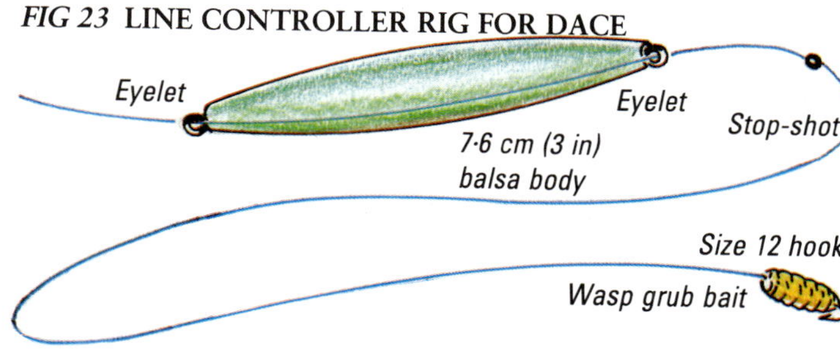


*FIG 24* LAYING-ON FOR DACE

*FIG 25* FLIES FOR DACE FISHING

and across and is allowed to drift only a short distance before the fly is lifted off and recast. (Fig. 25, p. 35)

For downstream work I use weighted nymphs which I tie on Size 12 hooks. A cast is made across and slightly downstream and movement is imparted to the nymph by a slight lifting of the rod tip. This gives the escaping-prey movement to the fly and the fish usually hook themselves in their eagerness to grab it. The dace is a free-riser in the summer months, though it is at its best in winter.

To catch dace in the winter I find that laying-on or very light ledgering tactics are best. An effective method on small waters such as the Little Alne, in Warwickshire, is to work quietly upstream flicking a maggot-baited hook, weighted with a single, non-toxic swan-shot into the run of the current. The rod is then held high so that the bait is carried down and under the near bank. This is particularly effective below hollow banks and tree roots. No float is used and the bite, which is generally deliberate, is felt as a pluck on the line. The sprightly dace is a fish for all seasons but because it takes the fly with such dash, for me it is a prime species for the summer. (Fig. 24, p. 35)

Pharyngeal teeth of the bream

## LATE SUMMER: THE GYPSY-LIKE BREAM

The bream is a roving, gypsy fish. Each year, if spawning has been successful, vast shoals of tiny fry gather and begin to move in a glittering mass around the perimeter of waters across Ireland, England and Southern Scotland. It is absent from the far West Country, West Wales and the far north of Scotland. These shoals represent food-on-the-fin for predators of all kinds, including the larger bream. Predation is great and large numbers of little fish are eaten. The search for food, aided no doubt by the herding action of predators, sets a wandering style of life on the shoal, which patrols a set beat and so its movements become predictable. Feeding as they go, each year-class moves off and, for the casual angler, the meeting points of these shoals of differing sizes of bream become hot-spots. It must be said, however, that the continual catching of small bream is a pleasure which soon begins to pall for the serious pleasure angler; for the matchfisherman, of course, it is a different matter.

The angler seeking quality bream must try to locate the feeding paths of the smaller shoals of much larger fish, and this is specialist's work. On large expanses of water, where its clarity is not always impaired by the feeding actions of the bream, the larger specimens can be found by observation. On the smaller areas, where the bream have coloured the water with their constant rooting for food, the job of pin-pointing larger fish becomes more difficult, although it is a good idea on the clear waters of canals to look for the roiled-up sections and I have prospected many miles of the Grand Canal in Ireland, where discoloration inevitably betrays the presence of bream.

Once the fish have been located the fishing becomes something of a ritual in which the sacrificing of large quantities of groundbait becomes an important part. This may be on the once-and-for-all principle of the casual angler but it is much more effective if fed in regular, smaller amounts. The aim is not to attempt to hold the bream in the swim but to condition the fish to finding an angler's bait in a set place at a set time. In both cases the groundbait should be the same: mix breadcrumb and bran then lace it with blanched maggots, chopped worms, sweetcorn or crushed hempseed.

The choice of hookbaits is wide and both flake and paste breadbaits are effective; so too are worms, maggots, sweetcorn and some of the mini-boilies. In the summer, bream will take large baits but as winter sets in it is better to fish with smaller offerings, and the single maggot or caster has accounted for plenty of large bream.

A bream does not fight strongly but its bulk will test out weak tackle. Add to the fish's slab-sided body the fact that it may be necessary to cast a long way to lay the bait before the bream and it can be seen that the use of very fine tackle does not make sense. In stillwaters, line with a minimum of 1.8 kg (4 lb) b.s. should be used. With running waters, where large fish may be encountered, this breaking strain may be too light. Hook size will vary with the bait but for breadflake and paste a Size 8 is not too large. Bunches of casters and maggots, or a couple of grains of sweetcorn, may be fished on a Size 12.

A 2.7–3.0 m (9–10 ft) ledger rod with a built-in quivertip is ideal when allied with a fixed-spool reel. The bream is not a shy biter, so a butt-indicator will work satisfactorily. When using this type of indicator it is an advantage to have two rod-rests. One of these should be

## BRONZE OR COMMON BREAM

*Abramis brama*

A deep, slab-sided fish of sluggish rivers and most stillwaters. The species predominates in the Midlands and South of England and throughout Ireland. The bronze bream has a small mouth but a voracious appetite. Living and moving in shoals, these fish can rapidly denude a river or lake-bed area of feed. Consequently, bream can be hard to find and anglers have to rely on heavy groundbaiting to draw the shoal towards their pitch. An awkward fish, the bronze bream lacks a smooth, rounded shape to the curves, which are angular, this feature becoming more pronounced as the bream becomes older and larger.

The body is keeled between the pelvics and anal fins. Bream of 2.2 kg (5 lb) are common, especially in Ireland, the species capable of reaching weights of 6.8 kg (15 lb) and more.

**Bait:** Bread baits, worms and most grubs.

## SILVER BREAM

*Blicca bjoerkna*

A smaller and more silvery fish than the bronze species and found rarely and locally in a number of waters in Eastern Britain. Although slab-sided, its body curves are more rounded and gentle than the bronze species. A fish of 0.45 kg (1 lb) is a specimen.

**Bait:** The silver bream will take all baits as for the bronze bream.

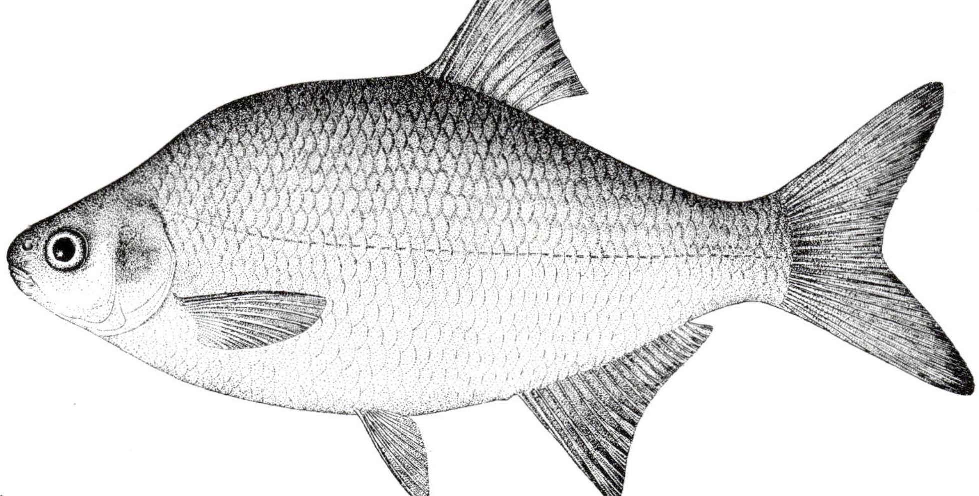

Pharyngeal teeth of the silver bream

*A*

*FIG 26* THE LIFT-FLOAT

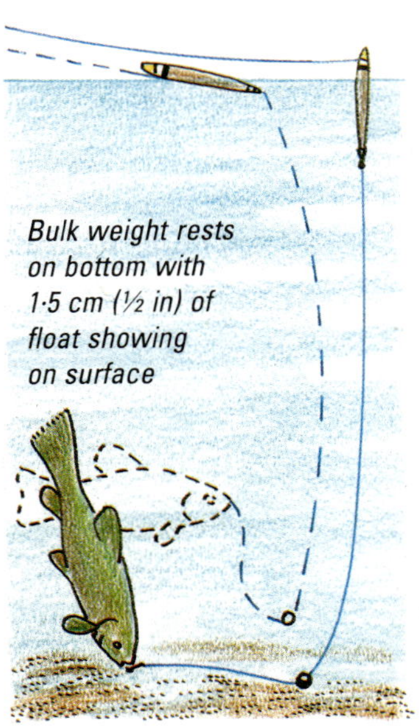


*FIG 27* BUTT INDICATORS

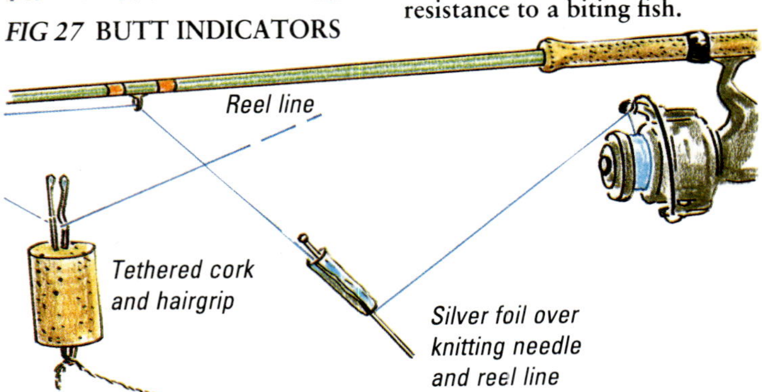


*A* The fenland lakes of East Anglia can provide some of our best bream fishing. *B* Quality fish from a fenland lake. Common bream to 3.2 kg (7 lb), a beautiful tench and a plump bonus roach.
*Fig 26* The lift-float technique depends not on striking as the float dips but when it suddenly rises to lie flat on the surface, due to the fish lifting the bait (and the weight) off the bottom. *Fig 27* There are many highly complicated electronic bite-indicators, but the simplest are balls of dough, silver-paper twists, paperclips – anything that will supply just enough weight to create a sag in the line but which will give no resistance to a biting fish.

*B*

set directly behind the other with the front rest being set lower than the rear. The rod tip may then be set below the level of the surface and this helps to combat surface drag set up by wind and currents. (Fig. 27)

On stillwaters, the bait should be fished hard on the bottom and conventional ledger or laying-on float tackle may be used. Part of the attraction of float-fishing for bream lies in the leisurely way in which the fish appears to take the bait. It stands upon its head, lifts the bait, causing the float to rise and lie flat on the surface before submerging and sliding away. It is fascinating but it can be avoided, together with false line bites, by using a longer trail between the bottom weight and the hook. On moving waters a bottom-fished bait may take bream but there are times when the fish are taking on the drop. At such times careful plumbing of the depth is required to ensure that the bait runs through just tripping the bottom, or is just above it when the float is held back. (Fig. 26)

All of this presupposes that the bronze bream is the quarry. Ordinary roach-fishing gear will suffice for tackling the much smaller and rarer silver bream.

The bream, then, is an important fish for the pleasure

angler. It is not the greatest fighting fish in the world but it is abundant and accommodating. Be warned, however, the gypsy-like big, specimen bream is not that simple to catch.

### LATE SUMMER: THE EEL

The eel is loved by a few and loathed by many. But this ought not to come as a surprise because most anglers' experience of the eel is based on the mini-mayhem created when tiny bootlace eels take the bait intended for other species and then knit-one-slime-one until the line is tangled into a horrid mess. Bigger eels, anything over 0.9 kg (2 lb), are an altogether different proposition and are worthy of respect.

There are few waters in the British Isles which do not have a population of eels. The fish may stay in a given water for 12 years or more, so most waters hold some large specimens even though anglers may not be aware of it. In waters where the eels become trapped because of falling water-levels, large eels become enormous and fishing tackle for these larger ones must be strong, with a capital 'S'. The hooked eel must be hauled up and away from snags as quickly as possible; a fish that is allowed to back away from the angler in its corkscrewing, sinuous manner is almost certain to be lost. This is because the eel lodges itself under rocks or roots or simply wraps its body round a snag. In these circumstances there is no point in being under-rodded, under-lined or at any other kind of disadvantage.

Lobworms are the most commonly used baits but on the tidal Trent eels have taken to boilies, of any flavour, with enthusiasm. The trouble with worms and boilies is that they are not selective and practically invite a confrontation with the smaller nuisance fish. A freshly killed roach, bleak or gudgeon is much the best bait to tempt the larger eels and the trick with these baits is to pierce the fish's swim-bladder so that it both rests on the bottom and also exudes traces of blood. Eels hunt by scent, in the way sharks can, detecting minute traces of blood at a distance.

The tackle for presenting the deadbait consists of a stepped-up carp rod, a fixed-spool reel loaded with 4.5–5.5 kg (10–12 lb) b.s. line, a light swimfeeder, a swivel and a flat-forged Size 2 carp hook. The technique is to use a baiting needle to thread the line through the bait from tail to head, then the hook is tied on and pulled back so that the point is just outside the corner of the mouth. A non-toxic swan-shot is placed on the line at the point where it enters the tail to prevent the eel from blowing the bait up the line as it attempts to eject it. The small swimfeeder is placed about 0.46 m (18 in) above the bait and is stopped from running down to the bait by a swivel. Dried ox blood, obtainable as fertiliser from garden centres, is packed into the swimfeeder. (Fig. 28)

When it comes, the take is usually felt by a few tugs at the bait, followed by a run. This run must not be impeded. The eel will stop for a moment or two and then begin with a second run, when a strike and instant bowed-rod pressure should be made. The fish must be kept on the move by maintained pressure and if it can be slithered up the bank so much the better.

Eels are nocturnal but I have had very exciting daylight sessions with them, particularly when thunderstorms have been building up. On one particular day dozens of big eels came to the net and it became quite impossible to take any other species. At one time almost every eel that was caught was killed but this is no longer the case. Most anglers return them, recognising that whether we love or loathe them they have their place in the natural scheme of things and should be treated with respect.

### AUTUMN: THE BOLD AND PREDATORY PERCH

More than any other fish, the perch is responsible for the life-long pursuit, perhaps bordering on addiction, which fishing becomes for many people. This fish's bold stripes and flared vermilion fins, its pugnacity, fix a sense of wonder in the hearts and minds of small boys everywhere. The sharp spine at the front of its two dorsal fins and the sharp edges of the gill covers give the clumsy youngster good reason for an enthusiasm which he may never lose. A perch of any size looks exactly what it is: bold, boisterous and predatory. There are large shoals of small and medium-sized perch in most waters of the British Isles and they grow large on a diet of cyclops, mayfly larvae and small fish of any kind including their own offspring.

The appearance of the perch is its main commendation. Its tail is small compared, say, with that of the carp or pike, and its fight is usually a short-lived affair. The fun is in the chase and in the admiring of the perch's bristling good looks, rather like an old-stager which at last has been hooked.

Perch may be taken in many ways including fly-fishing but the better specimens usually fall to a fish bait, or lures that simulate fish. Worms, too, have their place in the perch fisher's armoury and many specimens are taken on the maggot. These accidental catches illustrate the readiness of the perch to dart in with dorsal erect and mix with (or feed upon) any shoals of gudgeon or other baitfish working over the angler's groundbait.

Cloudbaiting techniques are used to encourage small fish to feed in a concentrated area and so attract the bigger specimen perch. Sooner or later these predators move in to harry and feed on the small species. This is the time to use scaled-down livebaiting tackle to present a lip-hooked gudgeon or minnow on a single hook in Size 8 or 10, tied

*FIG 28* **DEADBAIT LEDGER FOR EELS**

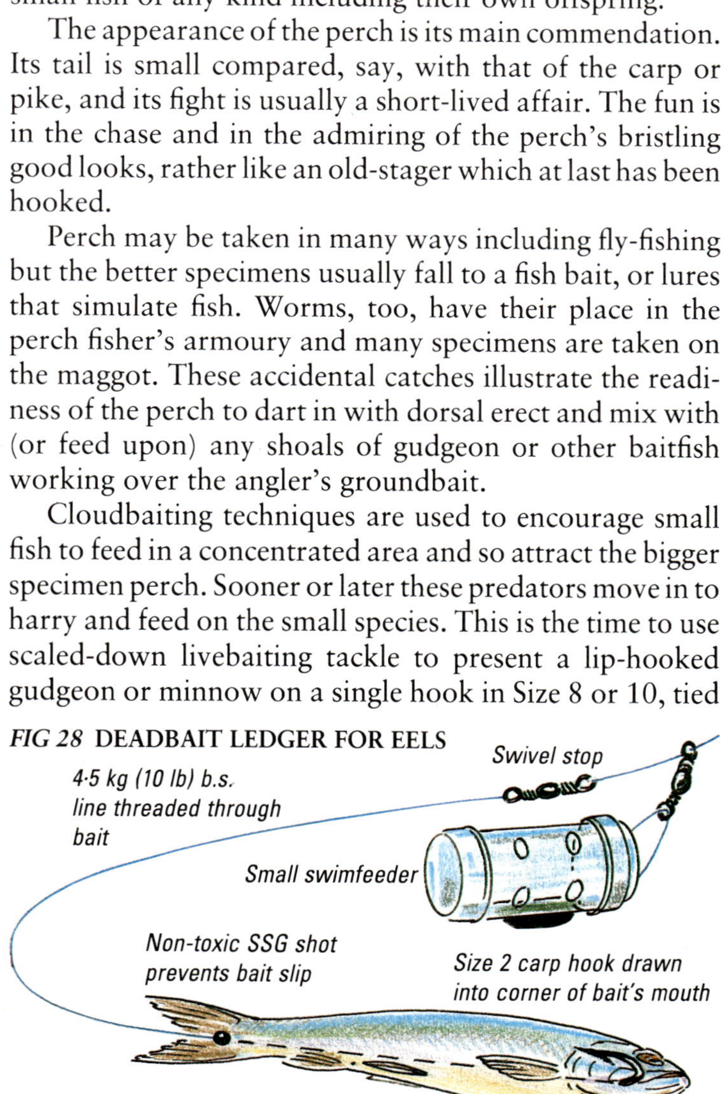

*A*

to monofilament line of 1.3 or 1.8 kg (3 or 4 lb) b.s. On stillwaters it is quite possible to present the baitfish beneath a small float with the bait being kept at the correct depth by a non-toxic swan-shot set about 30.5 cm (12 in) above the hook. Often, though, there is a pronounced surface drift which may move the bait away from the groundbaited area and in these circumstances it is best to use a paternoster rig, where the weight is placed at the end of the line. The hook-link is fished at right-angles to the main line by means of a three-way swivel. A paternoster is particularly useful for prospecting small, clear patches among dense areas of lilies. (Fig. 29)

The water in such gaps is often gin-clear and it is possible to watch the perch as it moves in to the attack but then, like a school-playground bully fearing a punch on the nose, backs off for a few seconds. Finally, however, it cannot resist the temptation of the little prey-fish, takes it, and down goes the float. There are times when a jack pike is in residence in these gaps and it is for this reason that I use an Avon-style rod for this branch of perch fishing. The rod may be a little too powerful for perch but will cope properly with a lively pike of 2.2 kg (5 lb).

In September and October the perch often become preoccupied with feeding on dense shoals of fry from the May or June spawning. When this happens the perch gather and drive in as a shoal. In the melee there are many

**_A_ A very sizeable eel from a fenland drain. Allen Edwards fishes the Great Ouse Relief Channel at Downham Market. Catches of prime eels can be made in the rivers and channels that drain the agricultural lands of the eastern counties and south Midlands.**

**_B_ Prime indigenous predators of the British Isles, both pike and perch are in any water for a reason, if only to regulate the balance that nature has set. Our other major predator must be the brown trout. Old, lone male trout exist wholly on fish, including their own species.**

*B*

casualties among the panicking fry and the perch pick them up from the bottom where they lie stunned or dead. When I see them I use a child's fishing-net to scoop out a supply of this handy bait from the margins; fished singly, hard on the bottom, they have accounted for many fine perch.

Locating the perch is the greatest problem on large waters. Mature gravelpits, for example, are perfect waters for the species but a lot of fishing time may be wasted in an area which, for reasons which may not be obvious, is devoid of perch. In these circumstances it is best to locate the fish by roving, spinning-rod in hand. Ideal tackle for this operation is a light 1.8 m (6 ft) spinning-rod with a fixed-spool reel loaded with 2.2 kg (5 lb) b.s. line. Small swivels and blade spinners complete the rig and with it every corner and every sand and gravel bar should be worked over.

The perch will respond to a steadier retrieve than the pike does and an even pace is an advantage. It is best to stand well back from the water's edge and care should be taken as the lure approaches the bank, where the perch will often be seen darting at the rear of the lure, making abortive and tentative attacks. Light spinning for perch is great fun.

Fly-fishing for perch comes into the same category as light spinning. Many fine specimen perch are caught from reservoirs by this style, often to the disgust of the game-fisherman who has paid good money in order to catch trout. The perch will take nymphs fished in a sink-and-draw fashion but they also respond to any of the fish-simulating lures.

The perch, then, is a fine sporting fish. Easy to catch as a youngster but difficult as a mature fish. A big perch is a real prize and looks, as I said earlier, bold, boisterous and predatory.

## AUTUMN: BARBEL

Strength, fitness, tenacity and fun are the words which come to mind when the barbel season begins. The fish thrives in the strongest of flows and is to be found in the Yorkshire Derwent, Nidd, Wharfe and Swale. It is also present in the Trent, Severn, Nene, Bristol Avon, Hampshire Avon, Dorset Stour, Kennet and the Thames, as well as being found in their tributary streams. Barbel move in shoals feeding and browsing on the bottom and it is this habit which dictates the most popular fishing style for this powerful species.

## THE OLD GROUNDBAITING RITUAL

In the old days it was considered necessary to prebait with a mixture of heavy crumb, bran and, most importantly, as many lobworms as could be obtained. This ritualistic procedure was followed through over several days so that the angler could begin to fish in the sure and certain knowledge that the barbel would be awaiting the baited hook. The trouble was that the barbel did not always oblige or, more likely, that the angler failed to put his hookbait in the baited swim. For the modern angler, swimfeeders have changed all this. The feeder, known to many anglers as the 'plastic pig' because of the speed with which it gobbles up the groundbait, ensures that a constant supply of bait is trickled downstream and round the hookbait. Sensing it, the barbel move upstream to meet this obliging food supply and sooner or later come in contact with the angler's hookbait.

The barbel's diet is catholic. Worms, sausage, luncheon meat, cheese, maggots, casters, hempseed will tempt the barbel and I have taken them from the Trent on tinned sweetcorn, but choice of bait determines the selection of swimfeeder. When using small baits such as maggots it is best to use the blockend feeder. An open-end feeder is more suitable for presenting stiff, cereal-based groundbait and in both cases I fix the feeder about 0.46 m (18 in) above the hook. A short link of lower breaking-strain line than that on the reel is used to connect the feeder to a swivel. The reel line is passed through this and is prevented from moving down to the hook by another swivel. In the event of snagging on the river-bed only the feeder and link line are lost. (Figs 30, 31, p. 42)

Correct hook selection is important for barbel fishing.

***Fig 29*** **There is nothing like a simple paternoster rig to hold a small livebait over an area which has been groundbaited. Perch often lurk in lilybeds and the paternoster will hold the bait in the clear patches among the lilies in just the right way to induce perch to come out, inspect it and then take the offering.**

***FIG 29*** **LIVEBAIT RIGS FOR PERCH**

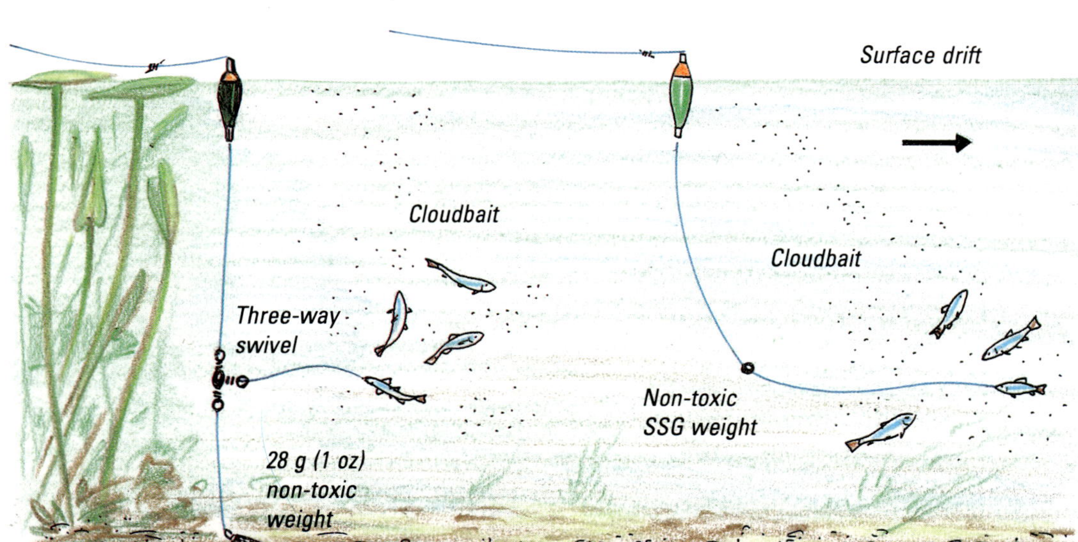

The fighting power of this species is tremendous and they will soon straighten out all but the strongest of hooks. My choice is for flat-forged 'in-line' straight-eyed hooks, which can be bought with eyes that are no longer than a spade-end hook, size for size, and when tied directly to the reel line they will not let the angler down. The hook size should be tailored to the size of bait. A good-sized bait of sausage needs a hook of around No. 2; a single caster might be fished on a Size 16. Breadflake and chunks of cheese will call for an 8 or 10 and in each instance it is important to sharpen the point before fishing.

To cast a heavy swimfeeder into strong-flowing water and, more importantly, to stand any chance of hooking and landing the hard-fighting barbel, demands that the correct choice of rod must be made. A 3.4 m (11 ft 6 in) carbon-fibre rod is ideal and this should incorporate a quivertip. The outfit is completed by a fixed-spool reel

## BARBEL

*Barbus barbus*

This is a fish of running water with a long, slender but powerful body. It possesses four barbules, two protruding from the tip of the upper lip and one from each corner of the leathery mouth. The snout has a drooping shape indicating that the barbel spends much of its time rooting about on the river-bed among weeds and stones for the aquatic larvae, weeds and worms that form its diet. The presence of barbel in any water is an indication of the degree of purity of that venue, the species not being able to withstand polluted surroundings. Barbel have been introduced to a number of rivers in England where they did not occur naturally, with a concentration in the Thames Valley, southern chalkstreams, Yorkshire rivers and the Severn.

**Bait:** Bread, cheese, worms, grubs and tinned meats.

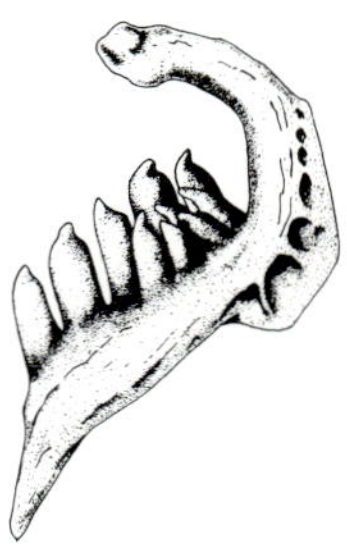

**Pharyngeal teeth of the barbel**

*FIG 30* SWIMFEEDER RIG FOR BARBEL

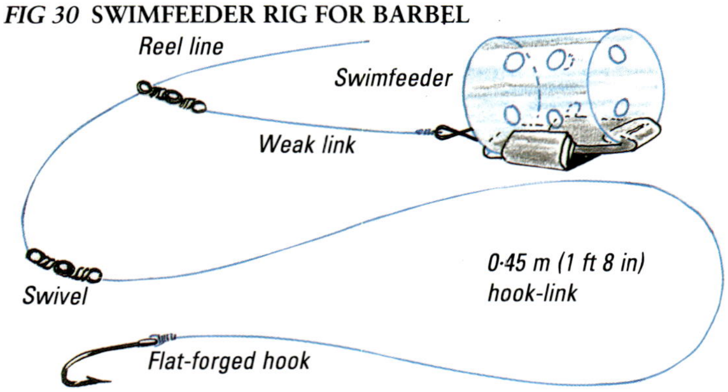


*FIG 31* TYPICAL LEDGER TERMINAL RIGS

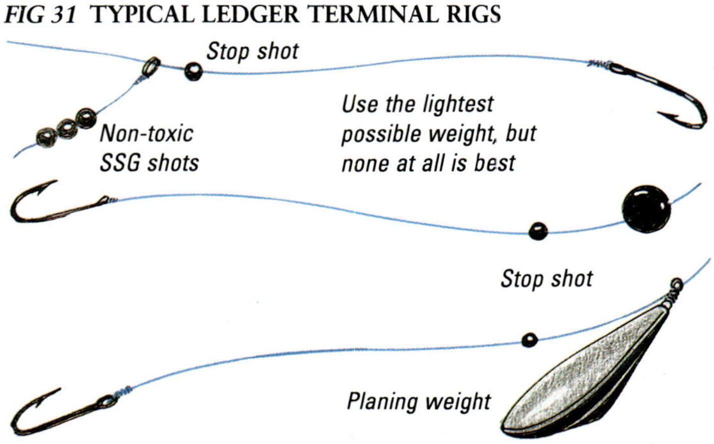


## SPINY LOACH

*Cobitis taenia*

This is not a common little fish. The spiny loach has no angling value other than to small boys who want it

for the jam-jar, a practice which is not recommended. The fish can be distinguished from its relative the stone loach by the backward-pointing double spine below the eyes. There are six barbules.

## STONE LOACH

*Nemacheilus barbatulus*

The stone loach is more widespread than the other species, the spiny loach (above). The stone loach prefers much cleaner water where it is found under stones and gravel in small streams and ponds. Look for the barbel-like snout that overhangs the fish's mouth. As with the spiny loach, this fish is of no interest to anglers.

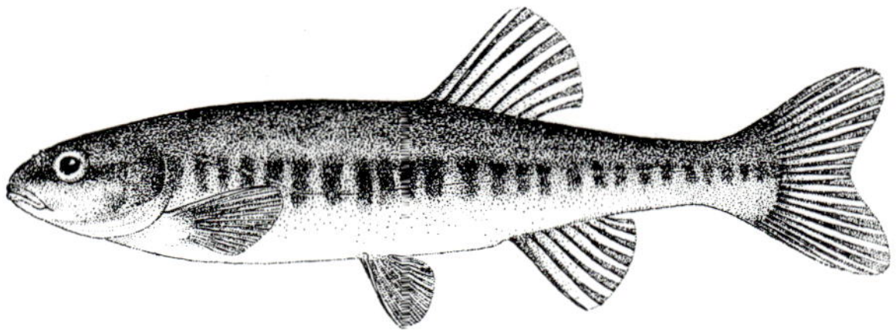

## MINNOW

*Phoxinus phoxinus*

This is one of the small freshwater species used as a baitfish. It is silvery in colour, with occasional dots or black stripes. The minnow has an incomplete lateral line and averages about 7.6 cm (3 in) in length. The shoals feed in running water.

## BLEAK

*Alburnus alburnus*

Easily recognised by its projecting, up-turned mouth, the bleak is used as a baitfish and also appears among the catches of match-anglers during contests on many major river systems. The silvery bleak can be caught on tiny hooks and single maggots, reaching 20 cm (8 in), with most specimens being very much smaller.

**Bait:** A maggot or tiny bread pellet fished near the surface.

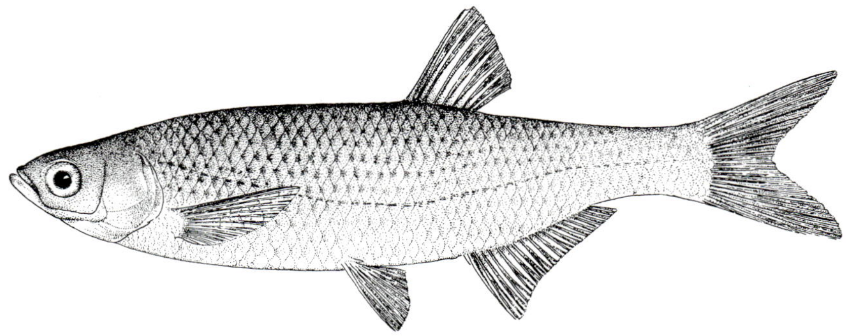

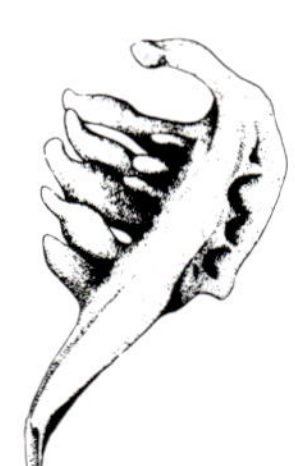

**Pharyngeal teeth of the gudgeon**

## GUDGEON

*Gobio gobio*

A small, pugnacious fish showing certain external similarities in body shape to the barbel. The gudgeon has two barbules, one at each corner of the jaws, while the fish's body is almost straight from the mouth to the anal fin. The gudgeon prefers running water over gravel and sandy bottoms where it feeds on small animal life. It can withstand some pollution.

**Bait:** Maggots and small worms.

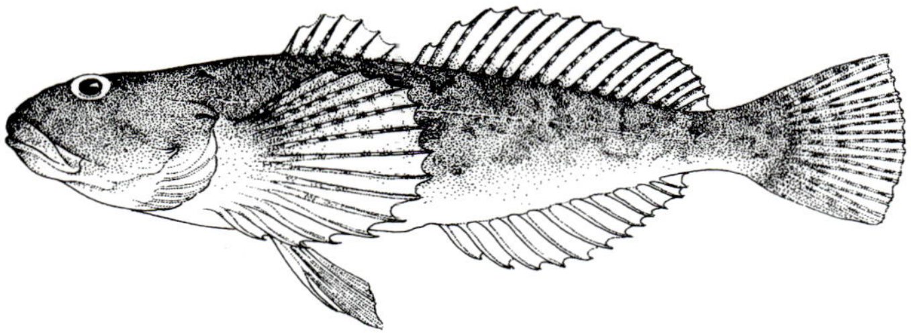

## MILLER'S THUMB

*Cottus gobio*

This small fish possesses two dorsal fins, the first six to eight spines and the anterior dorsal has soft rays that are almost joined. This species has a broad, flat head with fewer than seven spines on the gill cover, or operculum. The miller's thumb is found on the gravelly runs in small streams.

loaded with monofilament of 2.2–2.7 kg (5–6 lb) b.s. but a centre-pin is necessary for long-trotting. The basic requirements for float-fishing for barbel are much the same as those for chub. A good Avon-style float capable of carrying sizeable non-toxic weights is required and you must ensure that the bait is well and truly down in the swim. Maggots and worms are easy to get down but breadflake, because of its buoyancy, should be fished well over-depth and held back a little to make sure of correct bait presentation to the bottom-feeding barbel.

## KEEP CALM – DON'T PANIC!

Most anglers panic when a big fish is hooked. This is quite natural. The angler may have been at the waterside for a considerable time, there may have been blank sessions before. There may have been sown the seeds of self-doubt by the angler's inability to produce a genuine 'I caught a monster' story. Then, when the big fish is finally on, the panic sets in. This, however, is the time for calmness and self-discipline. It makes sense to remember that the fishing rod is in fact a spring and that providing it is kept at an angle of slightly less than 90 deg. it will absorb the force of the plunges of most species.

The most dangerous part of the whole operation comes when the fish sees the net. This should always be sunk into the water well in advance and it is absolutely vital that the fish should be brought to the net and that the net should not be poked at the fish. More fish have been lost at this stage than at any other as the fish is usually and quite simply knocked off the hook. Guide the fish over the rim of the submerged net and make a smooth lift to trap it. Remove fish and net from the water, using both hands if necessary. Once the fish has been landed it should be treated with care. Always have a wet cloth to moisten your hands and on which to lay the fish. If the fish is to be photographed and weighed do it quickly and then return it with care to its natural habitat to fight and give sport another day.

Once located, quite good bags of barbel may be made but it is a mistake to cram them into a keepnet. The spined ray of the barbel's dorsal fin often becomes entangled in the mesh, causing unnecessary discomfort and possible injury to the fish. A barbel which bites boldly and which always fights to the limit of its endurance cannot stand the additional stress of being cooped up in a net for long periods. It is better by far to unhook the fish, then to nurse it on an even keel until it is ready to swim away to fight another day. Tenacious, strong and fighting fit, barbel live in much the most attractive areas for the pleasure angler. To catch them is fun.

## AUTUMN: ZANDER

Like the wels, the zander is not native to the British Isles. This species was introduced to the Great Ouse Relief Channel at Downham Market in 1963. From there it spread into the Great Ouse itself, the Old Bedford River, the Delph and the Cut-off Channel. The species is now

*A*

**A This barbel, the first fish of the 1989 season, was a lucky catch. Mike Prichard was fishing seriously for a carp from a Trent hotspot! B Barbel from the River Severn, below Arley. They form a massive population in the river and result from a 'seeding' by an angling newspaper in the early 1950s. C The zander feeds best in dull, turbid water**

*B*

firmly established across the whole of Fenland. Their colonisation continues. In 1988 small zander were taken from the screens in the inlet to a power station on the Tidal Trent. The fish is a rough, tough predatory survivor and is destined to spread right across the country. To say that this is regarded by many as a mixed blessing is to understate the case. In the first full flush of a population explosion the zander soon creates havoc among the fry and immature second and third year stages of a fishery's stocks of fodder fish which upsets the matchfishermen since they have been accustomed to winning competitions by building up large weights of small fish.

Following the introduction of zander the main concern of the pleasure angler was the effect which it might have on one native species of predator, the pike, but time has shown that this concern was misplaced. The pike haunt the margins in a solitary way, except at spawning time. On the other hand the zander move in packs in open water, so the element of competition between them and the pike is reduced.

The fish takes well in coloured water and dull light conditions and is definitely at its most active in the twilight. Zander do not grow to the same heavy weight as the pike and it is an advantage to scale the tackle down accordingly. This is because the zander is quick to eject a bait if it detects tension on the line so lighter running-time and terminal rigs produce more profitable runs. A good combination is a soft-actioned rod with a test curve of 0.7 kg (1½ lb), a fixed-spool reel loaded with 2.7 kg (6 lb) b.s. line and the terminal tackle which is based on the use of very fine multi-strand steel wire to combat the needle-sharp teeth of the fish. I have known zander to be caught on both worms and maggots and they have also fallen to spinners but in general the bait should be a fish of some kind. Fishbaits, live or dead, are a matter of conscience for the angler but deadbaits are as good as live ones in attracting the feeding zander.

This predator will feed at all levels in the water and it is a mistake to concentrate on one method of angling. An effective and simple style is the ledgered deadbait slightly off the bottom. The bait, which should be slit open so that it exudes blood and scent, is injected with air or lifted off the bottom by the use of a small polystyrene ball; 2.7 kg (6 lb) running line is first taken through the eye of an Arlesey bomb and stopped with a swivel. The bomb's size is chosen to suit water-flow conditions so that when the rod is lifted the bait and bomb will move a short way downstream. It is illegal, however, to use a lead weight of less than 28 g (1 oz). A 30.5 cm (12 in) long trace of monofilament is then joined to the swivel and then threaded through the buoyant ball to another swivel. To this is attached the fine-wire trace on to which two Size 12 or 8 treble hooks are placed 76 mm (3 in) apart. The deadbait is hooked through the lips and into the wrist of the tail, with the bait being kept straight. Some anglers choose to reverse the position of the hooks but I believe that it does not matter a great deal since the zander is usually moving quickly. The fish is in competition with fellow-members of the pack and the take is very much a smash-and-grab business so there is little time for the zander to inspect the bait. Even though the fish is in a rush it will drop the bait instantly if it becomes aware of drag. For this reason I prefer to sink the rod-tip well into the water and to use a butt indicator, striking at the first sign of a bite. (Figs 32, 35, p. 46)

**conditions. It takes live and deadbaits, fished at all depths, but is wary of line drag and quickly drops a bait if it feels any resistance to its attack. Small hooks are vital. Zander can be found in Norfolk waters, into which they were introduced in 1963 and have rapidly spread to many East Anglian rivers and fenland drainage systems.**

There are many variations on the terminal rig. Float-fished livebait will take its share of zander; link-ledgering with live or freshly killed baits hard on the bottom are effective. Very slow twitch-retrieving along the bottom catches zander too. Baits in the 57–113 g (2–4 oz) size are ideal and should be as fresh as possible. (Figs 33, 34, p. 46)

The British list of freshwater fishes is short when compared with that of many other countries. The zander, in the short term, creates problems; in the long run it is my belief that this fine fish is welcome to our waters and that old mother nature will keep it in check.

### EUROPEAN CATFISH OR WELS

In October 1880 70 'cats' were released into the lakes in Woburn Park, Bedfordshire, the home of the Duke of Bedford. These fish thrived and in 1951 when the fish stocks were thinned out, fish in excess of 27.2 kg (60 lb) were killed, with one weighing over 31.7 kg (70 lb). Since that time the fish has been introduced, illegally for the most part, into about two-dozen good fishing waters, mainly sited in the Bedfordshire/Buckinghamshire area, but there are catfish to be found in Shropshire too.

The fish is a predator and can be caught on small live and dead fish, as well as lobworms and freshwater mussels. The fishing can be dour but the truly repulsive catfish becomes active in periods of high water temperature. The species has two long feelers on the upper jaw, four short ones under the lower jaw, small eyes, a single very small dorsal fin and a very long anal fin. There is a growing band of specialist anglers interested in catching the catfish and there is much lobbying to persuade the authorities to

*C*

extend its range. But remember – a Danube specimen is recorded as having reached the alarming weight of some 317 kg (700 lb)!

## AUTUMN: THE GUDGEON, RUFFE AND BLEAK

In the eyes of the non-angler the pleasure angler is a fool, dozing the hours away beneath a green brolly with mind, and sometimes eyes, closed to the harsh necessities of life. Non-anglers imagine that the thought processes grind to a halt once the waterside is reached but they are wrong. The pleasure angler is never rendered insensible by his sport. Indeed, many anglers put more concentration into their fishing than they do while earning a living. The hours flash by as the angler asks himself countless questions, ranging through bait presentation, weather conditions, water flow, the strength of tackle, anything that affects his prospects for sport. Some anglers ask and answer these questions by instinct and are called lucky by the envious

## ZANDER

*Stizostedion lucioperca*

A predatory species that came to British freshwaters over 100 years ago as an introduction from Eastern Europe. The zander has some of the appearance of both the pike and the perch, some anglers referring to it by the species couplet pike-perch but the fish is not related to either and is a separate species. The first dorsal fin is composed of sharp spines with the second formed of soft rays. Some specimens exhibit broad, dark vertical bars along the flanks. The species grows to 11.4 kg (25 lb) weights in Europe, but a fish of 4.5 kg (10 lb) is good for the East Anglian waters throughout which it is spreading.

**Bait:** Zander take live or deadbaits that are worked to attract the predator. On the Continent, small artificial spinning lures are used by fishermen with great success.

*FIG 32* BUOYANT LEDGER RIG FOR ZANDER

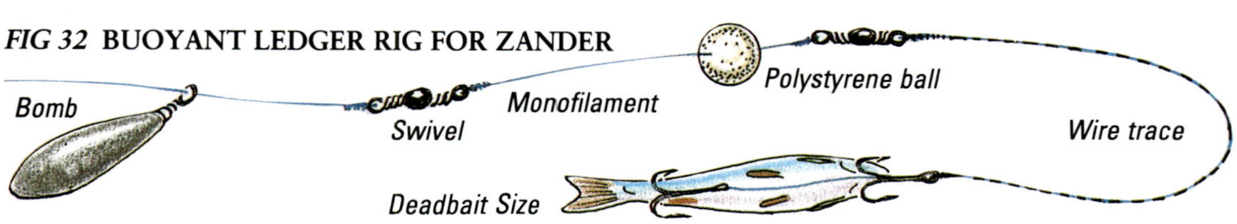


*FIG 33* LINK-LEDGER RIG

*FIG 34* TWITCH-RETRIEVE METHOD

*FIG 35* PATERNOSTER RIG

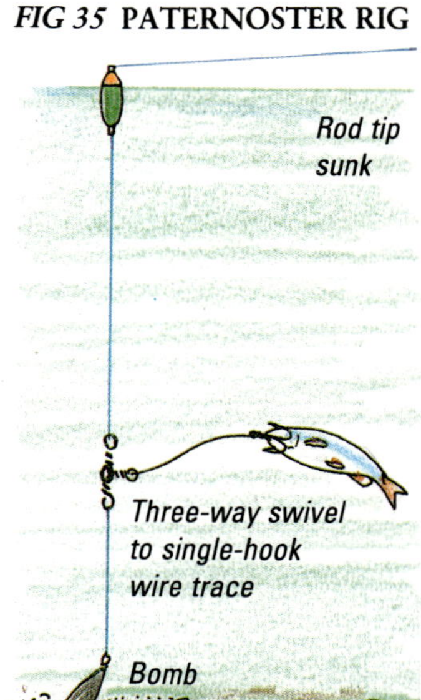


**Since the zander is not wholly a bottom-feeder any rig should be capable of fishing the bait off the bottom. *Fig 32* This is a buoyant rig for zander, the polystyrene ball acting to keep the deadbait just off the bottom. *Fig 33* With this rig an Arlesey bomb is free to slide on the reel line, while the ledgered bait is mounted on a wire trace. *Fig 34* Often, zander will be enticed to take if the bait is twitched, so a direct contact is kept by use of a short wire trace and a lip-hooked bait. *Fig 35* The classical float-paternoster again, ideal for mid-water roving zander.**

## RUFFE OR POPE

*Gymnocephalus cernua*

This small fish can easily be distinguished from the much bigger perch by the presence of two dorsal fins which are virtually joined together. The spiny little ruffe, rarely sought by anglers, is considered a specimen at 57 or 85 g (2 or 3 oz). It shoals in deepish water that is coloured or shaded from direct light.

**Bait:** Those who want to catch the ruffe should use small worms, fish fry and insect larvae.

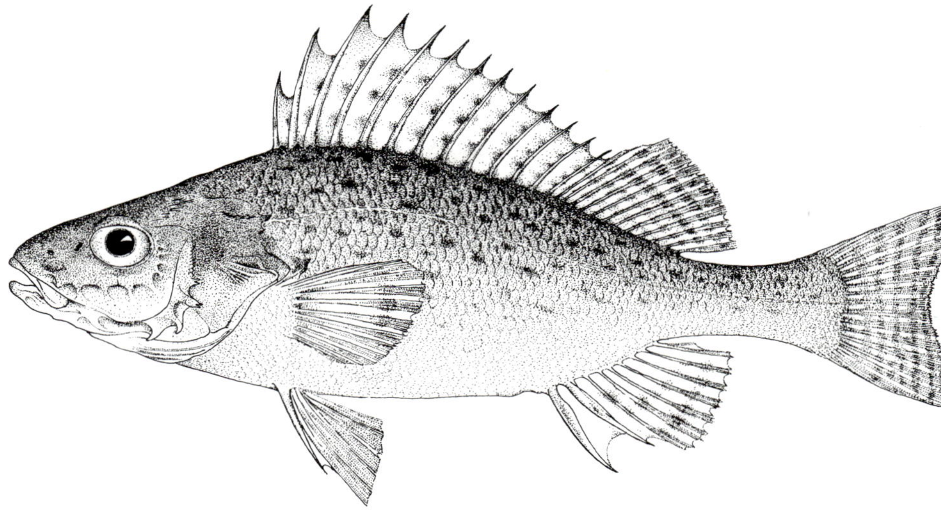

## PERCH

*Perca fluvialitis*

This is a striking predatory species possessing two separated dorsal fins, the first bearing 14 stiff spines and the second a few short spines followed by 14 soft rays. There are often one or two black spots on the base of the first dorsal. Perch are probably found in every water in the British Isles, with a preference for the slow-running stretches of rivers and streams where there is cover from overhanging trees and banks. The species adopts a more brilliant coloration for the spawning period. The species does not reach massive weights, a fish of 1.8 kg (4 lb) being regarded as a specimen.

**Bait:** The perch will take almost anything edible that the angler, or nature, offers – fish fry, insects, freshwater molluscs, worms, maggots and grubs, and bread. This fish will also rise to an artificial fly and many forms of twinkling spinning lures.

majority. Others build up a computer-bank of experience and are happy to take their modest share of fish. For the pleasure angler, fishing means constant thought and subsequent action, but there is a group of little fishes whose capture is of little significance so the mind may wander at will; they are the gudgeon, ruffe and bleak.

In Victorian and Edwardian times the gudgeon was an excuse for family parties to take their punts on the Thames. Careful groundbaiting and the raking of the bottom by the boatman assured a steady feeding shoal and fishing was a pleasure. Times have changed, but the gudgeon still abound and are best taken by tripping maggots or a small redworm along the bottom of a gravel-bedded swim. Tackle should be scaled right down with the float so weighted that just the tip is above the water. But it still makes sense to muddy the water and a simple method of creating this is to wade about in the shallows stirring up the silt and gravel by shuffling the feet.

In these circumstances the angler's mind can wander to other aspects, perhaps of trouble and concern to the sport. What, for example, about problems generated by anglers themselves? It is reckoned that more than four million people participate in angling and of these, 50 per cent are below the age of 25. Today's anglers have been raised in a throwaway age and this, in itself, creates problems.

### LOST WATERS

Waters are lost to fishing because anglers open and discard luncheon-meat, corned beef and sweetcorn tins and leave them on the bank. Their sharp edges cause injuries to cattle and the farmer can hardly be blamed for stopping the anglers using his land. The same may be said about plastic bags, which are a constant and possible lethal hazard to cattle and should never be left behind on the bank, although the presence of fertilizer sacks suggests that farming people, in their turn, add to the problem.

Some anglers forget that the cover of vegetation at the front of a pitch is a good rather than a bad thing. It is a mistake to hack about with landing-net handle or scythe to clear the ground completely. But there are more serious pollution problems than the litter left and damage caused by too many unthinking fishermen.

The angler may have difficulty in finding a clear patch of gravel from which to fish. He may have to contend with a thick carpet of blanketweed which prospers to the detriment of the fish, because of the over-enrichment of the water. Quite literally, the weed is fertilized by the run-off of nitrogenous fertilizers applied to the land by farmers. Its growth is also boosted by sewage effluents from inefficient treatment works. The odd gudgeon may be missed while it occurs to the angler that in 1988 742 sewage works broke the law by pumping illegal discharges into Britain's waterways. In some areas, and the South West is a good example, rivers are in decline because of a devastating combination of the effects of farming practices and poor sewage treatment. Thirty per cent of the sewage treatment plants set among the lush farmlands of the South West Water Authority's area were not complying with the law in 1988. Fish will be missed, too, while the angler considers that too many discharge consent conditions are set at the capability of the treatment works and not to the requirements of the receiving stream.

No fish can survive the fearful effects of pollution imposed upon the environment by the farm industry. In 1977, pollution by farmers was rare, it is now, sadly, common. The pollutants are slurry and silage, the latter being used as foodstuff for livestock. Silage is made from grass, cut and stored when fresh and green, and it produces a strong liquid. Stored properly, this causes no problems but too few farmers cover their clamps to exclude rainwater or to drain the liquid into sealed tanks for disposal. The effects of a silage pollution have to be seen to be believed. A typical 400-tonne silage clamp produces the same pollution load as one day's untreated sewage from a town of 150,000 people. Even small quantities of liquid silage kills the fish.

Slurry is the manure of pigs and cattle and has become a problem because of the growing practice of keeping animals under cover and together. Farmers are adept at placing feed in front of rows of penned animals; but in too many cases they are not so clever at dealing with what comes out at the other end of their livestock. On some farms, slurry is stored in vast quantities. In one instance a farmer kept 40,000 gallons behind a wall some 29 km (18 miles) up from the mouth of the River Axe, in Devon. The slurry weakened the foundations of the wall and it finally collapsed to send the whole stinking mass on a sinister slither down a slope and into the river. The Axe was very low and it took this evil plug of pollution three days to kill everything in its path to the estuary. And so, in those waters in which fish can survive, and to return to the gudgeon, here is a fish which is often sought for bait and can hardly be bettered as a perch and chub bait.

### GREEDY LITTLE RUFFE

Another small species which might feature in the often mixed bag of the pleasure angler is the ruffe. This is a greedy little fish the appearance of which in the swim is dreaded by some anglers because they know that its capture and removal from the swim will not be taken as a warning to other ruffe. Catch one and you will probably catch dozens. The ruffe shares the double dorsal fin characteristic with the perch. In coloration it is a pale ghost of the larger, more sought-after species but does not have its bold stripes. The ruffe differs from every other species in the colour of its eyes, which are violet. Care should be taken when handling this fish as the edges of the gill cover are sharp.

The ruffe falls easily to the presentation of maggot, casters or small worms. The fishing is easy, with bites impossible to miss. There is little skill needed or pressure felt by the angler in this kind of fishing and the thinking fisherman has plenty of time to consider the national situation of the over-abstraction of water from our rivers, thus compounding some of the pollution problems. The angler may also consider the ill-effects which the growth of fishing-farming is having. A clear example of this is the West Beck in Yorkshire. This is a beautiful chalkstream, but within the space of a few miles it is reduced from a Class 1 water, the home of mayfly and trout, to a Class 2 water, the home of midges and coarse fish. And it is due to the insidious polluting effect of fish-farm effluents.

There are those who consider that a decline in the quality of the fishing on the Hampshire Avon is attributable to abstraction. Time will tell, as the National Rivers Authority begins the task of 'policing' the 'burglar-style' activities of those who take good-quality water from the environment, use it to make profit, then return it to the watercourses. Even the 'unmissable' bite from the greedy little ruffe may well be missed as the significance of the problem of abstraction sinks into the angler's mind.

More anglers are appearing on the scene with each successive season. In May 1989 the Angling Foundation published the results of an independent survey undertaken on their behalf. The main findings from this showed that the angling population had shown a 3.5 per cent increase since 1986 and that 8.2 per cent of the total population of Great Britain fished for pleasure. Statistically, within the bounds of errors with such surveys, it is possible to claim that four million people go fishing. Of these, three-quarters are below the age of 35. This increase in anglers has to be set against the prospect of a decline in the quality of our rivers but, fortunately, an increase in the availability and quality of our stillwaters. Not one angler can afford to be complacent about the future of his sport.

No discussion of the pleasure angler's small-fish quarry would be complete without a mention of the bleak. This silvery little fish is regarded by many as an out-and-out pest. It swarms to attack the maggot, caster, flake or paste intended for the roach, chub and rudd. There are times, however, when the catching of a bleak assumes an importance not to be compared with its size. For example, there can hardly be a better fish for use as a live or deadbait. The competition angler, too, may bless the bleak which he sees topping in large numbers on a rapidly rising river.

To catch bleak intentionally means that one's tackle must be scaled right down to the finest of lines, the most sensitive float and the smallest of hooks. These fish are easily gathered into a surface-feeding shoal by the use of cloud-groundbait, casters and maggots. On a near-fishless day there can be a kind of repetitive pleasure in building up a catch of these little fish.

If any fish can be said to symbolise the ever-growing army of pleasure anglers it is the bleak. It is restless and sometimes infuriating; it is mobile and constantly trying to get into what it believes is the action. Taken singly the bleak has a character and an attractiveness of its own.

When raised in a sustained clamour the voices of four million very concerned anglers must be heard. The shouts must be directed at those who influence the environment by pollution and ill-considered abstraction. If the anglers will not do this, then so far as this country's rivers go he must face the fact that not for long will he be able to claim 'Angling is a pleasure!' And the sport will have died.

*A*

*B*

***A*** **A fish found in relatively few waters. This wels, or European catfish, took the scales down past 9 kg (20 lb) when it was caught at Jont's Point, Leighton Buzzard, Bedfordshire.**
***B*** **The laid-back angler, his stall is set out, his tactics thought about and decided upon.**

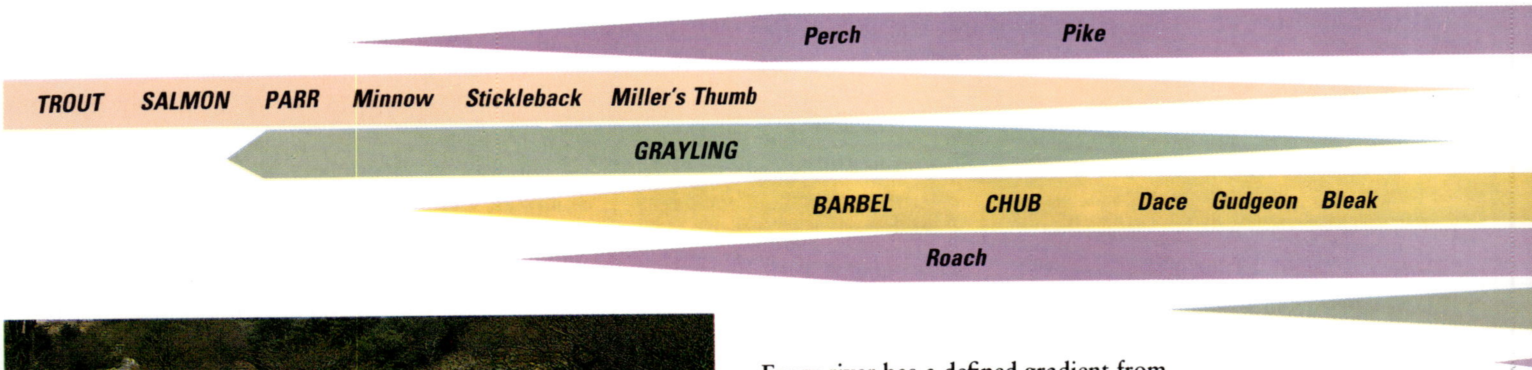

Every river has a defined gradient from source to the sea. The illustration depicts a classic highland, snow-fed river and its steep gradient. In broad terms almost all rivers of the British Isles can be divided into five zones: trout, grayling, barbel, bream and tidal or estuary. The zones cannot be regarded as clearly defined areas for there will always be overlaps, often many miles in length, where zones merge. Fish respond to basic, life-supporting conditions appropriate to their species.

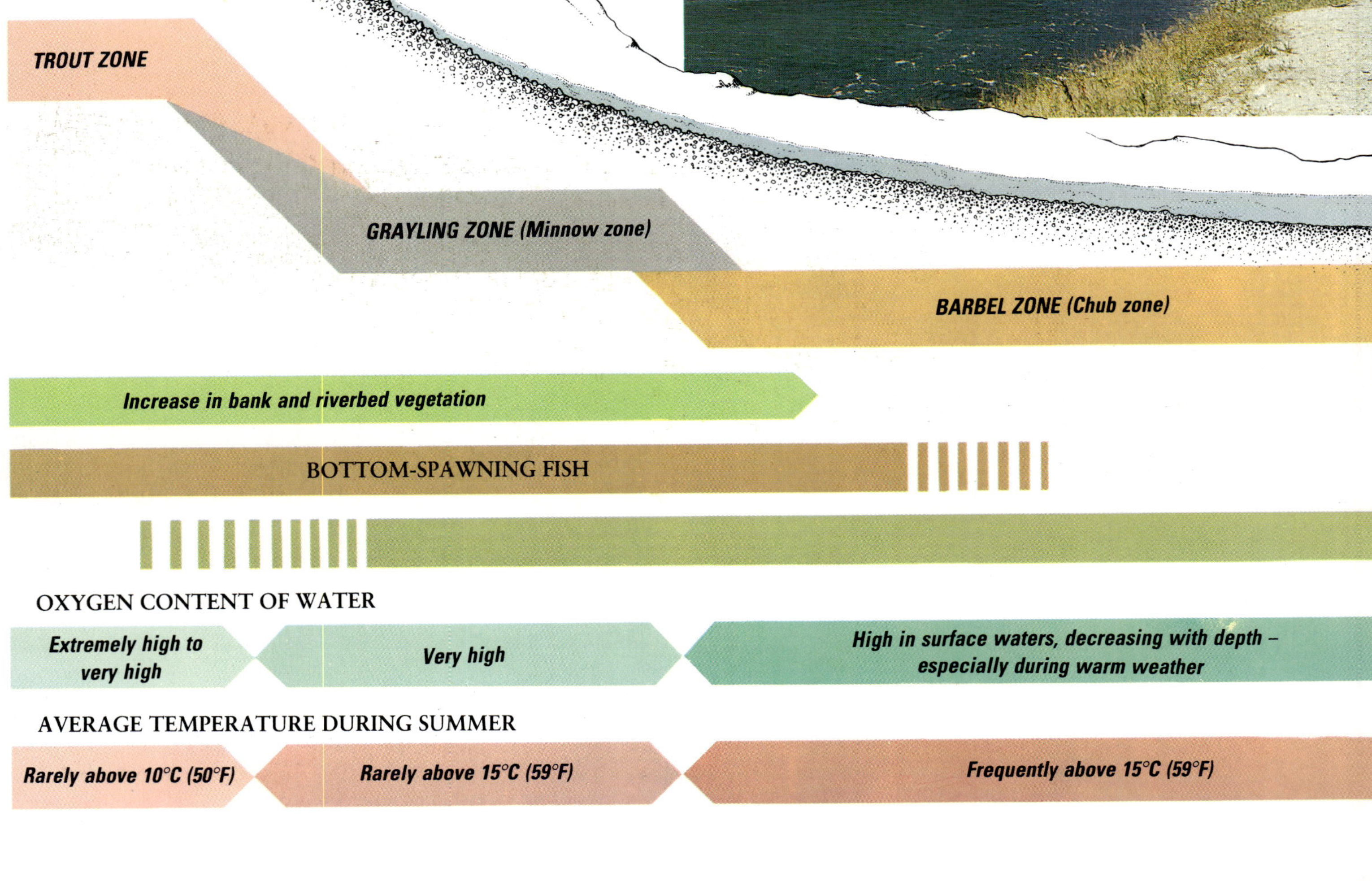

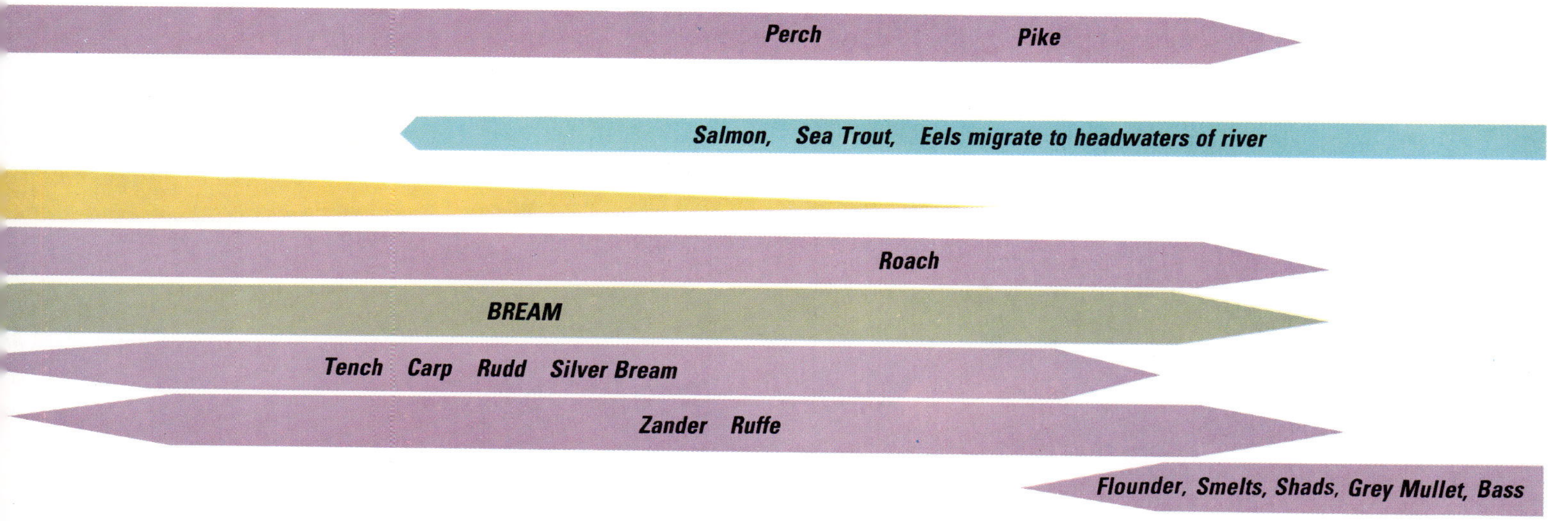


The oxygen content and temperature of the water, variety and type of vegetation, depth and speed of current all have a bearing on the species in residence. The chart tells an outline story of a river. To learn where to fish for specific species one must refer to the coloured bands at the top of the illustration.

Select a fish, then move vertically down to the lower colour bands for information about the river zoning, vegetation on riverbed and bankside, spawning behaviour, oxygen availability and average temperatures.

There must always be an overlap of zones, but a knowledge of the broad rules governing fish survival in the various conditions that a running water undergoes will be invaluable to the angler.

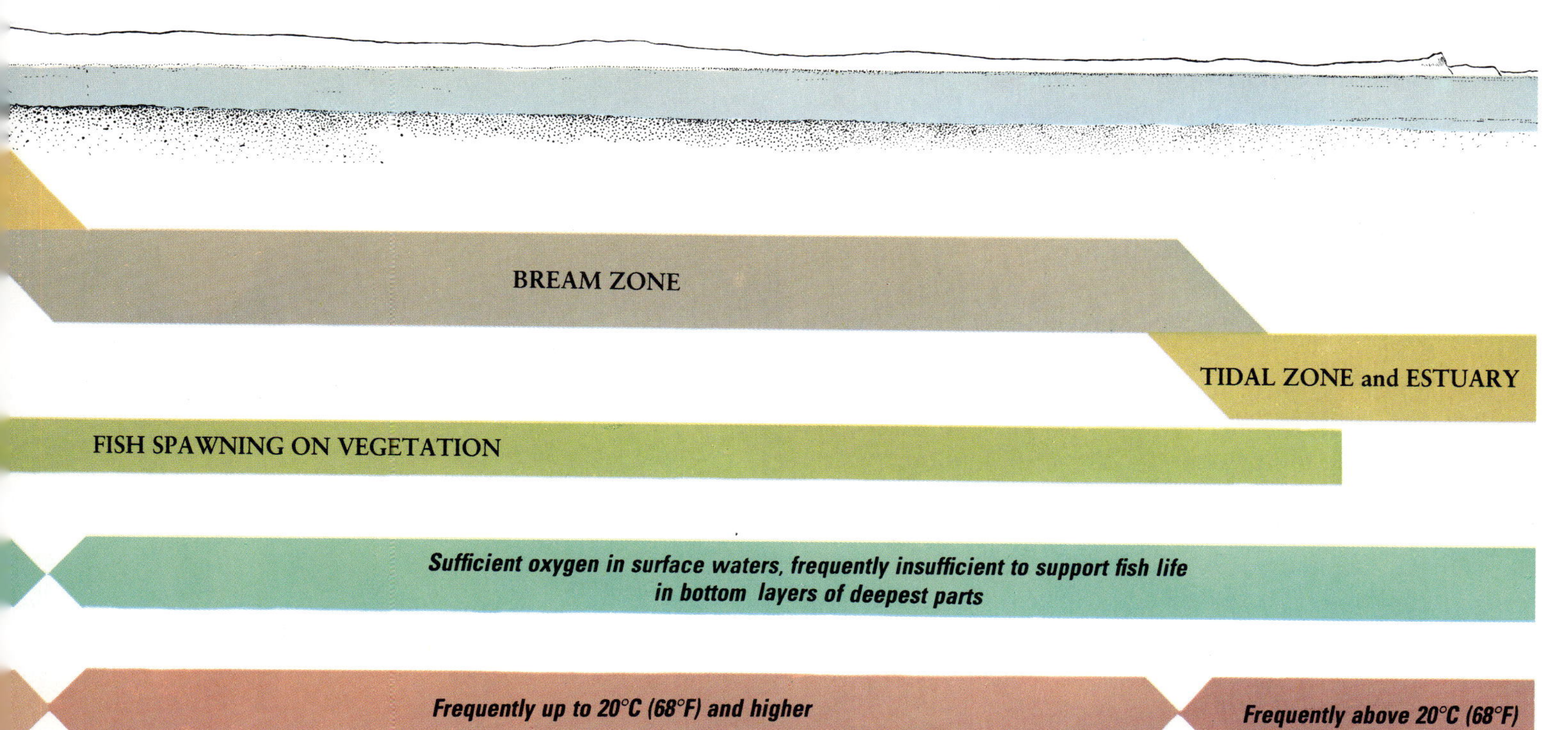

TOM PICKERING

# MATCHFISHING TO WIN

I do not consider myself to be another Ivan Marks or a Billy Lane, they were products of a different and certainly a much better era so far as the sport of angling is concerned. If Billy Lane could return from the grave and fish the way he always used to he would not win many matches until he had adapted to the many changes in technique and method which have taken place since his heyday.

Ivan Marks, of course, is still with us and still a masterly match angler. In Sweden in 1988 he stepped back in time to lead my Barnsley team to victory in the DFDS Seaways Challenge final. He did it with a superb display of long-range bream fishing, using the tactics and knowledge he had acquired decades before.

When Ivan Marks and Billy Lane were at the peak of their powers all the competitors in virtually every match had the chance to make big weights. Contests were fewer but much better then, especially in the Fenlands. If the angler did not take a big weight, usually of bream, he did not win – it was as simple as that. Ivan and Billy were adept at drawing the bream to their swim, making them feed, keeping them feeding longer than anyone else and then catching most of them. One felt that these two giants could think like bream, or whatever other species they were after. These two master fishermen were attackers; plunderers of fish shoals the presence of which were taken for granted. The top anglers of that decade were fish-catching machines.

Billy Lane reached the pinnacle of matchfishing fame

Master matchman and world-beater Tom Pickering at work with the pole on the River Trent at Stoke Bardolph.

by preaching and practising the use of enough weight to achieve perfect control of his tackle in any given situation. With the fish invariably present in numbers, and willing to have the feed piled in on them, that was virtually all he needed to do. But it is very different now, for the matchman of today has to live with the consequences of what was happening, undetected, when earlier generations were enjoying their matchfishing bonanzas. While they were winning matches our rural waterways were being poisoned with agricultural chemicals, and in so doing impairing the abilities of fish to reproduce in their former numbers. Cyprinid populations suddenly crashed on every fishery where Marks and Lane, and many others, earned their reputations.

For a few brief years the more urban rivers were improving as rural waters declined. Clean-up campaigns by industrial and sewage plants to eradicate pollution worked wonders for such rivers as the Trent and we enjoyed a decade of plenty which deflected our attention from what was happening in the Fens. Now all that has gone into reverse due to a lack of investment and the political will to fight pollution. The authorities now tell us that they are making the investment which will safeguard our future. Maybe, but today's matchman has to live with current reality.

Hopefully, one day someone will say that my approach to matchfishing is no longer relevant; that it *is* possible to fish heavier and to attack more. If he or she is correct it will signal the fact that our waterways are much better than they are today. Pollution, in all its pernicious forms, will have been conquered – if it happens.

But the reader must not misunderstand these words: the picture I have painted is not one of total disaster. Of course, there are fewer fish and drawing the right peg has become far more important than it was in the past. We have had to lower our sights and use a different approach. The name of the game is now finesse: we are no longer attackers and plunderers of huge shoals of fish because they are no longer there in such profusion.

In our favour is the fact that we now have superb fishing tackle with which to perform; our carbon rods have taken us light-years forward in ten years; and reels, line and hooks have never been better. Reel failure is almost a thing of the past and we have deadly methods about which our angling fathers and grandfathers knew little or nothing – pole fishing and the swimfeeder to name just two methods that Ivan Marks barely knew about and in fact he did not mention the feeder at all, probably not realising that here was a method which, once perfected, would negate so much of his skill. This will be understood when we discuss bream fishing.

Stillwater fisheries and some canals have escaped the ravages of pollution, and even the waters which have been affected are still quite good fisheries, but have to be approached in a different way. While the match-weights are different, the main objectives are precisely the same as always – to catch more fish than anyone else and win! I go out to win every match I fish and I don't care whether I do it with 0.9 kg (2 lb), 9.0 kg (20 lb) or 18 kg (40 lb). It is very nice to catch a lot of fish, and we often do, but the most important thing for the matchman is the winning of fishing competitions.

When I enter a match my first rule is to decide in advance what weight is likely to win on the venue and then I set out to achieve it. Follow me through a typical Tom Pickering season and you'll see how it's done.

## SUMMER TACTICS

For me, a new season always starts on the Stainforth and Keadby Canal. I am aware that all the readers of this encyclopedia will not be able to fish it but this venue introduces several methods which are relevant to many similar waters up and down the country. There is not enough space here to give comprehensive details about every single method, but I hope to cover as many different and effective styles as possible.

The 'S. and K.' is a real fisherman's water. We who fish it regularly do not expect big weights in matches but it is dependable, with 0.9 kg to 1.8 kg (2 to 4 lb) on every peg, and if you weigh-in 1.8 kg (4 lb) or more you are usually in contention. The three basic methods are waggler float, light ledgering and the pole, and sometimes we employ all three during the course of one match. I have caught a lot of fish here with what are possibly the newest methods in matchfishing. Certainly it employs the newest equipment, a 2.7 m (9 ft) 'wand' ledger rod, very slim and light, and usually equipped with two or three different quivertips, all

*FIG 1* LEDGER-LINK

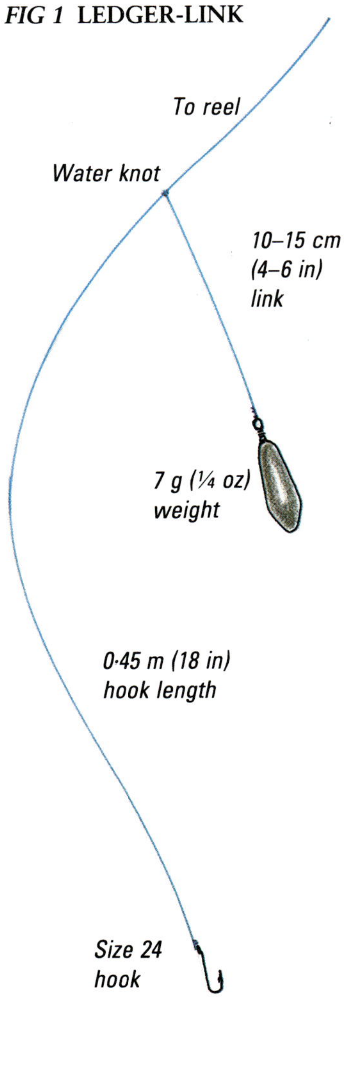


*FIG 1A* QUIVERTIPS

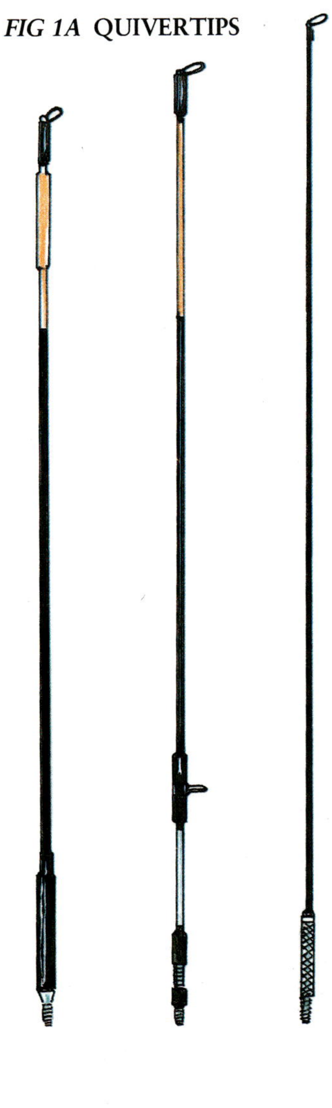

of them extremely sensitive by previous traditional standards. (Figs 1, 1a)

I rig mine up with a 7 g (¼ oz) weight and, usually, a maggot on a Size 24 hook to 340 g (12 oz) line. The weight will be on a 10 to 15 cm (4 to 6 in) link with a hook length of about 46 cm (1 ft 6 in). The bait is cast to a ledge on the far bank to catch mostly small chub and roach, although we can expect skimmer bream and other species.

Many anglers think that this is a method for the slightly cooler days of autumn, but it also works on those summer days when the wind is a bit too strong for easy float-fishing. With the 'wand' ledger rod you can drop the bait in exactly the right place and dip the tip under to sink the line. Dunking the reel-spool in washing-up liquid helps to sink the line quickly, without dislodging the bomb from the far shelf. Then all you do is prop the rod low and to one side, out of the wind, and watch for the bites. It is amazing how those little chub whip the quivertip round! These tips are so sensitive that they will register the tiniest of bites, but the early chub bites tend to be both spectacular and unmissable.

Every few minutes, loose-feed a few maggots with a catapult and for a while you will catch quite a few fish. It is surprising how many small roach, as well as eels and perch, will be taken on the wand, fish which would never register a bite on stronger ledger tackle. The fine, soft tips were designed to register all manner of bites and I deal with them all the same way, striking at the first indication, be it a big pull or a tiny tremor. Only if I miss a couple of bites do I consider ignoring the first slight indication and wait for something more positive.

## THE WAGGLER

Sometimes it is as easy, if not easier, to hit the small-fish bites on the ledger as it is on the float, though I prefer to use the waggler float if I can, at least for a while. On the narrower sections, which are about 15 m (50 ft) wide, I use a 3BB or 2AAA peacock-quill waggler with the fine insert in the tip. This float is weighted down so that only part of the insert is showing on the surface, and it will be cast to the far shelf, the same place as the ledger tackle. (Figs 2, 2a, p. 56)

Virtually all the weight the float takes is on the line, either side of the float, with very little down the line. If by plumbing the depth I find I have 0.9 m (3 ft) of water I will place a tiny No. 10 weight about 0.3 m (1 ft) from the hook. Any deeper and I will have a second No. 10 set at about half-depth, with the other still 0.3 m (1 ft) from the hook. Again, it is important to treat the line with washing-up liquid to help it sink. Immediately after the cast I let a little bow develop on the surface, and then without moving the float off-line chop the line under with a sharp sideways movement of the rod.

A lot of fish, especially chub, will be taken as the bait sinks slowly down along with the loose feed, although some bites will also come after it has reached bottom. The main reason for the float out-scoring the ledger is

***Fig 1*** **Matchfishing is a specialised and hard-learned skill based on much sensitivity of fined-down rigs. See how the bait on the Size 24 hook can act naturally.** ***Fig 1A*** **The lightning speed of quivertips aids the matchman to an extent unknown not very long ago. In all matchfishing, speed and accuracy are total necessities.**

**Tom Pickering strikes powerfully into a chub while ledgering on the Trent.**

*FIG 2* WAGGLER RIG

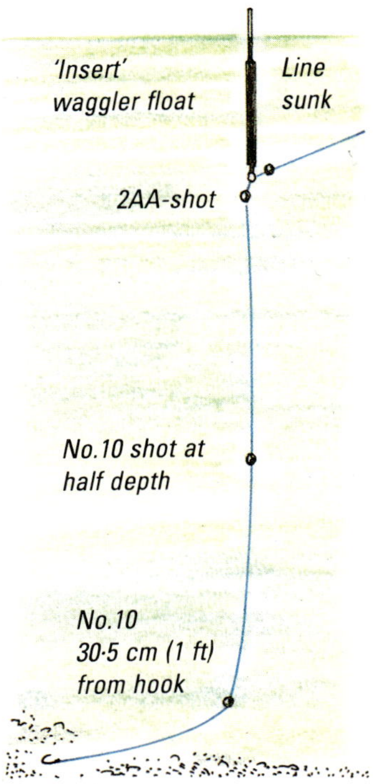


*FIG 2A* WAGGLER FLOAT

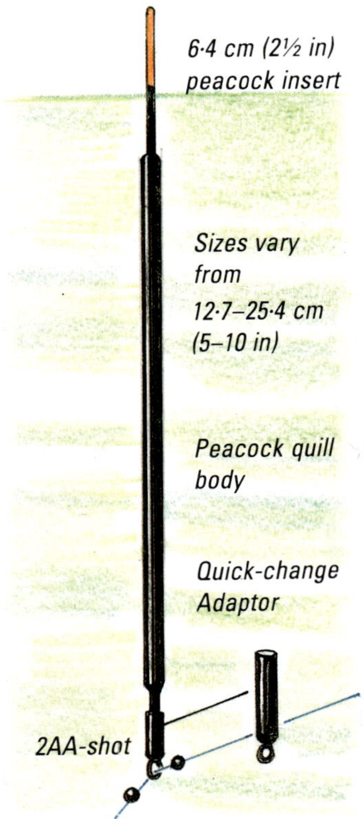


**Figs 2, 2A** One of the most sensitive float patterns, the waggler comes in many sizes. All are attached to the line by the bottom end only. Most are made from peacock quill.

**Fig 3** Groundbait and fish the far shelf at first. Some will trickle down the slope to the foot of the shelf. Fish here when bites begin to drop off from the original target area.

**Float fishing is the most used matchfishing method although in big rivers, where the feeder has proved a winning technique, ledgering has almost taken over.**

*FIG 3* FISHING THE FAR SHELF

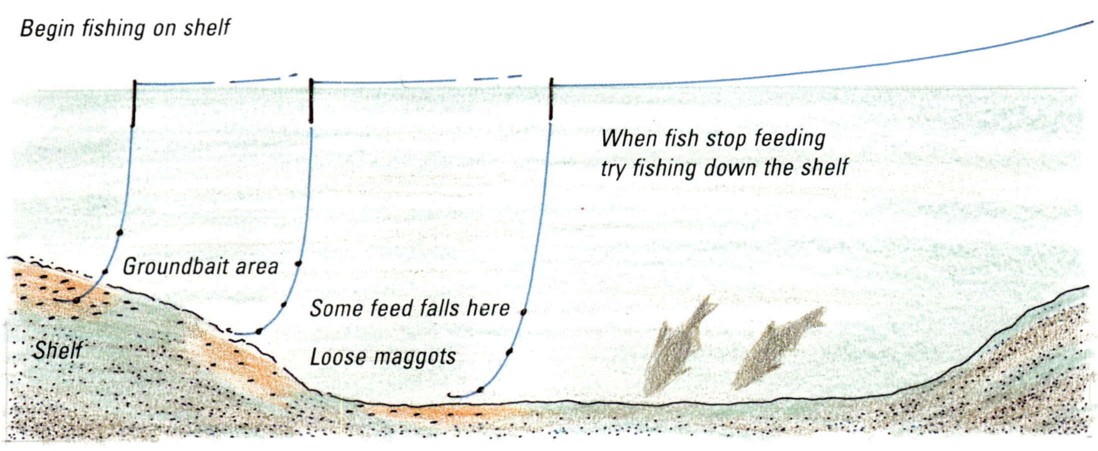


that you can twitch the float slightly, causing the bait to lift and drop down. This small movement often provokes a bite, but when you try this with the ledger the bomb will be pulled out of position. You are also likely to hook rubbish.

When you sprinkle loose maggots on the far shelf some will drop short, into the deeper water at the bottom of the shelf. This is quite all right, for I have found that the fish will find them and come down from the shelf, and then the bites will slow down. When that happens I deepen the float to fish right at the bottom, which usually produces a few more fish. It is surprising how many roach and skimmer bream are congregated down there, and at times chub can be found in the same place.

When the bites stop coming from below the ledge, shorten off again and go back to the ledge. On this water, and on a great many others, never persist too long with a method which has stopped working. Keep switching around and work for your fish. This basic approach will be the same on wider sections of the canal, but I might need a bigger float and more weight. (Fig. 3)

Do not seek for variations of the waggler float method. It works on a variety of waters, from canals, ponds and lakes to drains and slow-to-medium-flowing rivers, but it is virtually always used in the same way. You need enough weight locking the float on the line to cast the required distance, and very little weight down the line. It is a method for catching fish on the drop at any depth.

The wagglers are a big family of floats, all attached bottom-end only, which range in weight-carrying capacity from a couple of No. 4s right up to three swan and more. But I do virtually all my waggler work with peacock-quill floats taking from 2AAA to 3AAA lead-substitute weights.

## THE POLE

The third method which is vital on the S. and K. Canal is the pole, a style of fishing which can take thousands of words to describe. Here I can do little more than summarise why the pole is so deadly within a range of 15 m (50 ft), and give a few examples of the method in action.

The pole offers the angler a chance to fish with light tackle under close and perfect control. The bites are easy to hit, partly because the little floats offer very little resistance and partly because the end of the pole is directly above the float and a gentle lift is all it takes to set the hook. The pole fishes the float in exactly the same place every time, although you can go up to a metre (about 3 ft) farther out or in by adding or removing a section. Short poles can be rigged up with a length of line which allows a hooked fish to be swung directly to hand. With a longer pole you have to feed some of it behind you – usually using a roller – and take it apart ('unshipping') at the right length to either swing to hand or net your fish.

There are ingenious systems employing elastic, running through the tip sections of the pole, which act as a shock-absorber when you strike and play a fish. There are different grades of elastic to suit the sizes of fish you are expecting to catch and you have got it right if the fish you are catching are heavy enough to pull a bit of elastic out of the end of the pole. The stronger elastics are absolutely brilliant at controlling and playing out big fish. Even quite sizeable carp are in trouble against the stronger elastic but you see the system at its best, probably, when you hook a bream. The progressive power of the elastic will usually take the fight out of the bream on its first run, then the fish slows down, stops, and comes back to the angler's net, on its side and quite unresisting. Species such as carp and tench take a lot longer, many making ever-shorter runs before they are beaten.

Many anglers who took one look at the pole and decided they wanted nothing to do with the method are now dedicated converts. It grows on one, it's addictive, but the bottom line is that it is often *the* best way of catching the fish. The case for the pole is so overwhelming in the match-angling context that virtually every matchman now has at least one. Poles can cost several hundred pounds for good-quality carbon, with some reaching four figures, but as always in fishing, go for the best tackle you can afford. My advice is to aim for an 11 m (36 ft) carbon pole. Don't start with a glass pole, they are cheap but

**Modern, ultra-lightweight poles, even 14 m (46 ft) long, can be held throughout an average match. Perfect balance is vital.**

heavy, and you will end up buying a carbon in the long run. But let us get back to that canal!

The pole methods I use for the S. and K. Canal are fairly standard for a lot of waters. On all canals, drains, still-waters and even slow rivers one of the most effective pole methods is the slow-falling bait, just as described for the waggler on the canal. The big difference between pole and waggler, though, is that the waggler has to be reeled in and re-cast at regular intervals. With the pole you can just lift out and lay the line down again. It becomes an endless routine which puts the bait to the fish and keeps it where they are for vastly longer periods than can be achieved with the waggler. The equation is thus: More effective fishing time equals more bites, which equals more fish!

Within the limitations imposed by its length the pole is virtually unbeatable in many situations, though on the S. and K. it tends to be part of a varied approach. One rig I use has a small float taking three No. 8 shot, and a second float a bit heavier, taking three No. 6 shot. That is the overall capacity of the floats, anyway, but both are rigged with a No. 10 shot near the hook and an 8 above it. Whatever else is required to sink the float down on to the bristle tip is strung out evenly along the line above the No. 8. As before, the hook length will be 340 g (12 oz) and the hook probably a No. 24 or 22. (Figs 4, 4a)

I loose-feed maggot or caster to the 9–10 m (30–32 ft) mark and fish as described with the slow-falling baits. As before, the feed will be a bit scattered, so when the bites cease at, say, 9 m (30 ft), I either add another metre (or a few feet) and go farther out, or perhaps detach a pole section and fish nearer.

I share the time between the pole, the ledger and the waggler, trying all the variations I have described and in this way keep busy. I'm feeding pole and far bank swims constantly – an absolute must – but by switching from one method to another after catching two or three fish I rest one of the swims and increase my chances of keeping the fish coming to the net. Very low weights usually make the difference on this canal and the winner is usually the angler who keeps the fish coming to the keepnet right to the end of the match.

## THE RIVER WITHAM

The Witham, one of the waters which has declined through pollution, has a long and glorious history as a prolific bream and roach water and it still holds these species. For the matchman, at certain times and certain places the winner will need weights of one or the other of these shoaling species.

I watch the summer Witham match results in particular for bream catches, noting from where they have been taken. If bream have been winning recently and I have drawn a peg in the right place I will fish for them but I have to admit that I hope the bream have not been showing. When they are absent in summer the scene is set for my favourite summer sport – Witham eel fishing.

If the reader copies my Witham method on any water where eels can influence the outcome of a match he will

*FIG 4* LIGHT POLE RIG

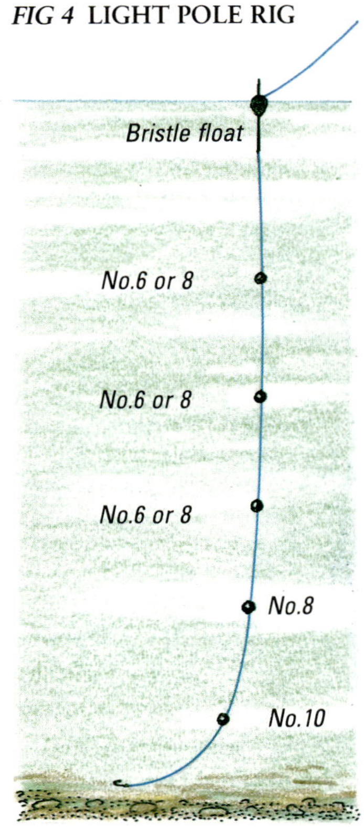


*FIG 4A* POLE FLOATS

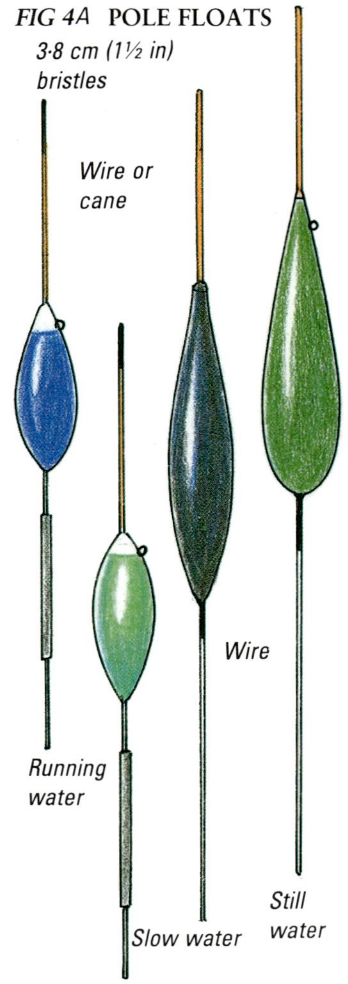


*Fig 4* Dace never need heavy treatment. This light pole rig for dace gives delicacy but sureness in detecting lightning-fast bites. *Fig 4A* A selection of pole floats.

find them easy to catch. In my experience fishing for eels is only difficult on the River Witham. After years of hard thinking I am not a lot nearer to understanding why this is so, but I do know a lot about the problems and how to overcome them.

The main difficulty lies in hitting the bites. While I am reasonably confident about virtually catching every eel that takes my bait on other waters it is totally different here. If I hit one in three I feel that I am doing very well. Sometimes I get it wrong and will be driven to despair, missing nine out of ten or even 19 out of 20. Why? Because the bites vary so much. Bites which come on the drop are rare, but hittable. So are the few which take the float under and keep on going.

More difficult is the bite which takes the float under and holds it there for a few seconds. You have to wait until it comes up and goes down again, and keeps on going before you can strike with any hope of success. One essential therefore is a float you can see under the surface. It must have a brightly coloured top or bristle insert, to be precise, for I almost always use the pole to fish for Witham eels. There is one impossible type of bite which takes the float under a short way and just holds it there. This bite is caused by tiny bootlace eels and if I get a lot of these bites I start to feed heavily, trying to fill these little nuisances with food and, at the same time, to attract bigger eels into the swim.

The tackle is simple enough; a pole rigged with No. 5 elastic, 0.9 kg (2 lb) main line, 5 kg (11 lb) hook-length and a small hook, usually a No. 22, but it can be a 24 if I am having more than the usual amount of trouble with the bites. Part of the trouble, I believe, is that the eels take the maggot sideways in their mouths and the smaller the hook the better is the chance I have with the strike.

The hook is usually a Mustad 90340 barbless, which is light but quite strong. I use barbless hooks because when they can be seen they are easier to remove. Taking a leaf out of the big-eel specialist's book, I break the line if the hook is not visible, because it is better to cut the line than to risk damaging the eel by poking around in its mouth with a disgorger. Eels can swallow hooks without harm and eventually get rid of them.

Float selection depends upon whether the water is still or moving. It will either be a river-float designed for slow flows (round-topped, tapering body) or a stillwater float (pointed-top body which fattens towards the base). In perfect conditions I prefer to use one taking about 0.5 g (1/50 oz) of weight overall, though it could be as big as a 1.5 g (1/20 oz) if the wind is tricky.

The half-gramme float is perfect and I use the equivalent weight in split-shot, three or four No. 6 shots together about 1 m (3 ft 6 in) from the hook, with a Size 10 0.3 m (1 ft) from the hook and a No. 8 0.3 m (1 ft) above that. There is also a No. 10 just under the float as a depth marker and it is all rigged to fish about 152 mm (6 in) over-depth. (Fig. 5)

At times this rig will catch eels when the bait is allowed to trundle slowly through with the flow, but I usually hold the float dead-still. When a bite starts to develop I move the pole toward the float to create a bit of slack line, for if the bite develops quickly the eel will feel the resistance and let go. That applies anywhere and to any species, but it is particularly important with Witham eels. Usually I have 0.9–1.2 m (3–4 ft) of line between pole tip and float which, given the average depth of the Witham, allows me to fish with a long-enough length of line overall, suitable for a 5 m (17 ft) pole.

Any more length I need is added to that and I unship the pole to 5 m (17 ft) to land the eels. As always in match-fishing it pays to feed two lines, whenever it is possible. When fishing the River Witham I feed at 11 m (36 ft) and 8 m (26 ft), expecting to catch the majority of eels from the far swim. The close swim is mainly used to give the far swim the occasional rest. It always produces a few fish, but on some occasions, for some reason, the near swim can yield more than the far line.

Feeding, always the key to match-angling success, is critical for Witham eels, but the formula is fairly simple. When you are catching eels go sparingly with the loose-fed maggots, for there is no point in giving them too much and filling them up. I have had my biggest totals, including four eel catches into double figures, by feeding only 1.1 l (2 pints) of bait over five hours.

Conversely, if the fish are not there, or are there but not feeding, I will feed much more heavily to attract them into the swim or to encourage them to have a go. Once they are feeding, I cut back to a rate of about 20 to 25 maggots per cast. The heavier feeding disposes of more than 1.1 l (2

Within the limitations imposed by its length, the pole is virtually unbeatable in many situations. Bait can be put out and held in a position where the fish are far better than could be achieved with a conventional rod.

*FIG 5* WITHAM EEL RIG

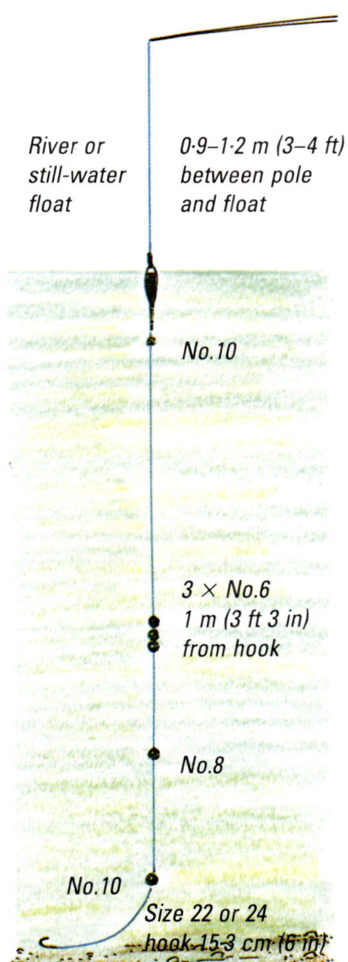


*Fig 5* Tom Pickering finds eel bites on the River Witham vary so much they are difficult to hit, they differ all the time. So he devised this simple rig and now has no trouble in adding eels to his match-weight.

pints) so it pays to carry 2.8 l (5 pints) altogether. And do not forget the closer-in swim, it needs feeding too, at about half the rate chosen for the far swim.

## DACE ON THE WARWICKSHIRE AVON

If there is one summer activity which rivals eel fishing for sheer enjoyment it is dace fishing on the Warwickshire Avon at or near Evesham. I have always loved dace fishing of course, but doing it on my favourite river is a pleasure doubled. I find plenty of excuses to fish this river, even making the trip for mid-week match series and taking the family along for the ride.

Some of the biggest successes early in my career came on the Avon and it would not worry me if I had to fish there and nowhere else for the rest of my time. It is so much like the Stainforth and Keadby Canal in two key ways – you need to keep really busy to win, and to use several key methods. Indeed there are four which are all relevant: the pole, the waggler, the float and the feeder. I rig all four up, every time, and usually use them all, feeding a line for each method I want to use, relatively close in for the stick-float or pole, farther out for the waggler and farther out still for the feeder, endlessly switching about between them.

Just like the S. and K. Canal, the winners on the Warwickshire Avon are not usually more than a little weight ahead of the place-men. The keys to success are exploiting each method to maximum potential, and knowing when to rest each swim. Usually I start close in, with light pole tackle, a string of evenly spaced No. 8s and a 10 nearest the hook. If you are going to catch fish close-in it is usually early in the match and on the pole I expect to take them on a slowly falling bait.

As soon as the tackle has sunk to full depth I lift out and lay the tackle on the surface again. It should be dropped in a straight line downstream, with the baited hook sinking among constant loose feed.

You can expect a bite anywhere in this river, from right on the surface to the full depth, so keep the eyes firmly fixed on the float, which will slowly cock as each weight registers and finally settle down so that only part of the bristle shows up top. Strike if the behaviour of the float differs in any way from the norm. It may not settle as soon as it should at any given point: it may flicker slightly or simply zoom away. Strike at any indication. Dace are fast biters which do not give too many chances. (Fig. 6)

I fish with the pole until the bites cease, then take up the rod and the stick-float rig to explore the same line but farther down, in the area which I cannot reach with the pole. The shotting pattern will be the same, aimed at catching on the drop until the rig sinks to full depth, and from the bottom or close to it. (Fig. 6a)

Success in stick-float fishing depends on several factors, including correct casting and good control as the float progresses down the swim. The aim should be to cast so that the tackle lands in line downstream, as described for the pole. If it lands in a heap the bait sinks too quickly and less naturally.

*FIG* 6 AVON RIG

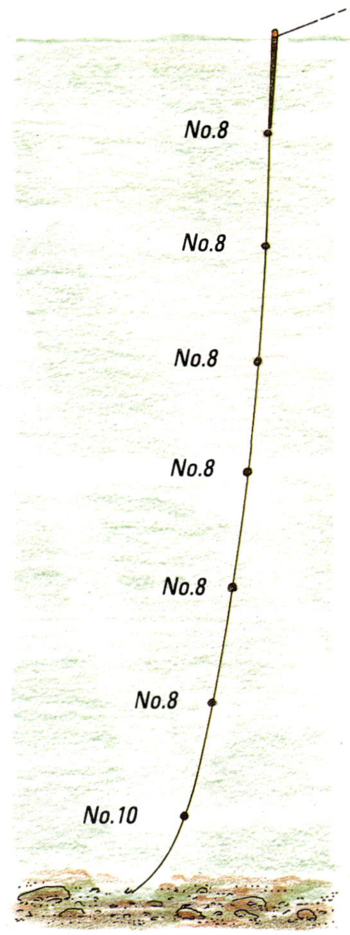


*FIG* 6A STICK FLOAT

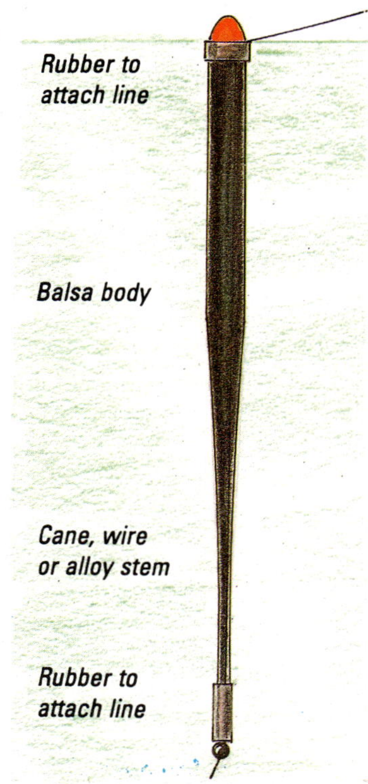


*Fig 6* The Warwickshire Avon is scene of many of Pickering's wins and this rig explains why. *Fig 6A* The stick float demands accuracy in casting.

At one time the need to slow the float down below the spread of the current was stressed, but I do not know a water these days which does not respond best to speed of current presentation. Just let the float run through, watching for bites on the drop, or lift-and-go-under bites after the tackle has sunk to full depth. The only control required is to keep the line as straight as possible between rod tip and float – tricky, sometimes, in a wind.

If you allow the bow in the line to develop the float will eventually skate off-line and you will not get a bite. Bows in the line are corrected by trapping the line as it comes off the spool and quickly lifting the line to straighten it. If you cannot correct a bow by doing that the chances are that you need a bigger float carrying more weight, a stick-float variation, one which has a wire stem instead of heavy cane, or an alloy-stemmed float such as the John Allerton stick. The wire stem is more stable, but designed really for more turbulent waters than the Warwickshire Avon offers and Allerton's float has a small shoulder near the tip which grips the current better.

Go for more weight or greater stability whenever stick-float control becomes more difficult. Always shot right down so a mere pimple of the tip is showing, for with too much sticking up you will miss bites. One tactic which unfailingly attracts bites is to check the float now and again by stopping the line coming off the reel spool, causing the bait to rise and often provoking a take. A pattern begins to emerge when you are catching plenty of fish on the stick.

**Building a catch is all about rhythm: feed the swim, bait up, cast out, fish through and repeat the sequence, all the time noting the catch rate to build a bag continuously through the match period.**

You will get to know where in the swim the majority of bites are coming from and checking the float at that point can be absolutely deadly; the float will stop and go under in the same instant.

It is doubtful, however, whether you will reach that situation in the near swim on the Avon, but it should be possible to add a few fish to those taken on the pole. Sooner or later you will be struggling for bites, and now is the time to switch to the waggler-float line, which should be fed by hand or catapult all the time you are feeding and fishing the near line.

The longer I can catch fish close-in the happier I am, for the waggler swim will be building up nicely with dace and, hopefully, species such as skimmers and chub feeding with ever-growing confidence. This is from where the bulk of the catch is going to come and I always feel a thrill of anticipation when I finally make the switch.

Although the methods are totally different there are similarities in the way the fish are caught on waggler and stick-float. While the latter float is attached top and bottom with silicone rubber sleeves it is rigged to fish a fairly slow-falling bait. The waggler, always attached bottom-end only, is rigged to fish an even slower fall. On the Avon it will probably be carrying no more than a No. 10 near the hook and one or two BBs above it.

The line is usually sunk when I am waggler fishing on stillwater and canals. On most rivers, it can pay to leave the line up on the surface, for this ensures a cleaner and more effective strike. Small-to-medium-sized bows which develop are not enough to drag the float off-line and they do not hamper the strike if the angler does it properly. It takes a long, smooth sweep of the rod to take up the bow and hit the fish. Sometimes you have to take the rod through a full 180 deg. and quite often you do not know if you have hooked the fish until you start reeling in.

Only if there is a very strong wind, especially one blowing downstream and in, is there a need to sink the line, but on the Avon this is rare. My float is not usually in long enough for bad bows to develop. In effect I am fishing similarly to the way the pole is used here, with a re-cast the moment the tackle has sunk to full depth. For some reason, Avon dace rarely take a bait at full depth, so for them one has to be constantly casting and striking. Occasionally I let the bait trundle through on the bottom in the hope of picking up another species, perhaps a roach, chub or skimmer bream.

All the time I am fishing the waggler line I will be trickling loose feed into the near line, preparing to give the main swim a rest if I sense that the fish are starting to become shy. Leaving the swim alone for a while rebuilds their confidence.

On the Warwickshire Avon and, indeed, the majority of other rivers, it is wrong to flog one swim to death, but it is a common-enough error. Only if I am struggling to catch enough from the first two swims will I resort to the feeder in the hope of connecting with some bonus fish such as chub, but this is a method I will deal with at some length, under different headings, starting with the next section which concerns summer bream.

## SUMMER BREAM

I like to think that a typical Tom Pickering summer will include at least one chance at a shoal of good-sized bream. With great respect to bream enthusiasts, however, I reckon this is the easiest game in fishing, though it used to be vastly more skilful than it is today. The great equaliser has been the swimfeeder.

Billy Lane and Freddie Foster could throw large balls of bait, packed with feeder maggots or casters, with pinpoint accuracy out to the distances often required on waters such as the Welland, Middle Level and Relief Channel. They therefore had to temper their accuracy with caution. Dropping big balls of groundbait on to the heads of feeding bream usually drove the fish away, so they tried to put the feed in when the bream weren't there and to get as much on the bottom as they could in order to attract and hold a wandering shoal.

Bream fishing in those days was a game of chess played by grand masters, usually with the pawns just there for ritual sacrifice, that plus the hope of becoming king one day, just as soon as they found out how it was done.

But almost overnight the pawns stopped being rookies, due to the arrival of a simple tube of plastic, dotted with holes, weighted with a strip of lead and rigged to fish on a link in place of the once universal Arlesey bomb. Enter the swim-feeder, and suddenly everyone who could cast with any accuracy was able to place feed in the right place, and for some reason the bream did not object to a falling feeder as they once did to a big ball of bait. Instead, the fish seemed mesmerised by the constant arrival of food.

Nowadays it is the matchman who can draw the bream, not he who can keep them the longest and catch the most. Everybody is a bream angler, with the quivertip usurping the role of the swingtip, which effectively died with Freddie Foster. Some still use the method which Freddie did more than anyone to popularise, and it is still deadly in the right hands and in the right places. But casting with the quivertip is easier, and it can do everything which the swingtip could do and more besides.

I cannot see what is difficult about bream fishing these days, certainly on still and slow waters. For good-sized bream of, say, 0.9 to 1.8 kg (2 to 4 lb) all you need is an open-end groundbait feeder on a 23 cm (9 in) link fixed to the main line, a hook length of 1.2 to 1.5 m (4 to 5 ft) and the patience to wait for the action. The long tail ensures that the bream will usually have the bait well inside its mouth before it swims far enough for a bite to register on the quivertip. By that time the strike is a mere formality. If you fish with a short tail for sizeable bream you will miss bites and even lose some of the fish you manage to hook. (Fig. 7)

Since bream do not fight very hard, light line of 0.45 to 0.7 kg (1 to 1 lb 8 oz) is all right, and hooks should be small. Size 20 or 22 are now the norm, with 24s if the fish are a bit on the shy side. Many of the modern Continental groundbaits are formulated for bream, so you can choose whichever takes your fancy. In my opinion they all work best used as half-and-half mixes with ordinary breadcrumb groundbait, the effect is the same and it is more economical. The ration of feed to groundbait is no longer critical, nor is the consistency of the mix, because feeders no longer break up in the air in the way those badly constructed balls of groundbait once did! Today, most anglers seem to mix feeder groundbait on the dry side to make sure that it is washed out more quickly. There is now no need for really heavy mixes to get it down fast.

Where to cast the feeder demands thought. If I do not know the swim I will cast around with an empty feeder, counting as it sinks to find a slightly deeper area or a shelf. If I do find some kind of feature, a hole or ledge, I will settle on that area and then concentrate on laying a carpet of feed on it. You can do this just by casting and retrieving a packed feeder for a while, and unlike those old-time matchmen I do not worry whether there are bream in residence to start with because these fish accept feeders as part of the scenery. (Figs 8, 8a)

If these bream were there at the start of the match they are there for a reason; they got to the peg long before I did and they are likely to stay. The constant casting and bait delivery simply encourages them to feed, and they no longer react adversely to a splashy bombardment of biggish balls thrown in by hand. On most bream venues I mix about six orange-sized balls packed with casters, unless I have reason to believe the bream on a given water do not like this bait. Most bream do, but there are some places, Holme Pierrepont, Notts, is one, where they prefer pinkies

*FIG 7* **SUMMER BREAM RIG**

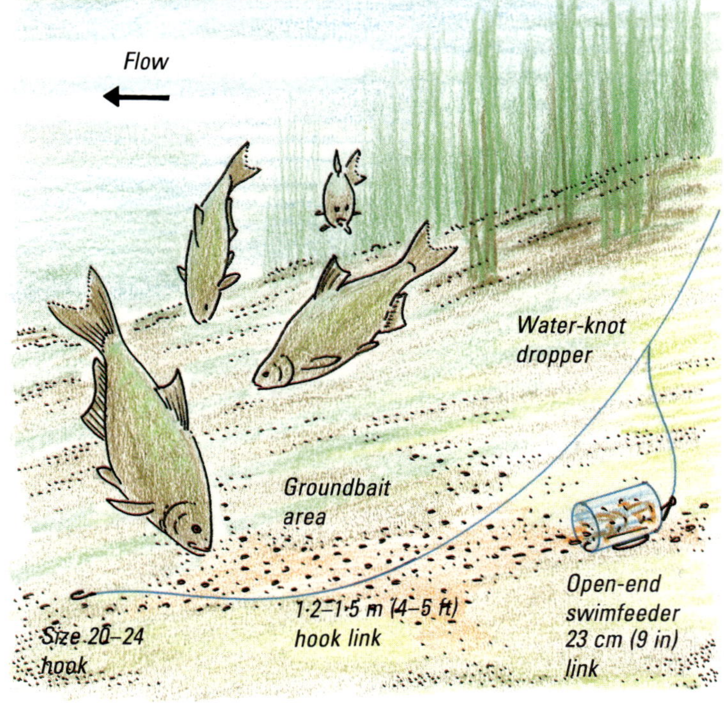


or squatts. I like a bit of everything as a rule, including samples of the hookbait.

Do not overload the groundbait with feed or it will not throw without breaking up. One useful insurance against this possibility is to wet the hands before throwing. Remoulding the balls with wet hands seals the outside and helps it hold together through the air. If you have a good-enough arm, throw them, or make the balls the right size to be catapulted if you know that you cannot make the distance by hand.

Pin-point accuracy may be the aim but you will never achieve it, nor is it desirable. After all, you will not get 22.8 kg (50 lb) of bream off a small pile of bait. A good shoal occupies quite a large area of water and it does no harm to spread the bait over a reasonable area.

Once the area is baited you will be adding to it with every cast with the feeder, but do not get too busy with casting. It is a matter of patience and we are looking, initially, for some positive sign of the presence of bream. As a rule, the first sign is a line bite – a quick rattle of the quivertip as a bream swims into the line. Try to avoid the temptation to strike at this, but you probably will, quite instinctively. To strike at the first movements is automatic, but when you have missed a couple and noted that the bait has not been touched you know what is going on. From then on you can ignore the little plucks and tweaks and wait for something more positive to develop.

When the fish are feeding well there is no mistaking the genuine bites. The tip will go round and stay there, whereas the line bite will take it round and let it spring back again just as quickly. One of the main attributes of a good bream angler is having the patience to watch the tip go and to wait for it to stay or spring back. Thanks to that long hook-link he will know that he is going to get the fish if he waits. He also knows that it is a time-wasting re-cast if he strikes too soon and misses. Recognising the true bites, and hitting them all, is what matchfishing is all

*Fig 7* **The matchman who can draw the bream can win the match and the quivertip will play its part. But the terminal tackle and particularly the feeder must be right. Keep the groundbait coming and include some hookbait with it. Bream nudging the line can cause the senses to flutter, but resist the temptation to strike at each pluck.**

*FIG 8* GROUNDBAITING TECHNIQUES

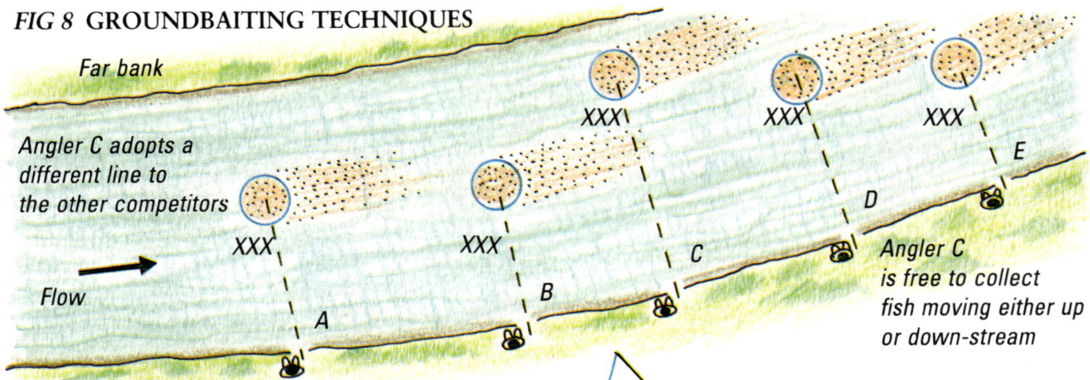


*FIG 8A* A DEFINED 'KILLING GROUND'

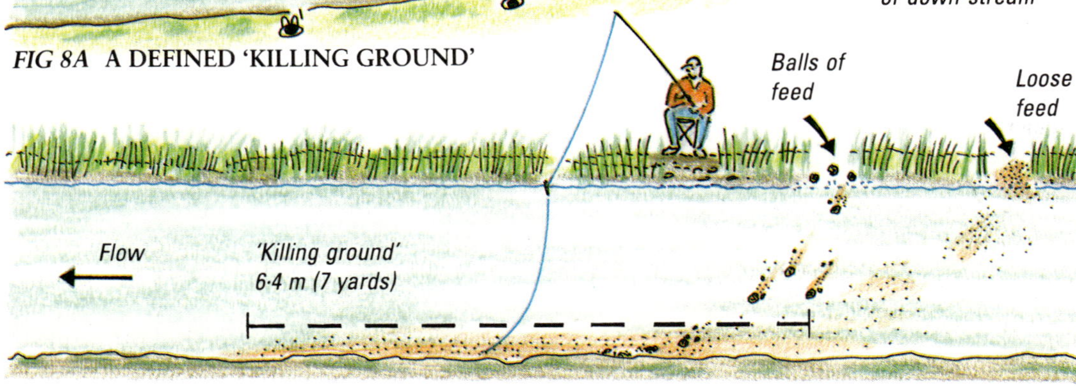


*Figs 8, 8A* **Aimlessly hurling in balls of groundbait will achieve little. Watch what the pegs either side are doing, then select your own spot. Their groundbait can well bring fish to your hook.**

about. Just as small weights win canal matches, one extra bream wins a lot of big-weight matches.

Given a swim full of feeding bream the foregoing is just about all there is to it, but if I have been sitting at the peg for a long time without any indication of the presence of bream I will try to attract some on to feed by adding one or two hand-thrown balls of bait. Sometimes the sight of groundbait clouding down will attract a passing shoal, or a single fish which may have been hanging about on the edge of the action.

Another tip is to fill the feeder from the bottom of your groundbait container rather than from the top, for the feed maggots work themselves down below the upper layer. Conversely, take it from the top for hand-throwing or mix it all up thoroughly. You can have too many feeder maggots falling in a ball for throwing but it can pay to add lots more to groundbait used through the feeder. Sometimes the extra feeder maggots falling through the water persuade the bream to feed. Often it only takes two or three to start feeding and then the others join in. Whoever compared bream with sheep was not far off the mark.

## WINTER BREAM

While the method described in the previous section is about right for summer bream it needs scaling down for autumn and winter, when these fish become more finicky. Very probably they will not take the arrival of six big balls of bait without being spooked. Instead, I usually have six casts with a large-capacity swimfeeder.

These bream do not usually feed so voraciously in the colder months, so overdoing the baiting can give them so much choice that your hookbait has less chance of being taken. You need to be in with a chance when a hungry bream is looking for food, but you have to tailor your approach and expectations to the venue.

You might be on a winner with two or three bream. What many anglers do not realise is that a bite every half-hour means, if you hit them all, ten bream in the net in five hours. If they are 0.9 to 1.3 kg (2 to 3 lb) fish the weights will total about 9 to 13.6 kg (20 to 30 lb), weights which are not usual in winter. Ten bites in a match is slow going, but it is usually a great deal fewer.

In winter, bites can be a lot less emphatic, too. You might just get the odd spectacular pull-round, but more likely is a tiny pluck. Do not worry about identifying line bites, the winter rule is that you strike at any indication. The fish do not move about as much, so the winter approach involves using a hook-length of about half the summer length and usually a shorter link-length as well.

## FAST-WATER BREAM

By fast water I mean rivers with more pace than the slow-flowing Fenland rivers such as the Witham and the Lower Welland. The classic example is the Trent, which on current form stands a chance of becoming the finest bream river we have seen for generations. Just about every match reported on the Trent on the opening weekend of the 1989–90 season was won with bream. The weights included 25 kg (55 lb) at Holme Marsh, 20 kg (44 lb) at Winthorpe, six weights over 13.6 kg (30 lb) and two over 12.3 kg (27 lb) in one match at Winthorpe/Holme Marsh and 21.5 kg (47 lb) at Shelford. Few matches were won with less than 9 kg (20 lb).

Virtually all these weights were taken on groundbait feeders, fished very much in the way I have described, except for one small detail: you have to be able to cope with the fact that the feeder needs to carry enough weight to just hold in the flow. It could be 14 g (½ oz) of lead strip (under legislation, lead is legal as an integral part of a feeder) for the non-tidal Trent in normal flow to 85 g (3 oz) plus in the tidal river or in heavy flows on the non-tidal. The light-to-medium feeder rods which cope on

*A* Probably the most significant advances in matchfishing have been the ledgering techniques applied and the use of swimfeeders, accessories which provide a continuous baiting process ensuring that both feed and hookbait lie in the same position on the riverbed.
*B* Removable weights of various sizes allow swimfeeders to be weighted to exactly suit the speed of current and casting distances needed to get the bait among the fish. *C* Fish clear up the feeder maggots but are still capable of sucking out the body juices of the hookbait.
*D* Tom connects and holds his chub at an alarming distance of 27 m (30 yards), drawing it carefully and with the minimum of excitement away

*A*

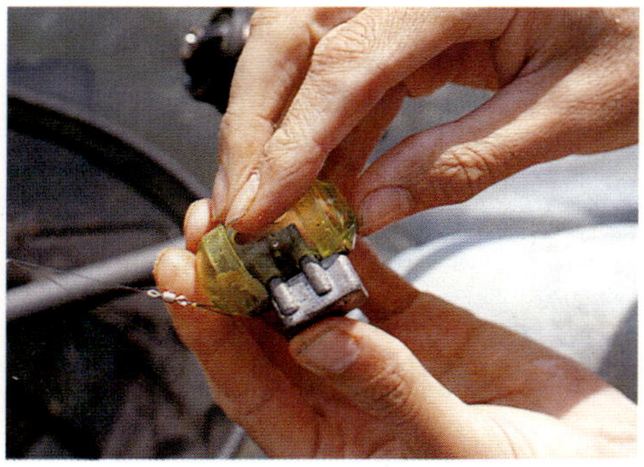

*B*

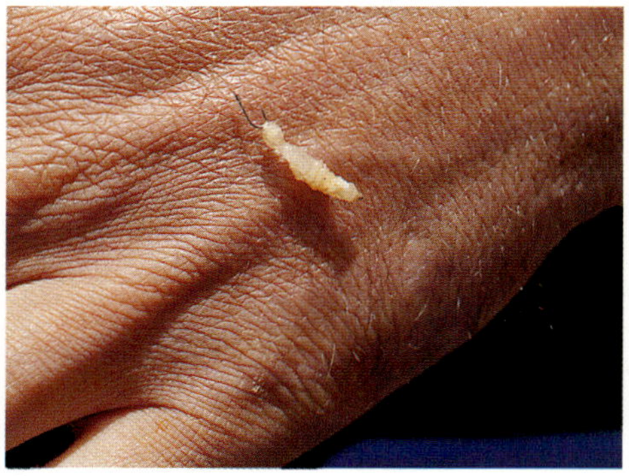

*C*

stillwaters and slow rivers are no use for casting more than 28 g (1 oz), so you need something with more power and a stiffer tip.

There are so many feeder techniques that the method rates a book on its own, something that I would like to do. In this book there is room only to discuss one or two methods ranging from the mere crude to the deadly clever. In the former category is the use of a very heavy feeder and a small hook to a shortish tail of about 0.6 m (2 ft). The idea is that when a fish of whatever species or size picks the bait up and turns downstream it is stopped immediately in its tracks by the weight of the feeder.

When fish feel resistance, they usually eject the bait, but in the case of the heavy feeder they have no chance. The combination of heavy weight and small, sharp hook ensures that the fish hook themselves. They rattle the quivertip and then get reeled in. It is effective, but whether is it proper fishing is a matter for debate! The method has accounted for some huge match totals of chub, bream and barbel, but it works better in the faster swims than in the slower sections. The main problem with this method is the smash-take from bigger fish which can break the hook-length against their weight. This led to the introduction of power gum shock-absorbers into the terminal rig.

The main, and more enjoyable alternative is to use a longer tail and a feeder which is more balanced to the flow. I cast-in with an empty feeder, trying to find what weight is just enough to hold bottom. There are clip-on weights of varying sizes if the feeder is too light, or trim weights down if it is too heavy. Do not make feeder selection with a loaded one. You need to know that the feeder will not move when its groundbait load has washed out, and that when it does move the probable cause is a bite. This can only be found out if the feeder is empty.

To some extent the type of bite registration is dictated by the flow. In the slower sections of a swim it is likely to be a pull on the tip, which could be slight or pronounced. Strike at either indication, but wait for more positive pulls if you miss when striking those little knocks. In the faster sections the bite is likely to dislodge the feeder, causing the quivertip to wag like the tail of a dog, and these bites are hard to miss.

In theory, the fish should feel resistance and let go the hook, but it does not seem to if the feeder is properly balanced to the flow. This is because the feeder is dropping downstream with the fish, which either does not feel it or cannot get rid of the hook anyway, due to the tension between hook and feeder making the bait impossible to eject. Whatever the reason, there are no smash-offs with this method, for there is not enough resistance for the fish to exploit.

## WINTER CHUB

Up to now we have discussed groundbait feeders only, and while chub sometimes turn up among the bream-attracting groundbait this feeding is usually a chub deterrent. The species does not like it, responding better to feed in the form of loose maggots. When the chub were more widespread in the Trent than they are today the killing method was blockend feeder with a maggot/hemp/caster mixture. This is virtually the same as the groundbait feeder but is sealed at the downstream end, with a removable cap at the upper end to enable the feeder to be filled.

When used properly the maggot feeder is deadly in its efficiency and it is just as effective in the streamier areas into which the chub seem to have retreated. They also congregate in slower areas where snags abound, and for the matchman drawing the peg adjoining a shoal of resident chub tends to be a frustrating experience. The fish will seldom take any interest. Barbel, too, have their preferred areas, though the experts say the fish will move around as the river rises and falls, looking for the pace of water which best suits them.

D

E

F

from the feeding shoal. Letting the fish splash about in the feeding area would result in fish rapidly leaving the swim.
*E* With a finger poised to check any last frantic dash and with the net well sunk, a chub is eased towards the net rim.
*F* A small chub, but they all count and if kept coming out at 0.34–0.45 kg (12 oz–1 lb) can contribute to a winning total.

The blockend feeder, preferably loaded with casters, is the best way to catch Trent barbel, and most of what I have to say about chub on the maggot feeder is also applicable to barbel. Indeed the method applies to both species in summer as well as in winter. Sadly, I do not get round to the Trent in summer these days, mainly because I am too busy fishing elsewhere, mostly with the all-important National Championship, invitation matches and other team events.

What feeders essentially do is to provide the matchman with the opportunity to place bait accurately in one place, while at the same time attracting fish from downstream. A feeder starts to lose maggots as soon as it hits the water and continues to do so all the time it is sinking. The bulk of the maggots stay in until it hits bottom but the early escapees drift to the end of the peg and beyond, bringing new fish to replace those being caught.

On good days this is an endless procession of fish. They will sometimes come right up to the feeder itself and shake it to release more bait! In the early stages, therefore, the fish can be caught on a very short hook-length, but you must be prepared to lengthen it if the bites slow down. That usually means that the chub have become wary and have dropped downstream. You need to get the hookbait farther away from the feeder, and a longer tail gives the bait a more natural fall and some bites will come before it hits bottom.

I usually cast to about a third of the way down the peg. It can pay in the later stages of a match to make the last few casts farther downstream to take the fish which have dropped right down. Do not try this too soon, for it eventually kills the swim, but the tactic is usually effective for a late burst of top-up fish.

Bites will vary from savage pulls on the short hook-length to less impressive indications on the longer lengths, but you should hit most of the genuine bites without much difficulty. You may get a few line-knocks when the fish are milling around the feeder early on, but most tip movements after that are caused by genuine bites.

Once again it can pay to balance the feeder to the flow to encourage drop-back bites caused by a dislodged feeder. In fact, this type of bite can be encouraged in the faster swims if you cast directly in front with a balanced feeder and allow a biggish bow to develop in the line between rod tip and feeder.

By experimenting with the weights and the size of the bow you can make a feeder bump straight downstream, holding and then moving. You are sending it in search of fish and the quivertip will move slowly in tune with each movement and when the bite comes the feeder dislodges completely, causing the quivertip to waggle madly. That is another unmissable bite. Those sportsmen who say the feeder is nothing but a crude method for crude anglers are quite wrong.

## CHUB AND ROACH ON THE FLOAT

Given anything like the right conditions in autumn and winter I much prefer to catch my chub on the float, and since roach demand a virtually identical approach I shall deal with both species at once. I have described stick-float fishing in the context of the Warwickshire Avon, and it is not all that different on the Trent and elsewhere.

The Trent was the river where the stick-float was first used, with caster the key bait. Later it proved adaptable for maggot fishing too and that is now the main approach. The basic shotting pattern has never changed, it is still the old 'shirt-button' style, evenly spaced shot gradually decreasing in size towards the hook.

Whatever size of stick-float I am using the bottom three shots are always the same, a No. 10 near the hook, an 8 above it and then a 6. What happens above that depends on float size and depth, but it could be one, two, three, even four No. 4s strung out evenly. The float itself will

*FIG 9* 'SHIRT-BUTTON' STYLE

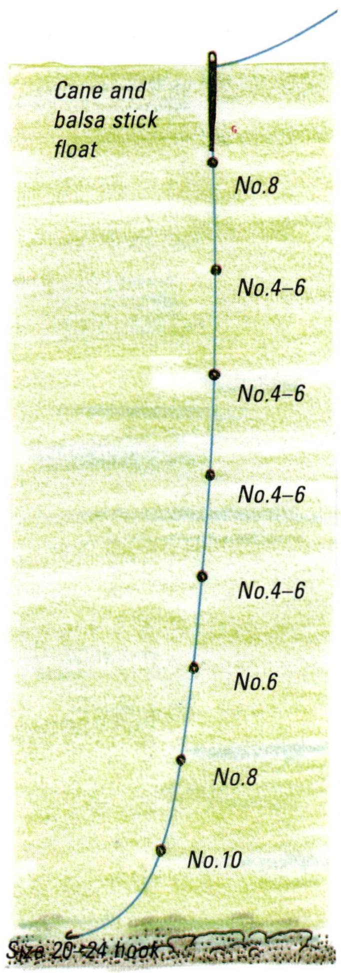


*FIG 10* TRENT CHUB RIG

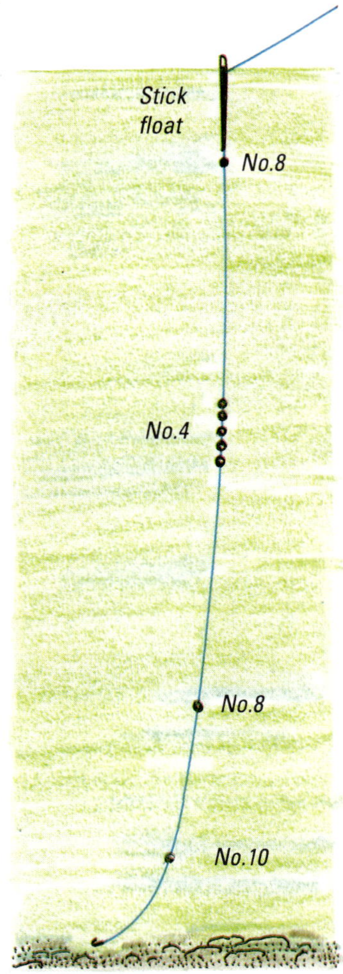


*FIG 11* WINTER CHUB RIG

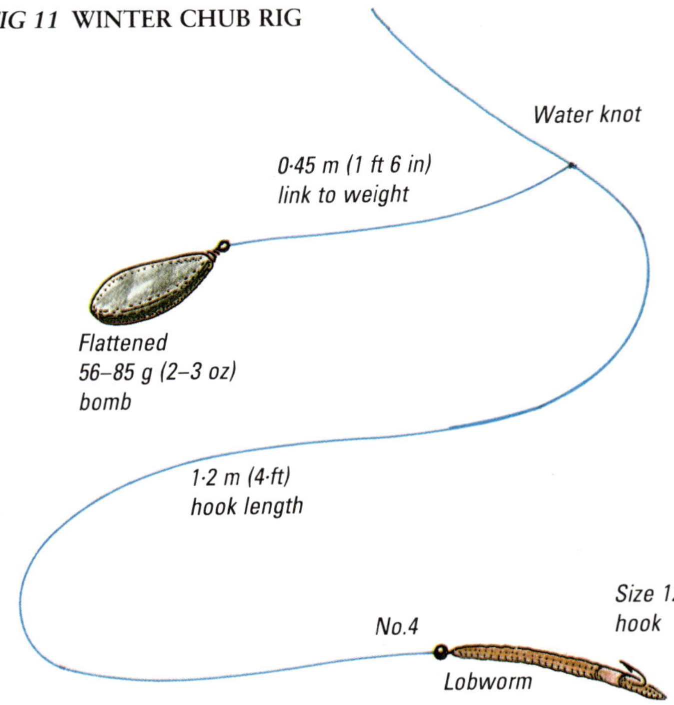


*Fig 9* The weight runs down the line evenly, ensuring that the bait drops evenly. *Fig 10* But chub take in middle or deeper water, so the weight is in the middle and towards the hook. *Fig 11* This worm rig takes winter chub.

Tom Pickering 'whipping' bleak at speed. Two top sections of a pole, a fixed line length and a small float which gives enough weight to cast the bait. Catch enough and many a match has been won with this tiny but prolific fish.

usually be the traditional cane and balsa model for the smooth, even-paced swims, or something a bit more stable for more turbulent water. Some anglers use the Allerton sticks with alloy stems all the time, but I think they are better for 'boily' swims. (Figs 9, 10)

Hook sizes have changed over the years. We used to think that 20s were small for the Trent and considered ourselves daring if we dropped to a 22. Now a 28–340 g (1–12 oz) line is standard for many Trent anglers, though I never start that fine. I begin fishing with a Size 20 to 0.45 kg (1 lb) line and catch what I can with that, and only when the bites stop will I scale down, but the move always works. It is very obvious that the fish are harder to tempt than they once were.

The stick-float is best fished at the speed of the current, with slowing down a useful tactic when you are struggling for bites. It is the feeding which is really important and that has to be constant, a given amount of maggots at every cast. A dozen at each cast used to be the recommended amount, but I feed double that nowadays, although it can depend on the situation. If I am not catching fish I will feed much more heavily, trying to make the fish feed or to attract fish. I use more feed when I am struggling to find fish than I do when I am catching them.

As soon as the fish start to bite I cut back on the feed to the standard feed-rate of about 20 maggots per cast and dropping the tackle into the feed in a straight line downstream, allow it to run through. It becomes an almost mechanical exercise after a while, although it pays to keep alert, I always try to work out what I will do if the bites stop coming.

One tactic which works (apart from checking the tackle and slowing down the speed of presentation) is to try casting farther down the swim. It is surprising how often this produces more fish, probably because the bait is sinking through a different, undisturbed area. Trying a little closer out or in also works well, as does the odd slight change to the terminal weighting. I find it mysterious how quite small alterations to weight patterns can lead to fish coming to the net.

Only change the weighting pattern when chub are in the swim. Roach like the evenly falling bait achieved with the 'shirt-button' shotting style, but chub are usually to be caught lower down or on the bottom. For them I try bunching the No. 4 weights where the 6 is, which makes the rig sink a lot faster, and fishing a little more over-depth.

Dragging the bait over the rocks is an effective tactic for chub, and another dodge which can pay on the Trent and elsewhere is to start hammering loose feed in towards the end of a match. This often catches good bonus chub in swims which have been producing only roach. It also seems to switch them back on, sometimes, when they have become wary. If you have a dying swim in the later stages of a match you have little to lose and potentially much to gain from trying it.

If conditions permit I always bait two swims on rivers, one close in for the stick and one farther out in the stream

for either the stick-float or waggler style, fished as previously described.

## HARDER CONDITIONS

While we often get normal flow conditions in winter, and, with luck, some mild weather too, we cannot always depend upon it. Very often matchmen find themselves struggling on rivers which are a bit out of sorts. It can be cold, with some extra water, or well up in near-flood. Some of our Winter League fishing seems to take place in such conditions too often for comfort and catching fish in team events is vital.

When the more normal approaches fail we have to try something else and there are one or two tactics which are well worth considering. In flood conditions, the first idea is a bait-change to the lobworm and at times it is that last-chance method!

A very important point here is to be sure that you have this bait when you need it. The conditions for collecting lobworms are often hopeless when you come to need them and I get mine in the autumn when the weather is both mild and damp. The lobs come up on to the surface of lawns, flower-beds and vegetable plots, beginning to emerge as darkness falls and the later you leave it the farther out they come.

On very warm, wet nights the lobs come out all the way and you can locate them with a shaded torch and simply pick them up. More often, though, they keep their tails underground and retract like lightning if disturbed by a heavy footfall or too bright a light. The trick is to grab them as far back from the head as you can just hold on. The worm will contract its body, trying to get back down its hole, but after a few seconds the contractions stop and the worm can be pulled out without further resistance.

In the right conditions it does not take long to collect a few hundred lobs, which can be kept alive for use weeks or even months later. I put mine into an old bath, sunk in the garden and filled with ordinary soil. Whenever collecting conditions are right I go out and top up the supply.

It may seem a lot of trouble to go to but I enjoy it, and when the time comes for lobworms to decide match and team results I am never at a loss for this bait. How to fish them is a matter for endless debate. Hitting lobworm bites seems to be as complex for some anglers as those baffling bites from Witham eels. But I think I have found the best way, certainly for Trent chub in winter floods.

At one time these fish used to come close-in to the bank in high-flow conditions but this is no longer the case, not as often anyway. The fish are more likely to be out in the flow, which demands the use of quite a big weight to hold the bait and tackle where you want it.

I usually hold it there with a 57–85 g (2–3 oz) bomb, flattened to help it hold bottom. This weight needs a strong rod to cast and of course stronger line than we would normally use. I have 1.3 kg (3 lb) reel line with a 2.2 kg (5 lb) shock-absorber tied onto it. This should run from the reel to about 0.6 m (2 ft) beyond the rod tip when the tackle is in the casting position. It ensures that I can cast the heavy gear without risking a break, but I still have fairly thin line offering little resistance to the flow.

The terminal tackle is fairly simple, a fixed bomb link of 0.46 m (1 ft 6 in) with a 1.2 m (4 ft) hook-length and a Size 12 hook. Critical to the success of the method is how the worm is mounted on the hook. We might be waiting for just one or two bites and when they come they must be hit. Some anglers have the self-control to sit there watching the little nods and bobs on the quivertip, waiting for the tip eventually to slam round and stay there. But sometimes they get nothing but the warm-up act and find that the main show has been cancelled! (Fig. 11)

This is puzzling, but I rationalised it this way: every movement of the tip is caused by a chub mouthing and testing the bait. If you reel in after several little movements which do not develop you invariably find that the tail of the lob has been chewed, the end missing, or there are several damaged areas along the worm's body. I decided that it should be possible to hook a chub if it has my bait in its mouth long enough to cause this kind of injury to the bait. Putting the hook in the worm's tail was the obvious answer, but if you do that the bait fishes head-downstream and loses its attraction.

What was needed was a method of rigging the lob with the hook in the tail and the tail pointing downstream. The problem was solved as shown in the tackle illustrated in the drawing. The hook is passed through the head of the worm, which is then pushed up the line. Depending on the length of the worm, a Size 4 shot is pinched on and the hook is put through the tail of the worm. The shot stops the worm sliding down the hook length and the bait is strung out, with the tail end waiting to be nipped by a chub. Striking with this rig is not at all complicated: watch for a tap and ignore it, but strike the second tap, and in the majority of cases you have your chub well-hooked and on the way to the net.

If you miss the bite you sometimes find that the worm is in two halves. That tells you that the bite did not come from a chub but an eel – and there is not much that you can do about that. I stick with the system of striking at that second tap. Very often it is no more positive than the first. It can be quite a tiny movement, but hit it anyway, it is surprising how often you will connect. It is also possible, though, to get a very positive first pull. You have to be ready to hit it, which is why I always ledger with my hand on the rod.

The reason for the long tail and the long bomb-link is that it creates a bit of slack in what is basically a crude and heavy method. It allows the chub to pick the bait up without feeling much initial resistance from the heavy bomb. In flood conditions and powerful streams, a shorter, tighter rig would be as taut as piano wire, and bites would be a lot more difficult to hit.

It is unusual to get many bites on lobworm, a bait which probably works in high and coloured water simply because worms are naturally washed into rivers in these conditions. Here, more often than not, we are fighting for bites and one useful tip is to try a switch-bait such as cheese. It is surprising how often a change to cheese, especially a smelly one – Danish blue is an example – will attract a bite.

I say 'a bite' deliberately, for that is what it usually is. Very often, in fact nearly always, cheese provokes a single bite and it usually comes straight away if it is going to come at all. I do not know why cheese is a one-bite wonder, and cannot even come up with a theory, but I have learned from experience that after hitting or missing a cheese bite I might as well go back to lobworm, there will be no more action with the cheese.

## THE BOMB METHOD

There is a stage between a normal river and high water/flood conditions. In winter the water can be up just a little, or normal but a bit cold. It can be fishable with a stick-float or waggler, but the fish are not active enough to chase or intercept a moving bait. In this situation a method of straight ledgering can produce a fish when nothing else will.

I use a weight as small as possible, usually 10.6 to 14 g (3/8 to 1/2 oz), fished on a short link of 76 to 100 mm (3 to 4 in) and a 0.46 m (1 ft 6 in) tail. Many match anglers resort to this tactic without really understanding what makes it work properly, and in my view it is the feeding method which goes with it that is the key. I feed the swim as though I were float-fishing, and that can be very difficult when you are not actually float-fishing! (Fig. 12)

It is so easy to trickle maggots in at every cast with the float, but it is a different thing altogether to maintain the same kind of frequency while watching a quivertip. Nevertheless it has to be done. Denis White and I have a saying which applies to several angling methods, 'Fish ledger, think float; fish feeder, think float'. The float is the ideal way of catching fish because it is completely in tune with the feeding which goes with it. When we cannot fish the float, or cannot *catch* fish on the float, therefore, we still try to feed as though we are float-fishing and in some instances make the terminal tackle behave at least for part of the time like float tackle.

*FIG 12* LIGHT BOMB RIG

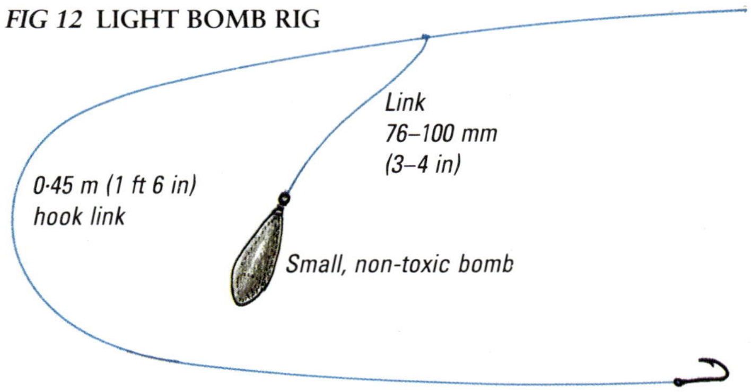


**_Fig 12_ With this light ledger the swim is fed as in float-fishing and it works!**

For example, a few moments after a feeder has hit bottom the hook-length is falling among feed just like a float-rig in the last 0.6 or 0.9 m (2 or 3 ft). Thinking this way helps us to imagine what is going on below and assist us to anticipate events. Sometimes, we are quick on to a ledger bite because we are expecting it at the exact moment when it comes.

In the case of the bomb method we assume that regular feeding, while not attracting float bites, is necessary because the fish are cleaning it up after it has hit bottom. They want it still, or moving more slowly than it can be presented with a float. They will take the bait 'nailed down' with the ledger tackle, but the fish need to be attracted and held in the right place.

I fish with my maggot bait in a side-tray, trickling it in all the time with the free hand. The other hand holds the rod, which is propped on a rest set just upstream of straight out. That way, bites register only on the quivertip. If the rod is angled downstream bites go through the tip and register on the rod, giving the angler much less chance of hitting the bite.

Usually, the right place to cast is about halfway down the swim. Close the bale arm of the reel as soon as the bomb hits bottom, and be ready for a bite in the next few seconds as the bait sinks to the bottom. The odd suicidal fish will take it on the drop but in hard conditions the bites are more likely to come after the fall of the bait.

I like to fish a line as tight as possible with as slack a tip as possible, which does not sound easily achieved. I am aware of this, but what I do not like is for my line to be too direct to the bomb, which causes much of the bend to be taken out of the tip. The current puts a bit of a bow in it, which eases the pressure on the tip. In effect, it creates a bit of slack for a biting fish to take up, which ensures that it has the bait well inside its mouth when the bite registers.

This may seem an immobile and boring way of fishing but I do not find it so, I am thinking all the time, concentrating on the feeding and watching the tip for bites. It is hard work for five hours and one obvious essential on cold winter days is to keep warm. If you are not wearing the correct clothing you will be too cold to concentrate properly. I sometimes wonder how the old-timers managed, sitting on a freezing, snow-covered bank without the benefit of good waterproof clothing and, above all, the modern thermal vests, longjohns and boots.

Matchfishing is tough in winter, but if you have a choice do not make it any tougher than it needs to be. In team events such as the winter leagues you have to take what comes, but it makes little sense for the accomplished match-angler to choose difficult and patchy winter venues. I hate matches in which anglers drawn in half or even three-quarters of the pegs have no chance of catching a fish.

While I love the River Witham in summer I loathe it in winter, when roach or bream are concentrated in one or two areas and the majority of anglers have no chance. I recall qualifying for one big competition final by catching a single stickleback on the Witham. It made more headlines than some of my big wins!

When the average matchman gets a plumb draw, a patchy venue does offer him the occasional chance to shine, but the ultimate aim of the ambitious matchman should be to compete regularly against the top performers. Watch them carefully when you get the chance. Learn from them and one day you will beat them. Angling is a truly great sport and the only one I can think of in which the newcomer can turn up and have a crack at a world champion. You can turn up and fish peg-to-peg with world champions Tommy Pickering or Kevin Ashurst, and you *might* beat them. Lots of anglers do and are inspired enough by their achievement to try even harder the next time.

Never take defeat hard: just try to analyse why it happened and learn from it. However good they are, no one is immortal on a riverbank. The real measure of a top matchman is how often he wins when the chance presents itself. Mastery of all the methods is the key and if you can absorb everything you have read here you will be a long way down the right road.

*A*

*B*

*A* Matchfishing is all about total familiarity with tackle and techniques. Complete mastery and control over rod and reel are absolute requirements.
*B* Completely different from the streamy River Trent, this placid stretch of the Grand Canal, at Ticknevin, in Co. Kildare, produces very good quality bream, tench and rudd in a more relaxed match atmosphere.

BOB CARNILL

# FLY FISHING FOR TROUT

Since the mid-1960s boom in stillwater trout fishing there has been a steady and continuous increase right up to the present day, making it now the most popular branch of the game-fishing scene. The tackle trade has responded by producing rods far superior to any other material hitherto known. Carbon fibre, Boron and Kevlar have almost completely replaced built-cane and fibre glass. Not only have rods improved but so too have the rod rings (eyes, guides, and so on), reels, fly-lines and to some degree, even the angler's clothing.

## CHOOSING TACKLE

RODS: To match one's tackle to a particular style of fishing is still sound advice though it is not as important as it used to be. Today's tackle is far more versatile if chosen wisely and a particular rod and line can be used to perform a wide range of duties. Not only have modern rods improved dramatically with regard to their lightness/power ratio, but they also offer the angler the action which will suit him best – as opposed to suiting the style in which he chooses to fish. A newcomer cannot be expected to know what his or her preferred 'action' will be, only experience will provide the answer.

For general fishing, a 3 m (10 ft) rod will take a lot of beating. However, for the matchman or a dyed-in-the-wool 'over-the-front' (loch-style) enthusiast, 3.2 m (10 ft 6 in), 3.3 m (11 ft), or even 3.5 m (11 ft 6 in) will be more acceptable. Such a rod allows the flies, particularly the bob-fly, to be dibbled in the surface at greater distances from the boat. In addition, true loch-style fishing does not

*A*

B

C

D

*A* Bob Carnill plies his trade on Lough Conn, a rugged, yet peaceful West of Ireland water. *B* A wild brown trout grabbed at the fly and tore off upwind under the boat, coming perilously close to the drogue used to lessen the speed of the drift. *C* A slightly more relaxed Carnill plays the fish toward the dinghy. *D* First of the fat-fleshed Lough Conn brown trout comes to the waiting net.

These illustrations show the gradual changes that are met in the trout family coloration, starting at the top with a sea trout from the sea, passing through to the illustration at the bottom showing a typical trout in breeding colour.

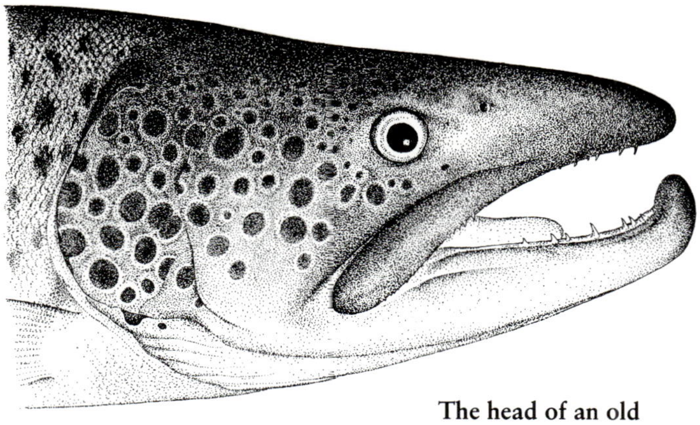

The head of an old or 'cannibal' male trout

## BROWN AND SEA TROUT

*Salmo trutta*

Like the salmon, trout are spawned in freshwater and live in brackish water. Some trout enter totally saline water, when they become known as sea trout. Brown and sea trout markings vary enormously, conditioned by their environment. At the parr stage, trout have vivid black and red spots, with a distinctive dark barring on the flanks. The adults retain this coloration, the bars disappearing in the smolt stage. Sea trout pass through a smolt stage when their parr colours change to a silvery livery. As adults, they exhibit black, cross-shaped spots. Trout are strongly territorial. As large fish they tend to be more solitary. Males and females undergo a marked change in coloration as the time for spawning nears. At the time of the coldest weather trout will move to gravel stretches in the smallest of feeder-streams where the males attempt to pair with several females. Depending on size, a female trout will yield up to 1,000 eggs. Trout can tolerate a high pH (alkalinity/acidity) range in water, making easy their introduction to a wide variety of waters both natural and man-made.

**Bait:** Live fish, natural and artificial insects, spinning lures, worms and crustaceans.

Trout parr

call for long distance casting so with a long rod the single roll-cast used to deliver just two or three rod-lengths of line can be made with one fluid movement as the flies are lifted from the water.

REELS: The 'receptacle to the hold the line' adage is neither true nor false, it depends on how one fishes. If the angler prefers to play a trout 'off-the-reel', then it becomes more than that. On the other hand, if an angler wishes to hand-line his fish the reel becomes a receptacle for storing line.

BACKING LINE: This is a narrow-diameter line spliced to the end of the much shorter fly line which allows a trout to run for distances far greater than a fly-line would otherwise allow. For all my trout fishing, I use a 8.9 cm (3½ in) diameter reel with a wide drum. Depending on the diameter of the backing, I can load between 45.7 and 91.4 m (50 and 100 yards) of backing, plus the fly line. Never stint on backing because you could lose the trout of a life-time.

Heavy monofilaments used as shooting, running and backing line for shooting-heads are more prone to 'memory' coils than fly lines. These usually require a good stretch prior to fishing although 10 cm (4 in) diameter, wide-hub fly reels help tremendously in lessening or even eradicating the problem and are widely used nowadays by shooting-head and lead-core enthusiasts.

FLY LINES: The choice in fly lines is enormous, not only in profile, but in colour, density, and to some degree, length. Serious stillwater anglers will often have at least five different lines enabling them to fish efficiently at almost any depth. Taking lines in their natural order of sinking rate, they are a floating line; an intermediate or 'neutral', both of which actually are very slow sinkers; a slow-sinking; a fast-sinking; and possibly a lead core or lead-impregnated line, the latter being the fastest of the fast sinkers. A sink-tip may also be carried though these are not nearly as popular as they were a few years ago.

PROFILE: 'Profile' is the overall 'shape' – or taper – of a fly line. Once you have become familiar with the different profiles, you will immediately relate the profile name to its expected performance.

LEADERS: A leader is the length of monofilament which is attached to the fly line, to which in turn is attached the fly or lure. Leaders may carry more than just one fly on the point position by way of adding one or more droppers at various distances along the leader. A traditional cast will usually have three flies: the point fly, a middle dropper and a bob-fly (top dropper). In Scotland some anglers fish teams of four flies.

The leader is tapered so that the power flow will be continuous from the rod through the fly line and eventually through the leader. This not only offers the best possible presentation of the fly but also helps to prevent tangles in the leader. I have found that a 0.9 kg (2 lb) b.s. differential between the joined lengths of a leader to be quite acceptable. This step-down does not make knotting

**Carefully applied finger pressure on the exposed rim of the reel brings the fight to a conclusion. Small fish are played on the line. This lightweight reel, the Leeda LC 100, with spare spools, makes changing lines easy.**

## RAINBOW TROUT

*Salmo gairdneri*

A species brought to the British Isles from the North Western States of the US. It thrives in stillwaters and has become the standard fish for man-assisted trout breeding both for sale as food and replacement stocks on fisheries. Anatomically, the fish resembles the brown trout in all but coloration. There is a vivid band of mauve-purple scales along the flanks roughly following the contours of the lateral line, and there are numerous black spots and blotches on the sides and back, extending to the caudal fin. The rainbow is not a successful spawning fish in our waters, indeed, most of the stocks in lakes and reservoirs will have been bred and introduced into them by fishery managements. There is some evidence to suggest that there are strains of rainbows that exist as naturally breeding populations in a few trout streams but it is not known if they will be viable over many generations. The rainbow is a useful addition to the angler's species; it seems more resilient to pollution and doubtful water conditions. It is a free-rising fish and with age does not become as predatory and bottom-living as the brown trout. Depending on the type of water, the rainbow is capable of growing to large weights, bigger than the brown and certainly faster. Fish of over 9 kg (20 lb) are known, and 4.5 kg (10 lb) is a specimen, but trout farms can rear them to double this weight before release into a fishery.

**Bait:** Natural and artificial flies, spinning lures, worms.

difficult, or too similar in diameter and strength.

Many brands of knotless tapered leader are now widely available, which can be spliced to the end of the fly line. There is a wide range of lengths, butt and tippet diameters to suit almost every requirement. Having attached the knotless leader to the fly line, the angler can fish a point fly, or he can 'tailor' the leader by cropping back into the steep part of the taper and then custom-build his leader by adding a different tippet strength, length, and/or droppers.

There are weather or water conditions where a level leader may be called for, particularly when lure fishing, and if one uses the wind to advantage, even long, level leaders can be used to good effect.

BUTT SECTIONS: These are short lengths of heavy nylon needle-knotted to the end of the fly line to which the leader is attached. Attachment to the leader can be by interlocking loops or a blood-knot. The butt section is a permanent fixture, replaced when it becomes damaged or too short to be of particular use. There is no set length for a butt section. The breaking strain of the butt section may also vary, some thick monofilament has been used, but this makes the step down into the leader material far too great, serving no practical purpose. I use 4.5 kg (10 lb) b.s. for my butt sections which is just 1.1 kg (2½ lb) greater than the 3.4 kg (7½ lb) b.s. first section of the leader; this gives a fluid power-flow with neat joining or knotting, whether using interlocking loops or a blood knot.

SHOCK ABSORBER: The Power Gum shock-absorber habit is becoming popular, especially among the ever-increasing band of stillwater dry and semi-dry fly enthusiasts. Because of the tiny flies often employed, coupled with a growing awareness that very fine tippets bring better results, the shock absorber will soon be an essential part of many an angler's rig.

Power Gum is an elastic monofil which stretches almost twice its length under maximum pressure, at which

*FIG 1* POWER-GUM SHOCK-ABSORBER

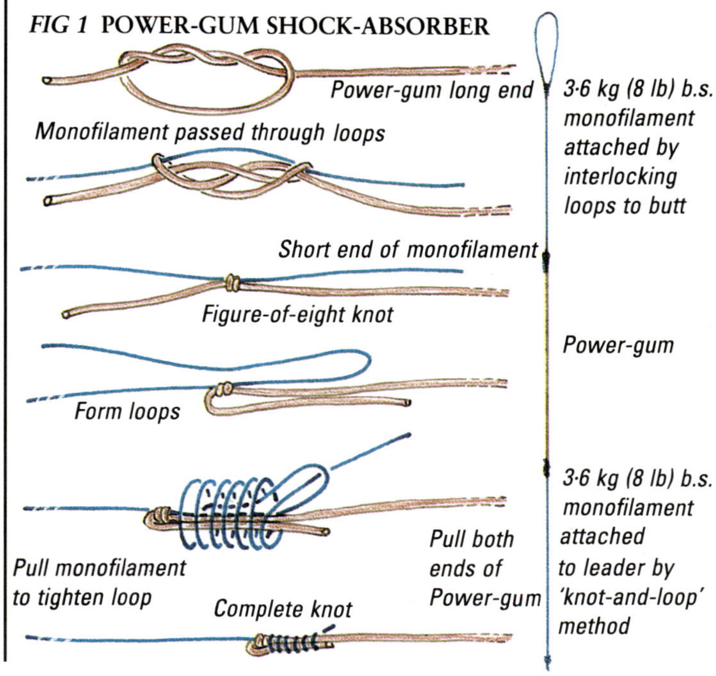

point it has a b.s. of approximately 4.5 kg (10 lb), depending on the brand. A Power Gum shock-absorber is usually inserted between the butt section and the leader. (Fig. 1, p. 75 )

THE FISHING BAG: When bank fishing I use a large, stout canvas bag that keeps out the rain and has plenty of storage space in the main inner compartment; it has another large pouch to the rear and two generous pockets on the front.

THE LANDING NET: I prefer a net that will be serviceable whether one is fishing from the bank or the boat. My net has quite a large, bow-shaped, rigid frame supporting a deep net. It has a collapsible head with a carrying clip making it ideal for fishing on-the-rove. The extending handle is suitable both for boat fishing or steep banks.

THE DROGUE: This is an underwater parachute used to slow down the speed of a drifting boat while maintaining a given position in relation to the wind/waves and is essential. (Fig. 2)

THE G-CLAMP: A G-clamp may be used in connection with both the drogue and the anchor. On the drift, or at anchor, most boats yaw, due perhaps to hull design and/or the effect of wind, waves or current. Yawing may occasionally be used to good effect, but it usually spoils a day's fishing. When this happens, reposition the anchor point of the drogue or anchor rope. The best way to do this is to attach a G-clamp to the side of the boat and take the rope around it. By moving the clamp, one can quickly have the boat lying true.

A suitable alternative to the G-clamp is a length of rope fastened at the bow and stern of your boat. Draw it tight, fastening the drogue or anchor rope with a tight sliding knot. This system allows the 'anchor point' to be repositioned by sliding the knot to the required position.

THE ANCHOR: Anchors are becoming increasingly popular as an essential part of every boat fisherman's tackle. Apart from being a necessity at times, an anchor also forms part of one's safety equipment. In the event of motor failure and/or extreme weather conditions, your anchor could save the boat from being blown onto a dam wall or mid-water sandbank.

Make sure that your anchor is substantial, and will hold a heavy boat with two anglers in high winds and waves. Choose something with either three large grappling prongs or broad, articulating flukes. But no anchor will work without the addition of at least 1.8 m (6 ft) of substantial chain (more if you can afford it for those larger waters). The chain's job is to pull the prongs flukes downwards, forcing them to gain a purchase in the lake bed.

Do not fix the chain to the anchor directly to the ring at the top of the shaft. If there is a ring at the fluke-end of the shaft the chain should be attached there, using a D-link. Then tie it to the ring at the top of the shaft with a piece of string that can be broken by a pull from one man. If there is no ring at the fluke-end have one welded on. This method of attachment is called a breakaway rig and it will save you many anchors over the years should the anchor become wedged on the bottom. It works by hauling on the rope until the string breaks, which reverses the lift to the rear of the anchor – and up it comes. (Fig. 3)

ANCHOR ROPE: When buying anchor rope, purchase as much as you can afford – between 30.5 and 45.7 m (100 and 150 ft) allowing you to anchor in the deepest of our larger reservoirs. It is also an advantage to purchase synthetic rope, which does not rot.

## THE STILLWATER SEASON

Trout can be caught on the fly on a fairly regular basis without one having the slightest interest in entomology; but not to observe and be curious about the trout's life is to deny oneself the very essence of what makes fly fishing so special.

## MID-MARCH TO MID-APRIL

My observations are based on the Midlands area; therefore certain regional adjustments may be needed with regard to weather variations and its subsequent effect on plant and insect life to the north and south of this central point. In most areas the trout fishing season begins around

***FIG 2*** **THE DROGUE**

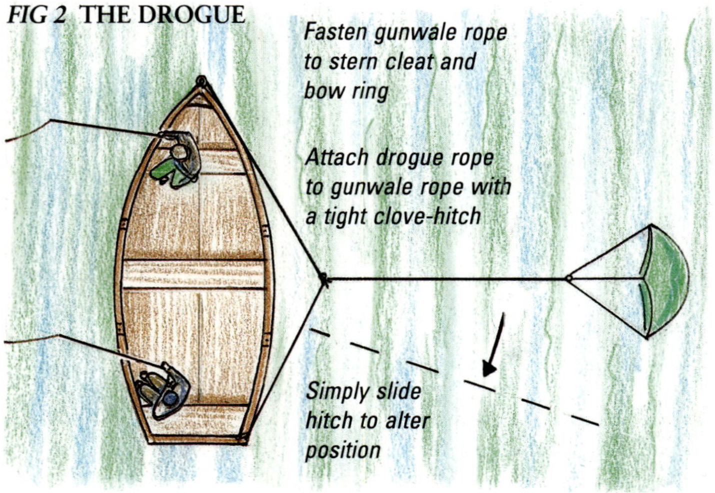


***FIG 3*** **BREAKOUT ANCHOR**

Bob Carnill's fly box. Every fly has been tied by him during the long winter months. Among these flies are many highly successful innovative patterns which he has designed and tied himself. Total conviction that a particular fly will work seems for some strange reason often to communicate itself to the feeding trout, with the result that an unexpected and 'bonus' fish comes to the net.

the middle of March. There is very little fly life in evidence and even less surface activity, but below the surface life will be stirring. Coupled with a gradual warming of the water, both insect life and the trout will become increasingly more active.

For most of March and into April the trout feed close to the lake-bottom, usually in and just beyond the deep margins. At this time, their diet will include bottom-dwelling invertebrates such as corixae, caddis larvae, shrimp, snails, chironomid (buzzer) larvae, water-beetles and their larvae, alder larvae, and occasionally daphnia.

Fish fry are occasionally found in the stomach of an early-season trout, but not in the quantities usually associated with the fry-bashing sprees of late summer and autumn. In addition, a few small, dark adult chironomids may be seen on or near the water, but the trout will usually ignore them and stay close to the bottom.

## EARLY SEASON TECHNIQUES

Whether we fish from the bank or from a boat, the location and techniques may be very similar. In either case, our most productive areas will be found in deep water, fairly close to the bank. In the early season avoid fishing over shallow, stone-bottomed areas, or at the mouth, or general vicinity of streams or land drains. Such areas are the haunt of gravid, out-of-condition, black cock rainbows, easy to catch but not a worthy quarry.

When fishing from the bank during this period, I prefer to have the wind coming over my back, it is much warmer and more comfortable and also crucial to the success of my favoured approach. The first thing I look for is deep marginal water within comfortable casting range where I expect to find concentrations of over-wintered, silver hen rainbows and perhaps the odd, large brown trout.

My rig would be the 3 m (10 ft) carbon rod matched to a WF#8 floating line. Leader length is 5.5 to 7.6 m (18 to 25 ft) with one or two droppers, the first spaced between 0.9 and 1.2 m (3 and 4 ft) from the point, and the top dropper at a similar distance.

My choice of flies for a two-dropper leader would be: for the point position one of the following: Pheasant Tail Nymph, Size 8, 10 or 12 long shank (L/S), Cased Caddis Size 10 to 14 L/S; Alder Larva 8 or 10 L/S, Worm Fly, tandem 2 × 10 or 8 standard shank, William's Size 8, 10 and 12 (standard shank) or a Shrimp 12 Yorkshire Sedge Hook.

For the first dropper: Black and Peacock Spider, Zulu, Mallard and Claret or Corixa. All are usually leaded for deep fishing in early spring – some very heavily. However, any pattern used on the dropper position ought to be smaller and lighter than its counterpart on the point.

When a top dropper is used, the following will be found useful: Mallard and Claret 12 and 14, Black Pennell 12 and 14, Black Spider 12 and 14, Buzzer pupa 12 and 14 (in black, brown or dark green). If there is any sun about try a small Silver Butcher.

A back-wind is not chosen just to aid casting. If one had

*FIG 4* FLOATING LINE-PATHS OF RETRIEVE

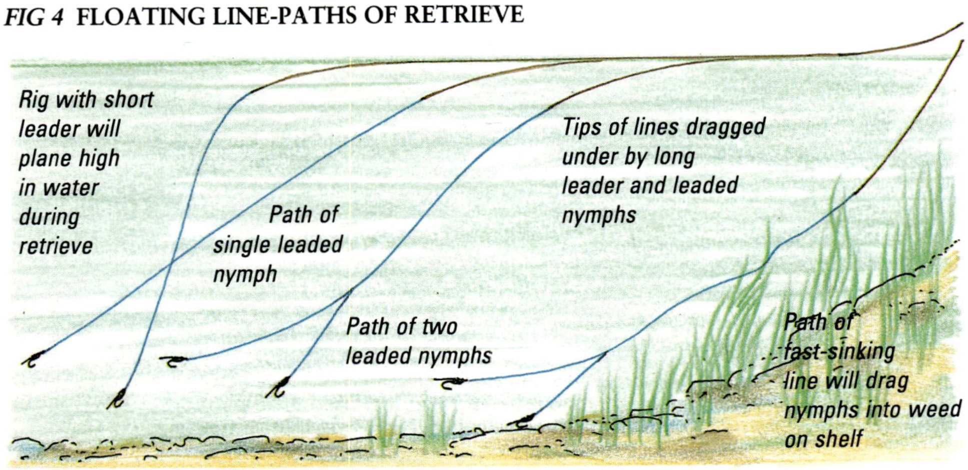


*FIG 5* SINKING LINE-PATHS OF RETRIEVE

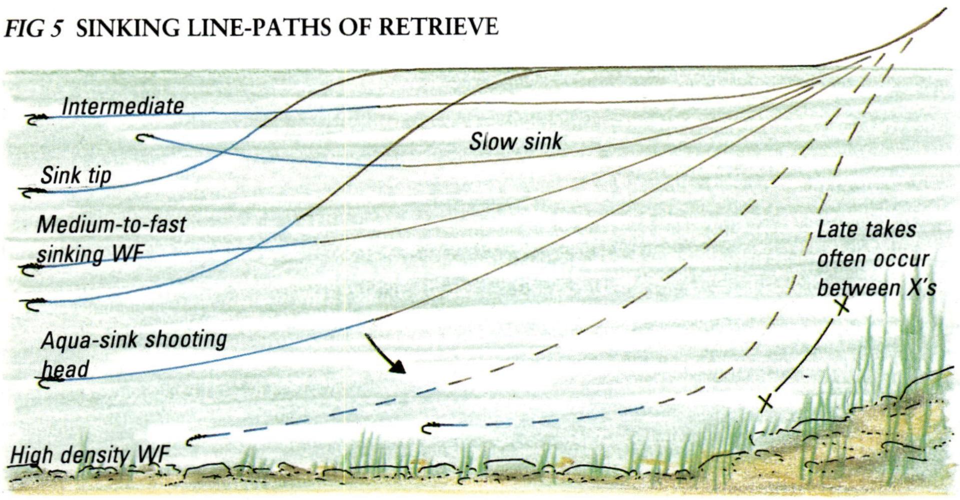

*A*

chosen to fish across the wind in some other location, it would soon be discovered that before the nymphs could sink to their effective fishing depth the line would be hanging in the bankside where it would not be fishing at all. With a square-on back-wind a fly line will lay straight out in front of the fishing position for as long as it takes for the nymphs to arrive near the lake bed.

The retrieve is something to experiment with. Sometimes a figure-of-eight may attract the trout, or short draws on the line prove to be the most effective. Avoid a fast retrieve when fishing floating lines and long leaders, all it achieves is to make the leader plane increasingly higher in the water the longer the retrieve goes on, thus making the flies fish far too high above the trout.

Takes are never vicious. The shallow angle between the long leader and the fly line acts as a cushion and one experiences a 'going-heavy' on the line which must be responded to immediately. Better to strike at weed than chance missing an offer! (Fig. 4)

Why do I not use a sinking line and a shorter leader to achieve the same or similar effect? Slow retrieval means sinking lines go on sinking throughout the retrieve and before the retrieve is completed the line is dragging through remnant weed and other debris on the marginal shelf. A floating line will fish the flies cleanly and effectively right back to the bank-side. (Fig. 5)

However, for lure fishing from the same location, then I choose a sinking line suitable for the depth of water in front of me The difference is that having made the cast and allowed the line to sink to the desired depth, the faster rate of retrieve usually associated with lure fishing would not let a sinking line sink farther; instead it would tend to plane at a given depth.

## BOAT FISHING IN MARCH/APRIL

Open water is not usually productive during the cold-water period. Whenever I take a boat out in the early spring, it is only used as a portable casting platform and I usually head for known deep-water marks close to the downwind shore, anchoring the boat no more than 45.7 m (50 yards) from the bank. The same tactics described for bank fishing can be used to good effect when fishing at anchor, and provided that there are no bank fishermen on the chosen stretch, the boat may be taken ever closer to the shore, and along it, in search of a likely fish-holding spot. If the sport to the deep-sunk nymph proves non-productive, I try the deep-fished lure. My standard rig for this kind of fishing is the usual 3 m (10 ft) carbon rod to which is matched a fast-sinking shooting-head.

Leaders need not be very long when fished on high-density lines; 3 to 4.6 m (10 to 15 ft) is adequate. Taper can be done away with, a straight-through length of 3.4 kg (7½ lb) is quite sufficient and will be delivered straight and tangle-free if the velocity of the shooting-head is utilised correctly. When fishing the Dog Nobbler, I use one lure; this ensures that its action is not restricted. However, when I choose to fish marabou or hair wing

B

*A* An English Midlands reservoir which provides the local population with good water and fishermen with an extremely fertile and rewarding trout habitat. Brown and rainbow trout stockfish are introduced, both species growing to large weights.
*B* Carnill's catch, rainbow trout from Eyebrook Reservoir. The largest was a fish of 1.8 kg (4 lb) plus, with the rest of the bag averaging 0.7 kg (1½ lb).

lures, I usually mount two, about 1.2 m (4 ft) apart.

## MID-APRIL TO MAY

Given a normal spring, mid-April to May brings a vast improvement in the fishing prospects. Lengthening days and the stronger sunlight quickly bring the water to life. We now expect to see the first of the 'proper' buzzer rises. In warm, settled weather, columns of these midges may be seen dancing above hedgerows, hot-surfaced tarmac and ash-pad roads.

Buzzers are the most important food form where lake trout are concerned. The larvae are often physically disturbed from their lake-bed tubes and eaten in great numbers. After pupation, on their way to the surface, they are preyed upon even more avidly. For those which have survived the rigours of the ascent and hatching, their eventual end will probably be in the stomach of a trout, having been taken during or after egg-laying.

Not all rises during this period are to the buzzer. A warm, settled day will get lots of small, shell-back terrestrial beetles on the wing, many of which fall onto the water where they are eagerly sought by the trout.

## TACKLING EARLY SEASON RISERS

THE BANK ROD: Casting to rising trout is considered to be the cream of the stillwater fly-fisher's sport. However, rises encountered during the early season period are most likely to come from small, isolated groups of trout.

At this time of year surface activity is not likely to get underway much before mid-morning – though it could be as late as mid-day to mid-afternoon depending on the weather. I set up two rods; one will carry floating line and deep nymphing rig; the other, a similar line (WF#8 F) but with a 4.6 to 5.5 m (15 to 18 ft) leader which is tapered 3.4, 2.5, 1.52 kg (7½, 5½, 3½ lb) if the trout do not run too large at the water being fished; or a 3.4, 2.5, 2.5 kg (7½, 5½, 5½ lb) if larger specimens are common.

The artificials mounted on the deep rig will be a combination of those already outlined; for the other rod, buzzer patterns would be my first choice. On the top dropper (bob-fly) I mount one of my Adult Buzzer (wet-fly) imitations; either a Blae and Black or a Black Duck Fly – this will fish just beneath the surface. On the middle dropper and point position, a buzzer pupa imitation. A Poly-rib Buzzer Pupa (own pattern) would be first choice, but at this point of the season the trout will take almost any buzzer imitation. Colour and size are important, Size 14 and 12 black, dark olive/green, claret and brown are among the most effective colours. I usually mount a Size 12 on the point, and a 14 on the dropper. (See seasonal chart for recommended A/B choice – Fig. 6, p. 80 )

The most favourable weather condition to encourage an early season rise is a light, south-westerly breeze which is both warm and humid. A touch of sun, peeking through broken cloud, will certainly help. Given these conditions I try to find a bank where the wavelets are lapping at an oblique angle, carrying pupae and hatching flies from deep, open water to within easy casting distance – and bringing with them a fair following of feeding trout.

Trout moving to ascending and hatching buzzers are renowned for travelling straight up-wind. It is therefore advisable to place one's imitations upwind of target fish, allowing the leader to sink momentarily just below the surface before commencing a slow figure-of-eight retrieve.

A final word regarding selection, or re-selection of the artificial fly; it cannot be over-stressed just how important and helpful an early examination of the stomach contents of a freshly caught trout can be.

If a fish contains a predominance of terrestrial shell-back beetles, it may pay to swap the buzzer imitations for small, dark-coloured, hackled flies, such as a Size 14 or 12 Zulu, Black and Peacock Spider or a standard Black Spider. Such a cast of flies should be fished extremely slowly just below the surface in the general vicinity of surface activity.

It may also pay to try a small 'semi-dry' fly fished static in the surface film, so that it mimics a small beetle trapped by the surface tension. A Size 14 Zulu, a Bibio, or a Brown Palmer, is an ideal pattern for this approach; being small, therefore light in weight, their palmered body hackles allow them to float in the surface film without the aid of a floatant which could make them stand too proud.

Boat fishing during the mid-April to May period is quite unpredictable; it may be like the preceding period if the weather is unkind; or, given conducive conditions, one may be fishing to buzzer rises either at anchor or even on the drift. The most productive areas will be the same as described for the bank rod, though they could be a little farther out on open water and a boat drifted or anchored in such a spot during a buzzer rise will offer the chance of good sport. Resist the temptation to take the boat closer in to where bank sport is seen, observe etiquette and do not approach within 45.7 m (50 yards).

## MAY: THE MONTH OF PLENTY

Buzzer hatches are prolific and varied, and the trout's appetite insatiable. Given the right conditions, the fish may rise all day. Without doubt, although buzzers are the most important food form during May and June there are many insect species appearing throughout the month. Perhaps the most important of the new arrivals is the lake olive dun; an up-winged fly. Lake olives may hatch the whole season through; but the largest hatches usually occur in May and June, and at the 'back-end' from about the third week in August, through to the end of September. Both the bank and boat fisherman can take full advantage of a rise to the lake olive.

A well-balanced rig usually has a nymph imitation on the point (occasionally lightly weighted), a winged fly on the middle dropper to represent a casualty of the hatch or a drowned adult and a 'hatching' imitation on the top dropper. Useful artificials include: for the point – a Pheasant Tail Nymph, a Border Angler's Nymph or the Grey Goose Nymph all dressed in Sizes 14 and 12 – some lightly weighted. For a drowned adult imitation on the middle dropper, a winged-wet Greenwell's Glory and its yellow-tagged variation will take some beating, but I experience good sport with my winged-wet Gold-ribbed Lake Olive. For the top dropper (bob-fly) position I use the winged-wet White Tailed Gold Ribbed Hare's Ear. This fishes well at almost any time and it is a superb hatching lake olive imitator. I use the standard darkish fur for early season, getting progressively lighter as the season progresses.

Trout feeding on ascending olive nymphs and the freshly hatched duns tend to quarter the water as they feed and although one casts ahead of a moving trout, the fish will not always cross the path of the leader. During the early part of a rise, cast in the general vicinity of moving fish, allow the artificials to drop-in and then commence a fairly steady figure-of-eight retrieve in the hope that a patrolling trout will come across the offerings.

If the rise intensifies I fish a full team of three winged imitations, casting them centrally over the boil of a rise, retrieving instantly by quickly hand-lining a short length of line at a time. In a frenzied feeding mood, trout take a fly savagely. This technique is particularly effective when one follows the wind-blown duns out over open water, fishing from a broad-side drifting boat.

Sometimes the trout feed steadily and confidently on the freshly hatched dun on the surface. A prime area for this activity is usually fairly shallow, becalmed water of an upwind shore. The rise form associated with this is an

*FIG 6* SEASONAL BUZZERS

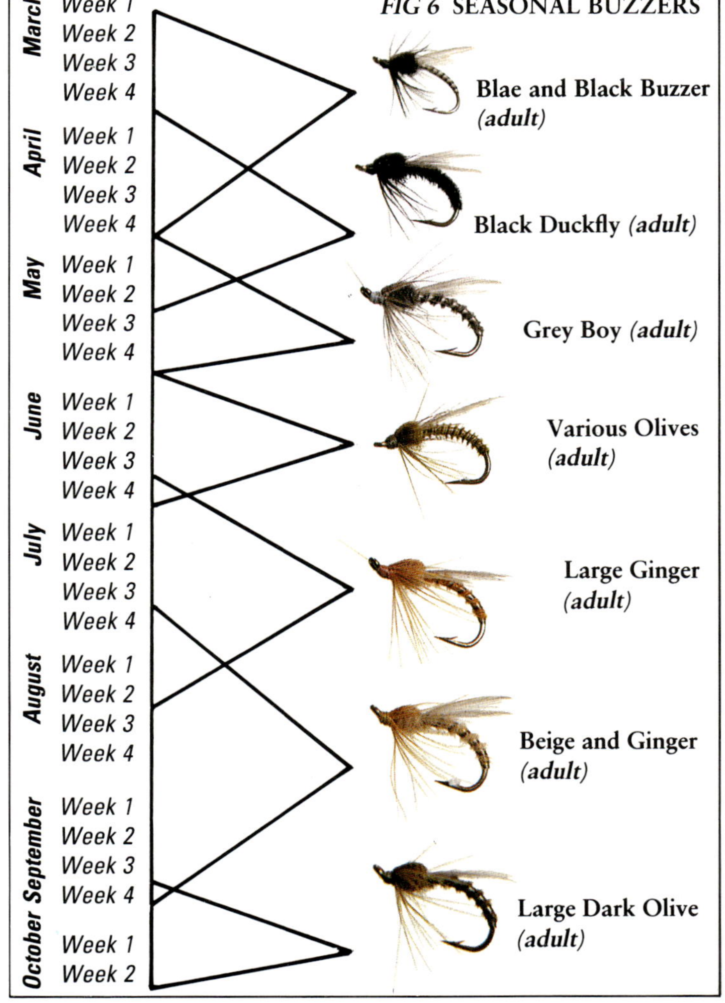

unmistakable, unhurried rise where just the neb of the trout breaks the surface.

Here, I usually cast a single dry-fly fished on a very fine, degreased tippet. On some days the best results come from casting to individual risers, on others the fly is best left undisturbed in an area of trout activity. In either case, when the trout takes the fly one must allow enough time for the fish to turn down before attempting to set the hook. An instant response usually results in a pricked fish, or no resistance at all on the line.

Not all surface activity in May will be due to aquatic flies, nymphs or pupae. There are two highly important terrestrial flies of which trout are very fond. The hawthorn fly can induce good rises when blown onto the water in large numbers. An appropriate dry-fly imitation is usually the best way of tackling such a rise, though I have often had good sport fishing a sunk imitation quite slowly just under the surface. In the absence of a suitable imitation, try a Size 12 Mallard and Claret, Connemara Black or Black and Peacock Spider.

Another important terrestrial, which appears about mid-May, is the tiny black gnat. Both the black gnat and hawthorn fly have a tendency to swarm in vast numbers in warm weather. The black gnat seems to be attracted to water and dances in columns low over the water, just a short way out over the margins. Trout become preoccupied with black gnats when large numbers are blown onto the water. Both the wet and dry-fly approaches are successful. A simple hackled pattern dressed on a Size 16 or 14 for both methods usually works. However, I have a special winged wet pattern I turn to when the trout are well and truly 'on' the black gnat.

The end of May and first half of June see the appearance of the mayfly. Trout take time to get used to the adult fly, perhaps intimidated by its large size. During this period the ascending nymphs are heavily preyed upon. So as soon as mayfly duns appear anglers should be searching the water with a suitably sized Mayfly Nymph or, as I prefer, a similar-sized Pheasant Tail Nymph. Recommended hook sizes for mayfly nymph imitations are Size 8 and 10 L/S – 2, 3 and 4X L/Ss are useful. (Fig. 7)

Once the trout have accepted the freshly hatched duns and spent spinners, good sport can be assured for a week or two. Casting an imitation dun or spinner into the path of a cruising trout and then watching it sucked down, can be heart-pounding. In all dry fly fishing, give the trout time to turn down before attempting to set the hook.

## JUNE: THE WATER WARMS

Perhaps the most significant change in June is the water temperature and the effect this has on the trout's feeding pattern. As the water temperature rises, day-time activity becomes less intense, giving way to excellent early morning and late evening rises. There are also three new, significant food forms to interest the fish, two fitting in with the evening feeding pattern – the caenis and the sedge. The other important species is the damsel fly nymph, which fills the usually quiet mid-day niche.

The first half of June must not be ignored, it can provide the best buzzer fishing of the season. Points of land overlooking bays are the real hot-spots. Most buzzer hatches in June are usually widespread and given a ripple excellent sport can be had from a drifting boat. However, established water currents, created by waves being pushed around a point of land, often hold large numbers of feeding trout and should not be ignored. (Figs 8, 9, 10, p. 82 )

If the wind speed reaches 16 kph (10 mph) or more, wind-lanes will form out on open water if the fishery is large enough. These can be highly productive areas, yet not all lanes will be used by trout, and the angler must search for the most productive drifts.

*A*

*B*

*FIG 7* CAPTAIN HAMILTON NYMPH HOOKS

*Medium-length hooks for large nymph patterns*

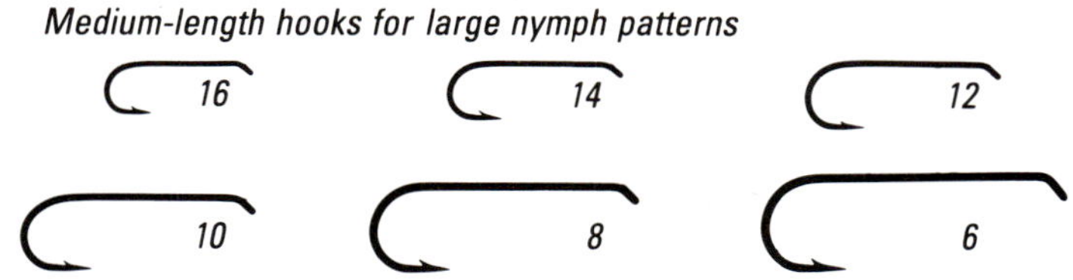


***A*** **A medium olive male dun. A very important fly as far as the trout fisherman is concerned. Extends throughout the season from April to October. A fly eagerly taken by trout and grayling alike. *B* An artificial medium olive fly, tied by John Goddard.**

By the middle of the month caenis and the sedge are well established, fitting perfectly into the summer feeding-pattern of the trout. Few anglers welcome the arrival of the caenis, the fisherman's curse, because of the frustratingly difficult rises they create. But the best caenis hatches occur during perfect summer fishing conditions, and they bring the trout to the top and in a feeding mood.

I do not worry over trout feeding on a soup of duns and spent spinners; on the contrary, I begin to fish in the late afternoon with a cast of Caenis Nymphs (own pattern), prospecting in and around sheltered and somewhat weeded bays. I fish the Nymphs until the surface of the lake is littered with the natural, creamy-coloured, freshly hatched duns and the trout are feeding madly. Then, rather than trying to get a trout to accept my dry imitation from among millions of naturals, I set up two rods to deal with the last two 'acts' of a typical summer evening's performance.

I mount sedge imitations on the first rod, usually a sedge pupa imitation on the point and first dropper, with a winged wet sedge, Invicta or Silver Knicker on the top dropper. On the other rod I fish buzzer imitations, usually two Size 10 black or dark claret buzzer pupa on the point and first dropper positions and a 10 Large Ginger Adult

*FIG 8* BANKSIDE HOT-SPOTS

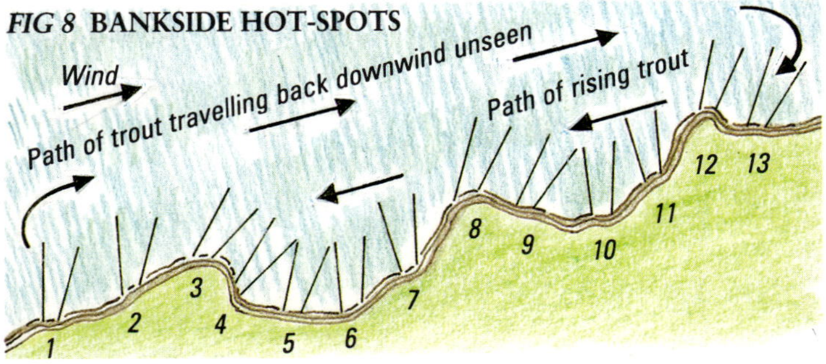


**_Figs 8, 9, 10_ Rods 1, 2, 3, 8, 9, 12, 13 occupy the hot-spots and can cover rising fish with ease. Rods 4, 5, 6, 7, 10, 11 will have great difficulty – or even find it impossible – to do likewise. Pre-season visits can supply information about prevailing winds, the nature of the bottom and its contours, the various depths, the position of feeder streams or natural springs – all can be assessed and remembered when the time comes to cast a fly.**

*FIG 9* HOT-SPOTS ROUND A SHARP POINT OF LAND

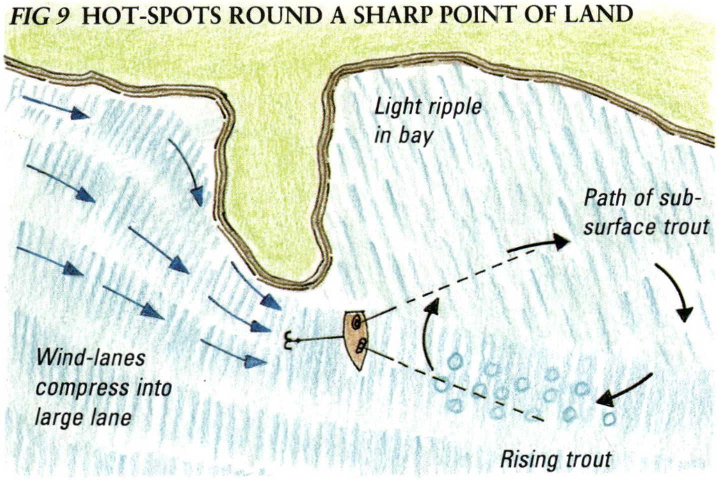


*FIG 10* HOT-SPOTS ROUND A SMALL BULGE OF LAND

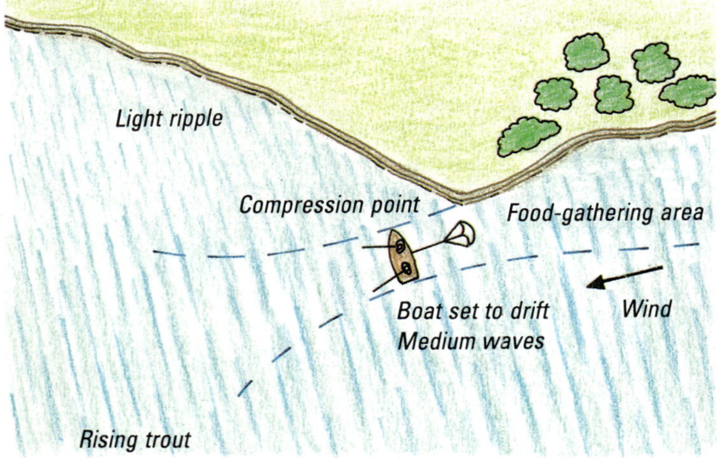

## CHARR

*Salvelinus alpinus*

A minutely scaled member of the salmon family found in a few waters of the British Isles, where the charr population can be considered as land-locked, these are migratory fish that were stranded in a number of locations after the last Ice Age. Charr are found in some parts of Scotland, the north-west of England, Wales and Ireland. They inhabit deep, cold glacial lakes where the lack of rich feeding prevents them from growing to sizes attained in other parts of Northern Europe where the species is often sea-dwelling for part of the year, returning to freshwater to spawn. Resembling the trout in shape, there is a white fringing to the pectoral, ventral and anal fins. In the winter a vivid red breeding colour appears on the fins and belly. A charr of 0.9 kg (2 lb) is a specimen.

**Bait:** Artificial flies and small spinners.

The stomach content of a pot-bellied trout taken on Lough Conn produced hundreds of minute charr fry.

MAP SHOWING DISTRIBUTION OF CHARR, *SALVELINUS ALPINUS*, IN THE BRITISH ISLES, BOTH EXTINCT AND EXTANT

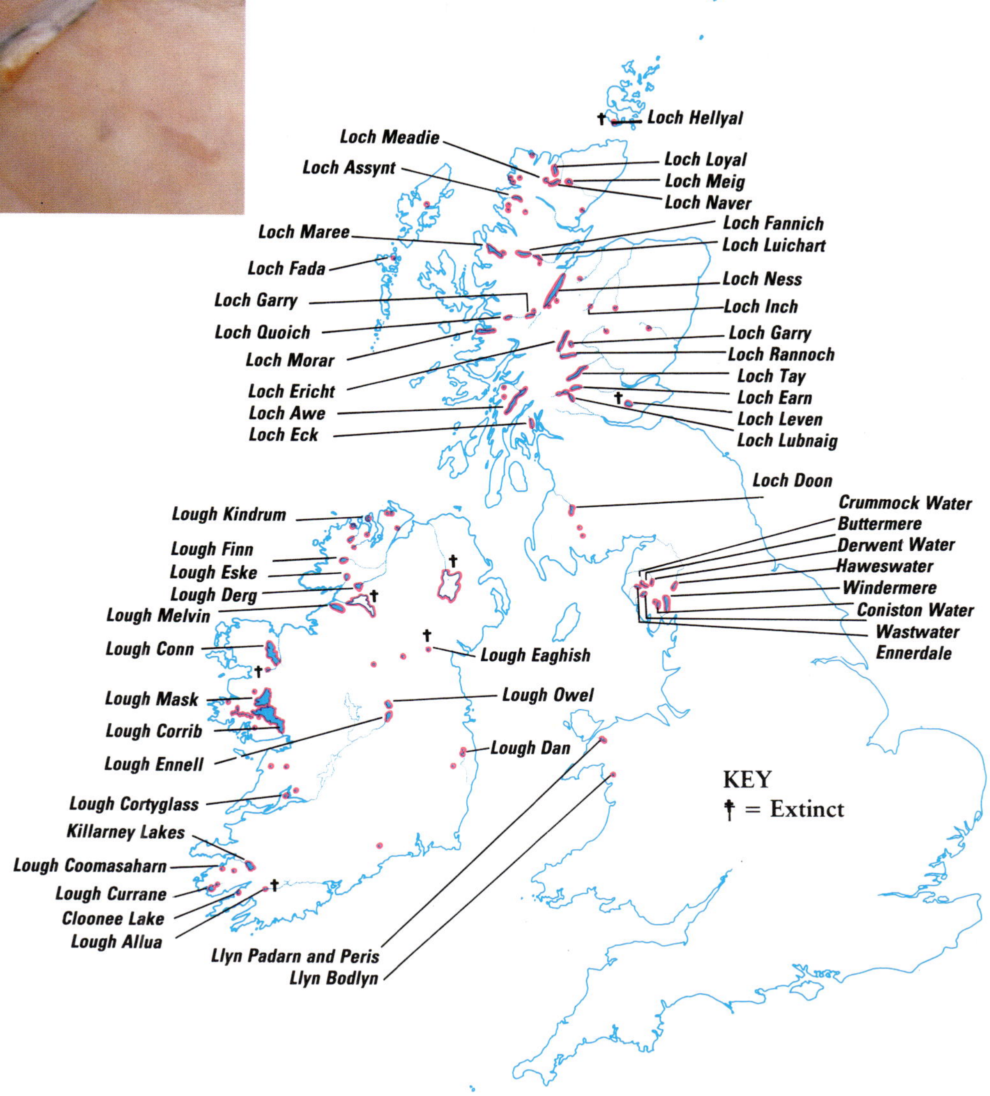

## NORTH AMERICAN BROOK TROUT

*Salvelinus fontinalis*

This species was introduced into British freshwaters from the eastern States of the US in 1884, at about the same time as the rainbow trout was brought to Europe. Another introduction was made from the Continent, in 1869. The brook trout is not a trout but a charr and is sometimes called the speckled trout or speckled charr. The species does not seem to have survived the initial introductions, although there are a few fisheries that have more recently established a thriving population of this fine fighting game fish. A specimen of 2.65 kg (5 lb 13½ oz) is recorded.

Bait: Artificial lures and worms.

buzzer on the top. In this way I am prepared in anticipation of the switch.

On a text-book evening, while the trout are still gorging on caenis, a steady stream of mature sedge flies will trickle out over the water. Often, a new hatch of sedge flies commences at the same time. The first switch of the evening is made as soon as there is enough sedge activity to divert the trout's attention away from the caenis.

The trout's rise to the sedge in its various forms may last into the dark, providing fast and exciting sport. But, as suddenly as it started, it can cease. The sedge-suggesting patterns which have proved so successful are ignored, even though rising fish can be seen and heard all around. The third and final switch has now taken place and it is time to pick up the other rod, already rigged for a buzzer rise.

The trout are still feeding on large buzzers when most anglers are leaving the water. Now, anglers can fish by sound for rising trout, or by instinct if they can. Or they can position themselves facing the western sky-line so that the rise forms are silhouetted.

Not all anglers can fish at the prime times, many find themselves at the water-side in the worst period, mid-

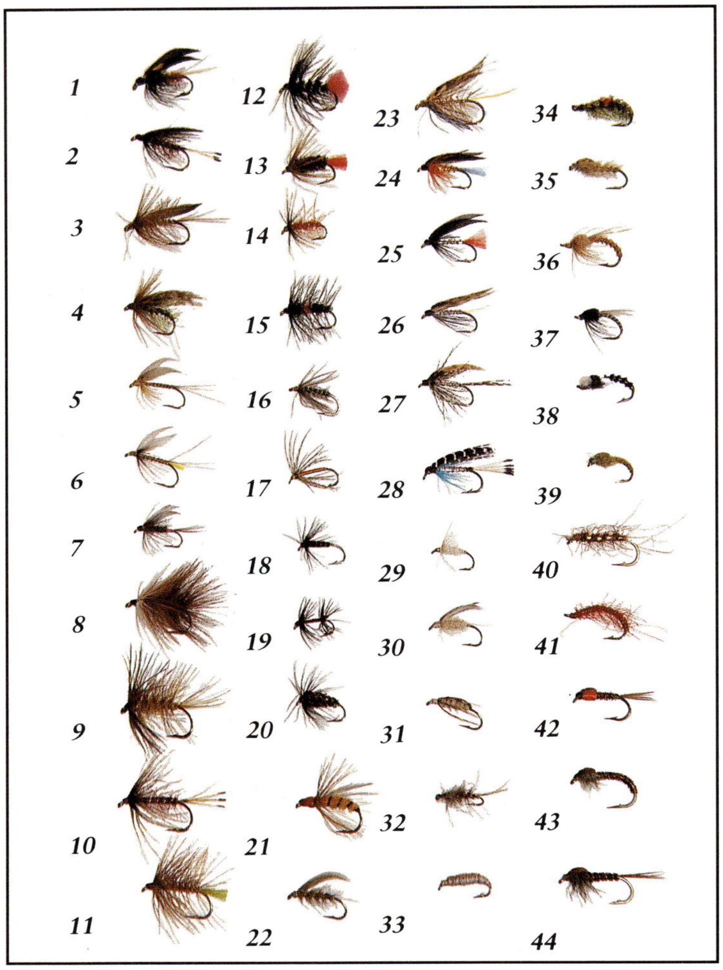


morning to mid-afternoon. Yet, given favourable conditions, there is a very good chance that fair numbers of damsel fly nymphs will be migrating shorewards to hatch (transform, being a better term) affording the chance of some unique sport.

These sightings tell the angler to fish a single damsel fly nymph imitation through the marginal waters. Whenever I fish the artificial in a situation like this I use one on the point of a very long leader, say 4.6 to 6 m (15 to 20 ft), depending upon conditions. In a calm or near calm, the leader is lengthened, and in a reasonable ripple or light wave it may be shortened. The most productive retrieve is a long, steady draw on the line, keeping the nymph just beneath the surface, where the trout will be.

## JULY: THE PATTERN IS ESTABLISHED

Fishing can be easy, it can be difficult, it can be frustrating or even heart-breaking, it all depends on the weather and the adaptability of the angler. One thing is certain, the summer feeding-pattern is well established, with early morning and late evening providing the bulk of our sport. The trout's menu is much the same as it was in June, with sedges and buzzers rating high on the list. Daphnia have been available all season; it is now that trout tend to feed on them seriously.

Another form of food which tends to keep the daytime period alive are the millions of coarse-fish fry. Most hatched out around the first week in June, but it is only now that trout take them really seriously. Fry-bashing

TROUT WET FLIES, NYMPHS AND BUZZERS

*1* Watson's Fancy
*2* Mallard and Claret
*3* Wickham's Fancy
*4* Green Peter
*5* Ginger Quill *(winged wet)*
*6* Greenwell's Glory
*7* Iron Blue Dun
*8* Loch Ordie
*9* Golden Olive Bumble
*10* Claret Pennell
*11* Wingless Wickham's *(amber tag)*
*12* Zulu
*13* Red Tag
*14* Grenadier
*15* Bibio
*16* Waterhen Bloa
*17* Partridge and Orange
*18* Black Spider
*19* Knotted Midge
*20* Black and Peacock Spider
*21* Drone Fly *(T. Saville winged wet)*
*22* White-tailed Gold-Ribbed Hare's Ear *(winged wet)*
*23* Silver Invicta
*24* Kingfisher Butcher
*25* Silver Butcher
*26* Silver Knicker
*27* Silver March Brown
*28* Teal Blue and Silver
*29* Wingless Cameo Lady
*30* Cameo Lady
*31* Corixa
*32* Gold-Ribbed Hare's Ear *(original)*
*33* Killer Bug *(Sawyer)*
*34* Red Spot Shrimp *(N. Patterson)*
*35* White-Tailed Gold-Ribbed Hare's Ear Nymph
*36* Large Ginger AB
*37* Black Duckfly Adult Buzzer
*38* Poly-Rib Buzzer Pupa
39 Olive Buzzer Pupa
40 Shipman's Buzzer
41 Seal's Fur Bloodworm
42 Hot-Spot Pheasant Tail Nymph
43 Cove Nymph
44 Pheasant Tail Nymph

***Wet flies, nymphs and buzzers tied by Bob Carnill***

## VENDACE AND POLLAN

*Coregonus albula*

## POWAN, SCHELLY AND GWYNIAD

*Coregonus lavaretus*

## THE COREGONIDS OR WHITEFISH

Fishes of the Salmonidae: *Coregonus lavaretus* (powan, schelly and gwyniad); *C. albula* (vendace and pollan); *C. oxyrinchus* (houting), but Unesco (1984) recognises only the vendace, *C. albula*, and houting, *C. lavaretus*. All six fish have similar characteristics, like a herring with small scales but possessing an adipose fin. With the exception of the vendace they have pointed snouts with protruding upper jaws. They share a feeding behaviour on plankton and small animal-life feeders and inhabit stillwaters, mostly in the north and west of the British Isles. In Europe the coregonids live in rivers and lakes, with some migratory species. In Eastern Europe the houting is partially sea-dwelling.

trout are notoriously difficult. Having had every lure offered them the trout become conditioned to it and more subtle methods are required to take these easily accessible trout. Fishing a floating-fry imitation is one method that is extremely popular nowadays, though this approach peaks during August and September.

The technique is simple enough. Locate an area of activity. If fry-bashing is taking place there will be agitated fry in the surface film. The shoal swims away from the predator by fanning out on the surface, and showers of tiny fry leap from the water as a trout closes in, then a slashing attack leaves many injured and struggling on the surface.

The floating-fry was designed with these casualties in mind. After an attack, the trout will return to feed on dead and dying fry as they float in the waves. Rise forms, as trout take fry from the surface, are reminiscent of a nymphing fish.

Most floating-fry patterns these days use a white expanded foam of some kind or another to form the fish-like shape and provide the necessary buoyancy. It is advisable to match the size of the artificial fry against that of the natural fish.

Fishing the floating-fry is not unlike fishing a dry fly. It is cast out into an area of activity, allowed to float unrestricted on the ripple or wave or simply left static in a flat calm. Once the floating-fry is taken, setting the hook should be delayed just long enough for the fish to turn

## HOUTING

*Coregonus oxyrinchus*

MAP SHOWING THE DISTRIBUTION OF THE *COREGONUS* spp IN THE BRITISH ISLES

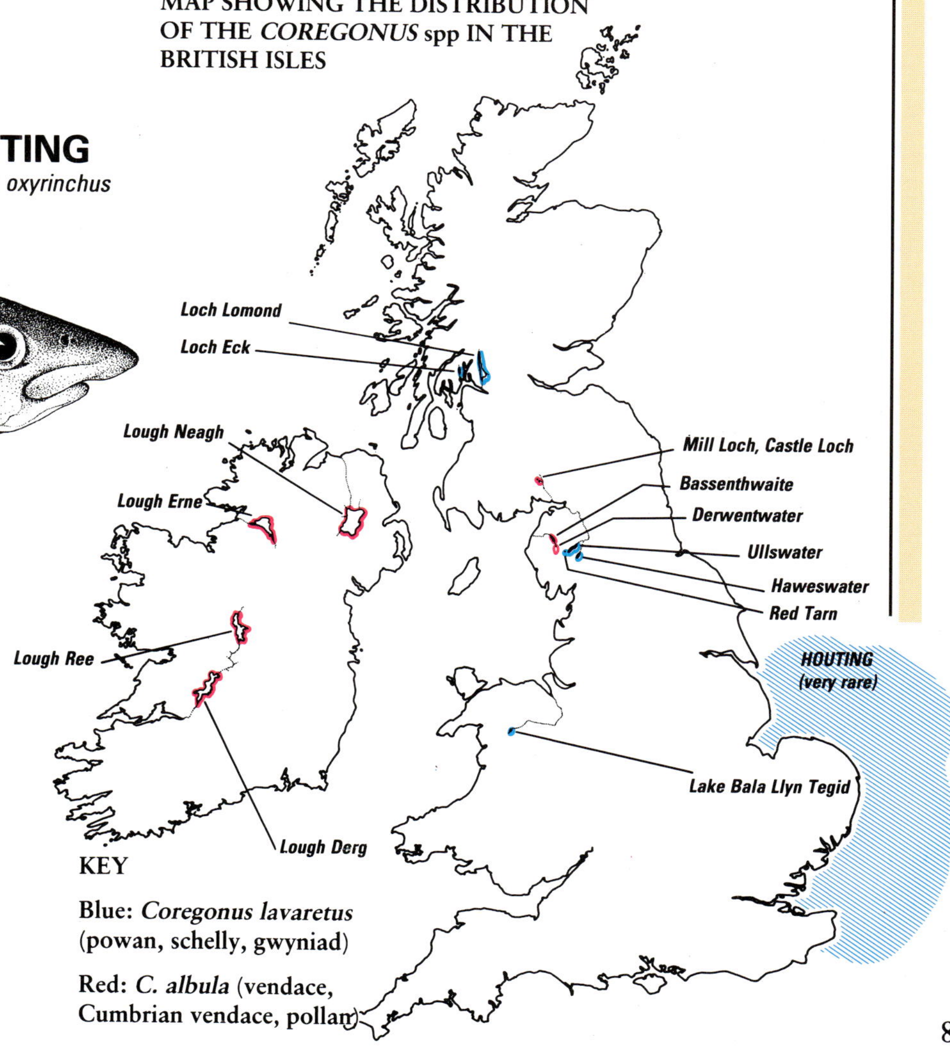

down and properly close its mouth. Most anglers will use just the one fry on the point, but I often use two. The second lure is on a 10 cm (4 in) dropper, about 1.2 m (4 ft) from the point. Sometimes a twitched fry will prove more attractive to the trout than one fished static. As with all trout fishing, experimentation is a must.

## MID-JULY TO MID-AUGUST: THE DIFFICULT PERIOD

These are the dog-days when the trout are fat and summer-fed, and water temperature is at its highest. Early morning and evening are the most productive periods of the day. Sometimes the dog-days get a reprieve when a high wind stirs, cools and oxygenates the surface layer of water, which can make it very attractive to the trout, even during mid-day heat.

During a good blow, one of the most exciting methods is to fish the wake-lure over the front of a drifting boat. Since the late 1960s, the Muddler Minnow has become synonymous with this style of fishing. Its highly buoyant spun deer hair head makes it ideal but many variations have been tied on the basic theme. In some cases, cork and hard foam have replaced the traditional spun deer's hair. One thing that cannot be changed is the principle that makes this type of lure so attractive to the trout.

Most wake lures are what might be called water-movers, they do not skim lightly over the water, the rear-end sits within it while a broad head ploughs a furrow of disturbance in the surface. One may fish a wake-lure as a single lure on the point, or as part of a team. For team work, the wake-lure is fished either on the point with two dropper flies above or, more popularly, on the top dropper, with the two droppers fishing behind. The latter combination is somewhat out of balance so far as casting is concerned, but of the two it is generally recognised as being the most effective.

The theory is that any disturbance made by the wake-lure homes the trout on to the trailing nymphs or flies and it works, for it is common to see a trout appear from nowhere to chase the lure for quite a distance before turning down and taking one of the trailing artificials. There are days, however, when all the attention and takes come to the wake-lure.

## AUGUST: THE SPORT CONTINUES TO IMPROVE

August starts right in the middle of the dog-days. Whereas the sport went from excellent to difficult in July, it can now be expected gradually to improve. Sedge flies, large buzzers, daphnia and fry still form the basis of the trout's food but from the middle of the month through much of September there is a swing to corixae feeding where this species proliferates. Large numbers of chironomid (buzzer) larvae may also be found in trout stomachs. Several species of larvae may be present in the autopsies but the red variety, bloodworm, appears to be most favoured by the trout.

The appearance of bloodworm and other larvae during

**A TROUT DRY FLIES**

*1* Tup's Indispensible
*2* Pale Watery Dun
*3* Gravel Bed
*4* Brown Palmer
*5* Wonder-Wing Alder
*6* G & H Deer Hair Sedge
*7* Red Sedge *(Walker)*
*8* Little Red Sedge *(Skues)*
*9* Winged Black Gnat
*10* Hackled Black Gnat
*11* Knotted Midge
*12* Winged Rough Olive
*13* Ginger Quill
*14* Orange Spinner
*15* Grey Duster *(parachute hackle)*
*16* Grey Duster

Flies to be fished in surface film:
*17* Amber Spinner *(T. Clegg)*
*18* Ginger Spinner
*19* Terrestrial Beetle *(Carnill)*

**B RESERVOIR NYMPHS AND STREAMERS**

*1* Blue and Silver Terror
*2* Brailsford's Green Nymph
*3* Cased Caddis *(Carnill)*
*4* Wormfly
*5* Damsel Nymph *(Carnill)*
*6* Montana Nymph
*7* Wadham's Floating Fry
*8* Baby Doll
*9* Sweeney Todd
*10* Goldie
*11* Muddler Minnow *(original)*
*12* Breathalyser
*13* Leprechaun
*14* Appetiser
*15* White Marabou
*16* Zonker
*17* Black Dog Nobbler
*18* Vulture
*19* Hanningfield Lure

warm, settled conditions appears to be directly linked with the gas-inflated mats of algae which regularly break away from the lake bed and float up to the surface. During August the floating fry really comes into its own. It can be a day-saver and regularly produces some of the heaviest bags of trout to be recorded for the whole season. The best sport from corixae-feeding trout is usually to be found in the areas of heavy fry-feeding activity.

For many years, trout stomach contents have proved that during August there is a marked preference for the immature, larval corixae. Many are taken from the surface where they rest briefly after shedding their outer skin in order to grow-on. Trout taking these tiny corixae often do so with head-and-tail rise, which suggests that they are feeding on nymphs or pupae.

My favourite way of tackling trout feeding in this manner is to position myself so that I can cast across the ripple, upwind of a feeding area. Mounted on my leader will be a trio of Size 16 buff-beige hackled flies, a smaller version of my Cameo Lady minus the wing. When wet, these patterns look remarkably similar to the translucent natural insect. The leader is usually given a light smear of Muscilin grease, though the short droppers and 5 cm (2 in) or so of the point are de-greased to ensure that the artificials work just below the surface. One final touch is to squeeze the flies below the surface of the water so as to soak them thoroughly.

Once the cast has been delivered upwind of a feeding area, the flies must be allowed to drift freely round and over the hot-spot. The slightest retrieve of the line will make the flies skate and ruin everything. A take will register as a pulling tight on the line, which only requires leaning into to set the hook. Should a take not occur, wait until the team of flies has floated clear of the hot-spot, before lifting off to re-cast upwind and letting it come round again.

The majority of corixa patterns are intended to imitate the adult insect and they do it admirably. Some are weighted to allow for deep fishing, while others will be

A

B

lightly dressed, ideal for shallow water and prospecting around weed beds.

What do I use when imitating the adult corixa? My Cameo Lady is not a cure-all during the corixae feeding period, but the winged-wet Cameo Lady is my first choice when the trout are eagerly feeding on adults of this species. It has little in common with the adult corixa, but the trout accept it, particularly when the artificial is retrieved quite quickly.

Fishing over-the-front from a drifting boat can be excellent during this month provided, as for July fishing, there is a good wind. With a good wave, bushy flies such as the Soldier Palmer and all its variants are ideal for top-dropper work; with straggly bodied seal's (or substitute) fur patterns on the point and middle dropper. Suitable patterns include the Grenadier, Shredge and the drowned Drone Fly.

August is also a good time for searching deep, open water for the daphnia-feeding rainbows and gaudy lures usually bring the best results. In August, however, one may be confronted with a pea-souper of an algal boom, making the need for bigger, even more gaudy lures that much more important.

The golden dun midge is the most important buzzer species for the month with the main hatches occurring during middle to late evening. Huge hatches of this fly frequently coincide with very settled conditions which often produces the dreaded flat calm few anglers can cope with. On evenings such as this the lake may be a mass of various rise forms. There could be trout slashing at sedges and/or egg-laying buzzers, others slurping and sucking down spent flies while other fish head and tail as they cleave the struggling pupae from the surface film.

The angler's fly line and leader are his main enemy when coping with a flat calm. Both stand out on the surface of the water and have trout-scaring properties. The use of an intermediate fly line can do the trick when using both imitative patterns and lures, which become increasingly effective the darker the evening, particularly for those larger-than-average brown trout which 'lift' in the water with the onset of darkness.

By the end of the month the quality of the fishing improves. The weather and water temperature are more conducive to good sport with the return of the black gnat and the lake olive. Both may appear in vast numbers, steadily increasing as September progresses. A few daddy-long-legs appear at the end of August.

## SEPTEMBER: TIME TO STOKE UP

This is the most favoured month for the fly fisher. The 'over-seasoned' trout are in absolute prime condition and their appetites voracious, giving the impression that they sense the onset of winter and are stoking-up for harder months ahead.

This is the time when every trout-fisher can employ his or her most favoured method, wet-fly, dry-fly, nymph or lure. In the mellow days of this month, trout may be on the move from sun-up to sunset. Throughout September, the trout will be fry feeding or taking even larger coarse fish. Sedge flies are still in evidence, still forming an important part of the diet, as do corixae, lake olives, black gnat and that giant terrestrial the daddy-long-legs.

Fry-feeding trout may be moving at first light or before, often very close into the margins, and another bonus is that the same trout which became conditioned to lures earlier in the season now seem to throw caution to the wind and will often attack them quite viciously.

From about mid-morning to mid-afternoon lake olives and black gnats can be expected and these are rarely ignored by the trout. The techniques described for these species for the May/June period will still apply and should produce excellent results.

Given anything like a stiff breeze to a good blow, some of the daddy-long-legs which hatched the previous evening will be blown out on to open water. As with the mayfly, it takes a little time in the early days of their emergence for the trout to get used to and accept this larger-than-normal fly. Nevertheless, once the trout have got the taste of the daddy good sport may be experienced from both the bank and the boat.

Out on the boats, and on the right day, the dapped daddy can produce fascinating and extremely exciting sport. Depending on the fishery rules, both the artificial or the live daddy may be used. For this fishing, a longer-than-average rod is a must, upwards of 3.6 m (12 ft) being the norm, but enthusiasts of the dap will usually use rods nearer to 5.1 m (17 ft). The principle behind dapping is to allow the wind to carry the fly aloft, well in advance of a broad-side drifting boat, then by lowering the rod the fly is allowed to settle lightly on to the surface without any part of the leader coming into contact with the water. The fly is then deftly bobbled along on the surface, punctuated by occasional pauses.

In order to use the strength of the wind and be able to control the artificial perfectly, a special line, often referred to as a blow-line, is necessary. Instead of floss silk, modern technology has given us an ever-increasing range of synthetic flosses. For moderate wind strengths, about 2.7 m (9 ft) of floss is usually sufficient, but should be considerably shorter in high winds.

The reel-end of the dapping floss is usually attached to a generous supply of about 3.6 kg (8 lb) b.s. monofilament and for the leader, a length of 2.2 to 2.7 kg (5 to 6 lb) b.s. mono. Whichever method of attachment is adopted it is vital that the uppermost knot passes easily through the top eyes of the rod. Leader length is a debatable subject; some fishermen will advocate one as short as 1.2 m (4 ft), whereas others will go for 1.8 or 2.0 m (6 or 7 ft). It is how a particular rig is performing in a given wind strength that matters, if one feels the need to lengthen or shorten a leader in order for it to be more controllable, then so be it.

For much of September evening fishing can be excellent, with sedges and buzzers often being taken simultaneously by the trout and all the early season methods are still good. Often it makes good sense to have two rods set up in advance, one carrying sedge-suggesting patterns and buzzers imitations on the other.

During a good season, excellent sport may continue right through to the month's end. However, from about the middle of the month and through into October, on some stillwater fisheries shoals of trout are beginning to take up residence in certain parts of the lake, usually within casting distance from the bank. This shoaling behaviour affects both trout species but it is more noticeable among the brown trout.

The favoured gathering grounds of brown trout are in fairly shallow water, over a hard, stony bottom. Shoals are evident by the restless leaping of the fish, rather than by rising in the recognised manner. Most of the trout are males in breeding colours and they have not gathered to feed. They may lack appetite, but they have plenty of aggression and a medium-to-slow retrieve of a lure through their territory will be chased or attacked.

## OCTOBER: THE WEATHER FACTOR

The right weather conditions are always a key factor to successful trout fishing, though October seems to be more finely balanced in this respect than most. Good sport can almost be guaranteed should mild weather extend into October. On the other hand, bitter north-east winds are to be expected and they can kill the sport. The season usually closes as the end of the month approaches, regardless of local rules which, in some areas, permit fishing for rainbows to continue throughout the winter. The close season for brown trout is variable throughout the different regions. It may be closed as from the 1st of October in one, or as late as the 30th in another. Nevertheless, tactics for brown trout remain the same as for the latter part of September.

Brown and rainbow trout are the two most common species stocked in our lakes. Of the two, the rainbow is the most desirable quarry as we reach the last week or so of October. Most rainbow trout reach spawning condition later than the brown trout and therefore retain their condition considerably longer. Many fisheries have now introduced Triploids (genetically engineered asexual trout) and similar all-female rainbows to their waters. This has a beneficial effect on the quality of the back-end winter fishing where it is encouraged and the early part of the following season. Triploids being asexual retain their condition throughout because the reproductive organs are undeveloped and the all-female stock fish either shed their ova or re-absorb it, and by so doing, they too quickly regain condition.

Given a normal October the stomach contents of trout will reveal an ever-decreasing amount of food with each passing week. In the early part of the month, fish fry and fingerlings will still be eaten, and so too will snails. During the more settled milder days, there may be rises to buzzers and the last of the sedges, the latter emerging in the early afternoon sunshine and not the evening, when the air-temperature usually drops very low, very quickly.

There are exceptions to the rule. Not all seasons are the same so we must always be alert and prepared to take advantage of the unexpected. In most years I have stopped

A

*A* **Fishing the wet fly across and downstream to a trout that had risen repeatedly, indicating its position, to take struggling, emergent flies on the streamy surface current.**
*B* **Fishing the dry fly upstream and across the River Suir in late afternoon. Flies hatched sporadically throughout the sunlit hours but emerged in thousands, to induce a feeding frenzy in the hungry trout as twilight came to the river.**



trout fishing by the middle to last week in October, preferring only to follow the traditional trout season from spring through to autumn.

## RIVER TROUTING

The seasonal behaviour of trout in running-water is very similar to that of lake trout: during the cold-water period of early spring they will be found close to the river bed, usually in the deeper and slower parts of the pools. Apart from their usual diet of bottom-dwelling invertebrates, spring-caught river trout are frequently found to contain bullheads, stone loaches and small grayling.

As the water warms in the spring sun, the trout move higher in the water and begin to feed greedily on ascending nymphs, hatching and freshly hatched flies. During this period fish quickly regain their former strength and condition, having been depleted by spawning and the winter which followed, and so they begin to occupy lies in the faster, shallow water. This will usually be at the head and the tail of the pools or close to the bank in the pool itself where the main current channels a steady supply of water-borne food to them.

Like the stillwaters, rivers also have their dog-days, although they usually arrive a little earlier in the season. From about the middle of June through to August, the day-time period can be very dour indeed. A fish or two may be found rising if one walks the banks in search of them. Evenings are now usually the most productive part of the day. In settled conditions an evening rise is to be expected and sport is brisk provided that the correct artificial fly is found in time.

Late August and all of September sees renewed daytime surface activity from the trout. This is due to several factors: (1) on many rivers, if not most, flies will be in an abundance, (2) the shortening days and cooler nights lower the water temperature and appear to re-vitalize trout, and (3) like their stillwater counterparts, river trout can sense the approach of winter and to survive the rigours of spawning and winter they must feed well.

Sport can be good to the end of the season if the weather is fine and water levels remain favourable. Where grayling occur they can provide excellent sport for the fly-fisher through the winter while the river is in good order.

B

## THE RIVER TROUT'S DIET

The nymphs and larvae of aquatic flies form a very important part of the river trout's diet, with the up-winged or 'day-flies' being the most important. These are followed closely by the caddis flies, the stoneflies and alder flies.

Not all waters will have the above insect species. Some will be rich with aquatic insect life, while others will be poor. Where scarcity occurs naturally, terrestrial flies and beetles will take the place of aquatic food forms. In areas where this occurs, the trout are usually very free rising and feed less selectively. Among the many terrestrials which the trout will take are the black gnat, hawthorn fly, cow-dung fly, heather fly, various crane flies, soldier and sailor beetle, bees, flying ants, aphids, bracken clocks (beetles), caterpillars, and others. On many waters, too, freshwater shrimp (Gammarus) and water-snails will also form an important part of the trout's diet.

TACKLE: For the larger rivers, stillwater (reservoir/lake) rods, lines and terminal tackle will be perfectly suitable. For the smaller rivers, streams and becks, particularly those generously canopied by overhanging trees, a much shorter rod and a light line are not only more desirable, they are a necessity.

TACTICS: Many of the dry-flies, wet-flies and nymphs used for lake fishing will be equally useful on running-water, but their application is different. The flow which makes rivers so appealing and inviting is the beginner's greatest enemy before it becomes his friend. To present an artificial fly correctly so that it attracts trout, as opposed to putting them down, we must be able to recognise and understand the different kinds of current and make them work for us.

## DRY-FLY FISHING

The classic dry-fly approach is to delicately cast the fly between 0.3 to 0.6 m (1 to 2 ft) upstream of a rising trout, without any portion of the nylon leader crossing the fish, and then collect the loose fly line with the free hand as it is carried back downstream on the current. The line may be collected in loops or by using the figure-of-eight method. Whichever is adopted, the speed at which the line is collected must match that of the current, but without disturbing the artificial. The angler must be in full control at all times and able to set the hook should the fly be taken.

Even on a glass-smooth glide it is rare for the current to run at one speed between the angler and his target fish. Trout are notorious for taking up feeding positions where the flow of the main current is altered. The usual reason for the fish choosing such a spot is because water-borne food is being channelled and carried quickly along on the swifter current created by the diversion.

Each rising fish must be approached on an individual basis and with an open mind for no two lies are exactly the same. The best results may come from carefully choosing an angle of approach which will allow a straight line and leader to be delivered. Where this is not possible or if the current is particularly tricky, then the 'snaky' (loose) line and leader approach may be the only solution.

The snaky-line not only comes in handy when fishing the up-stream dry-fly, but also when we need to fish across the current or even downstream. Turning one's back on the current and casting downstream may be considered unethical on some fisheries. However, for the majority of rivers where wet and dry-fly are the accepted methods, learning this technique can come in very useful in a situation where an up-stream or across-the-current approach is not possible.

To throw a snaky-line we must cast the fly in the usual way, but aimed to over-shoot the mark by about half a metre (1 or 2 ft) when fishing up or across the stream, or a metre (3 or 4 ft) when casting downstream. Then as the cast unfurls, instead of following through as normal, the rod is stopped rather higher. This has the effect of a shock absorber and a spring, i.e. it will stop the fly line while still quite high above the water, and the recoil of the rod will suddenly pull the fly line and leader backwards to fall lightly on to the water in a snaky formation. The recoil which creates the loose-line effect can be increased by pulling the rod tip back at the end of the cast, and then quickly lowering it. Any variation in the current between angler and trout will then work on straightening out the snaky line, thereby allowing the fly to float unhindered over the trout's position.

LEADERS: Presenting the dry-fly demands accurate and delicate casting. One of the surest ways of achieving this is to use a good-quality knotless tapered leader. Cast correctly, this type of leader will give a perfect turn-over and an accurate delivery, allowing the fly to alight gently. Knotless tapered leaders are expensive and not everyone would be prepared to buy a leader that costs approximately ten times as much as one made up by joining three short lengths of mono together. Sometimes I am caught without a knotless leader during a good wet-fly fishing spree, then the trout suddenly turn their attention to flies floating on the surface. When this happens I put a leader together myself. A taper of 3.4, 2.5 and 1.5 kg (7½, 5½ and 3½ lb) b.s. will be more than adequate. However, should the trout be preoccupied with really minute food forms, an additional short section of 0.7 or 0.9 kg (1½ or 2 lb) b.s. ensures that the artificial fly fishes correctly.

It cannot be over emphasized just how important tippet diameter is. Always err on the finer side rather than the heavy. If too heavy it will dominate the fly, preventing it from sitting correctly on the surface of the water; in addition it may also restrict the fly from following faithfully the small movements of the current.

Greasing the dry-fly leader has been a controversial issue for a very long time. For example, in a lively stickle at the head or neck of a pool it really doesn't matter. In this kind of water the fly passes very quickly over the trout and in any case leader-shadow, which is what we are trying to avoid, will be lost among all the other shadows thrown

A

*A* Verdant bankside growth and lush water plants create the perfect trout fishery. The streams draining surrounding hills ensure a plentiful, clean and continuous water flow to the Suir.

*B* Shallow margins on a limestone lake provide prolific weed growth. In these conditions one can expect huge numbers of invertebrate life. Wading is taboo and trout feed in very shallow water.

B

across the river bed by the action of the ruffled surface water. In this situation it usually pays to lightly grease-up so as to prevent a drowned leader from doing like-wise to the fly.

At the other extreme is a shallow, gin-clear chalk-stream glide over a light-coloured river bed where every speck floating on the surface throws down an exaggerated shadow. Here we would be advised to camouflage the leader's presence by encouraging it to sink just below the surface. This is achieved by rubbing the leader down with a proprietary sinking/de-greasing agent, a home-made concoction, or soft bankside mud.

## DRY-FLY FLOATANTS

Perhaps the greatest step forward in modern floatants was the introduction of silicone-based products. The beauty of Permaflote and others is that we can give the artificials a quick soak, after which they dry out very fast indeed leaving them thoroughly water-proofed well in advance of being used.

There are times when the trout show a distinct preference for a fly floating in the surface film, as opposed to standing on it. The more conventional patterns specifically designed for this type of fishing are parachute flies and those dressed with a wide variety of spent wings. There is, however, an ever-increasing swing to straggly bodied flies of dubbed fur. For buoyancy, these patterns rely solely on the treated, picked-out body fur.

## WET-FLY ON RIVERS

Wet-fly includes nymph fishing as well as the more traditional wet patterns, and like the dry-fly, wet-fly/nymph fishing can be practised up, across, and downstream. When fishing up or across the current many of the guidelines given earlier for the dry-fly will apply with equal importance to both the wet-fly and nymph. Any pattern fished in this manner, albeit sunk below the surface, must be allowed to ride freely with the current, unhindered by drag of any kind.

In very clear water the artificial and the trout may be observed at all times, allowing us to fish and react accordingly. On less clear or broken water, the tip of the fly line or leader must be watched where it enters the water and there must be instant reaction on seeing the slightest dip, falter, or stopping of one of them, by tightening into what will probably be a take. Sometimes a sub-surface boil or a silver or golden flash will be seen as the trout turns down after taking the fly and the hook should be set immediately, otherwise the fish may be lost.

## DOWNSTREAM WET-FLY AND NYMPH FISHING

Fishing the wet-fly or nymph down and across the current is perhaps the most under-rated and most criticized form of fly fishing. When fishing the down-stream fly or nymph, a trout may be indicating its position by rising, which makes things decidedly easier, or it may not. In the case of the latter, it may well be that trout are lying quite deep in the water and feeding on nymphs being carried along on the current. This may occur at any time throughout the season, but during the early days of spring it is often the norm. Whether we are presenting our fly just sub-surface to a riser or combing the depths with leaded nymphs in search of a feeding trout, the problem is to deafeat the speed of the river's flow and the various currents it creates, and maintain the depth at which we wish the fly/nymph to fish. If we fail in this respect the current will lift the leader and flies, and even heavily weighted nymphs, and make them skate unattractively across the surface.

Leader-lift and skating flies are two natural hazards which quickly become evident when we first start to learn the art of downstream wet-fly fishing. The power of the current constantly plays on the angle of the leader and tries to lift it to the surface. There are several ways of taming the current and making the flies fish at the correct depth. We could use a sinking line in any of a variety of densities, or a sink-tip, but I use neither. The former I dislike immensely in running water, the latter I prefer to do without. My preference is for a full floating line, flies and nymphs dressed to suit the occasion, and as much upstream mending of the line as is necessary in any given location.

For really deep fishing, mending the line and leaded nymphs go hand-in-hand and form a deadly combination which allows us to search the water very effectively in most currents. 'Mending' the line means throwing a loose upstream loop, or series of loops, in the fly line which momentarily prevents current drag on the foremost part of the line and leader, thus allowing the heavy nymphs to sink deep without restraint of any kind. The loose line which forms the mend(s), is held in a large loop below the reel. Having mended the line to our satisfaction, it is allowed to straighten with the pull of the current. This will make the nymphs suddenly spring to life and swim enticingly across the current, close to the river bed.

So far I have been referring to nymphs as opposed to 'the nymph'. The reason for this is that in heavy and/or quite deep water, it is advisable to use two leaded nymphs because their combined weight not only assists greatly in achieving the desired depth in the water, but their distribution offers a better profile.

Why do I prefer the floating line to a sinker? First, the sinking line vanishes from view and teaches us nothing so far as surface currents are concerned. In addition, trying to lift a lot of sunk line out of a current before each cast is made is hardly conducive to river trout fishing as I see it, and in no way can it compare with the sweet lift-off and fluent rhythm one experiences when using a floater. (Figs 11, 12, pp. 95, 97)

**Four well-fleshed brown trout caught from the Castle Fishery on the River Suir, a noted Irish game-fishing water in County Waterford. The brown trout there share this beautiful river with a fine run of good-sized salmon.**

**SOME AQUATIC FLIES AND THEIR IMITATIONS**

**ORDER: EPHEMEROPTERA**

*The March Brown* (Hook Size 12): Period, March/April.
NYMPH: March Brown Nymph (Skues)***; March Brown Spider**; Partridge and Orange; also, a standard W/W March Brown with the wings and hackle trimmed back to short stubs makes an excellent nymph pattern.
WET-FLY: W/W March Brown; March Brown Spider; Silver March Brown***; Gold March Brown***.
DRY-FLY (Dun): March Brown (winged); March Brown (hackled).
SPINNER: Not important.

*Large Spring Olive* (Hook Size 14): Period, March/April and Sept.
NYMPH: Sawyers Pheasant Tail Nymph***; Hare's Ear Nymph**/***; Waterhen Bloa; Greenwell's Spider.
WET-FLY: Waterhen Bloa; W/W Rough Olive***; W/W Gold Ridded Hare's Ear; W/W Dark Greenwell's Glory.
DRY-FLY (Dun): Rough Olive; Dark Greenwell's Glory; Gold Ribbed Hare's Ear; Blue Dun; Blue Upright.
SPINNER: Pheasant Tail***; Red Quill***; Red Spinner***; Lunn's Particular***.

*Small Dark Olive* (Hook Size 16): Period, March to September.
NYMPH, WET-FLY, DRY-FLY AND SPINNER: As recommended for the Large Spring Olive but in smaller sizes.

*Medium Olive* (Hook Size 14 and 16): Period, April to October.
NYMPH: As recommended for the Large Spring Olive but in smaller sizes.
WET-FLY: W/W Olive Quill; W/W Olive Dun; W/W Rough Olive (dressed 'medium'); Light W/W Greenwell's Glory.
DRY-FLY (Dun): Olive Quill***; Olive Dun***; Olive Upright***; Greenwell's Glory; Gold Ribbed Hare's Ear.
SPINNER: As recommended for the Large Spring Olive.

*Mayfly* (Hook Size 8, 10 and 12): Period, Late May for about three weeks.
NYMPH: (Hook Size 12, 10 and 8 long shanks): Walker's Mayfly Nymph**/***; Large Pheasant Tail Nymph.
Dun and Spinner; there are many patterns to represent the dun, spinner, and the spent fly, sometimes referred to as 'Spent Gnat', listed below are just a sample.
DUNS: Green Champion; Brown Champion; Irish Mayfly; French

Partridge; Goulden Favourite; Fore and Aft; Stragglebug; and J. R. Harris's Greendrake.
SPENT PATTERNS: Moneymore; Spent Black Drake; Spent Drake; and Little Spent Gnat (Lunn).
All the above Mayfly patterns (excluding the nymphs) may be found in A. Courtney Williams 'A Dictionary of Trout Flies' ***.
*Blue-winged Olive* (Hook Size 14): Period, May to end of season.
NYMPH: Poult Bloa; B-W. O. Nymph (J. Veniard)*;
B-W. O. Nymph (Preben Torp Jacobsen)*.
WET-FLY: Poult Bloa; W/W Blue-winged Olive (Skues)***.
DRY-FLY (Dun): B-W. O. Dun (David Jacques)*; B-W. O. Dun (Jim Nice)*; B-W. O. Dun (Reg Righyni)*.
SPINNER: Sherry Spinner; Orange Quill; Orange Spinner; Pheasant Tail.
*Iron Blue Dun* (Hook Size 14 and 16): Period, April to end season.
NYMPH: Iron Blue Nymph (Thomas Clegg)*; Dark Watchet; Waterhen Bloa; Snipe and Purple.
WET-FLY (Dun): Waterhen Bloa; Dark Watchet; Snipe and Purple; W/W Blue Dun; W/W Iron Blue Dun; Hackled Iron Blue Dun.
DRY-FLY (Dun): Iron Blue Dun; Blue Dun; Adams.
SPINNER: Rusty Spinner; Houghton Ruby; Pheasant Tail.
*Pale Watery* (Hook Size 14, 16 and 18): Period, May/June to end season.
NYMPH: Grey Goose (Sawyer)**/***; Pale Watery Nymph (Sawyer)**; Tup's Indispensable***; Poult Bloa***.
DRY-FLY (Dun): Tup's Indispensable; Little Marryat***; Enigma**; Daily Dun**; Goddard's Last Hope**/***; Ginger Quill.
SPINNER: Pheasant Tail; Lunn's Particular.

**ORDER: TRICHOPTERA**

Depending on locality, this family of flies may be referred to either as sedge, or caddis flies. In appearance they are very similar to small moths both in flight and at rest. Quite surprisingly, in view of the fact that there are more than 190 species of sedge present in Britain and Ireland (rivers and stillwaters), the dry-fly enthusiast needs but a few imitations to see him quite successfully through the season. Three sets of patterns similarly dressed to represent the dark, medium, and light coloured naturals will cover most eventualities provided that they are dressed on hook sizes 14, 12, and occasionally a size 10. Any from the following groups can be highly recommended.
*Dark Sedges:* Hambrough's Sedge*** (Hook Size 14, 12, 10): Small Dark Sedge*** (H/S 14); Gilbey's Little Dark Sedge*** (Hook Size 14 and 12).
*Medium Sedges:* Cinnamon Sedge (various); Little Red Sedge (Skues)***; Little Brown Sedge (Taff Price)**; Large Brown Sedge (Walker)**; Wickham's Fancy; Caperer.
*Light Sedges:* Grey Sedge (J. Veniard)**; Silver Sedge (Taff Price)**.

In addition, any of the patterns listed under 'medium-sedges' may be dressed in pale, 'washed-out' colours to represent the insipid, freshly emerged fly of most species. I find the most effective dressing for any 'dry' adult sedge pattern is a palmered body hackle from shoulder to tail, a wing dressed low over the abdomen and well past the bend of the hook, and a slightly longer, very full-wound collar hackle in front of the wings.

**ORDER: PLECOPTERA**

Stoneflies are of great importance to fly-fishermen who have access to fast, boulder-strewn rivers which sport plenty of good, clean gravel. Northern Britain, Wales and the West Country are well endowed with this particular type of river and it was from those areas that many of our stonefly patterns evolved. The most important members of this Order, so far as the fly-fisher is concerned, are as follows:
*February Red:* (Hook Size 14): Period, (Two species) Feb/April and March/July.
WET-FLY: Partridge and Orange; Old Joan***; February Red (Roger Fogg)**; February Red (J. Veniard)**.
*Early Brown:* (Hook Size 14): Period, Feb/May.
WET-FLY: Winter Brown (Pritt)***; Light Woodcock (Pritt)***; Dark Woodcock (Pritt)***; Early Brown (R. Fogg)**.
DRY-FLY: Early Brown (R. Fogg)**.
*Needle Fly:* (Hook Size 14 and 16): Period, Feb/April.
WET-FLY: Dark Spanish Needle (Pritt)***; Light Spanish Needle (Pritt)***.
DRY-FLY: Needle Fly (J. Veniard)**.
*Yellow Sally:* (Hook Size 14 and 16): Period, April/August
WET-FLY: Yellow Sally (Pritt)**.
DRY-FLY: Yellow Sally (anon)**; Yellow Sally (Henry Wade)****; Yellow Sally (Taff Price)**.
*Willow Fly:* (Hook Size 14 and 12): Period, Aug/November
WET-FLY: Partridge and Orange; Brown Owl; Dark Spanish Needle; Light Spanish Needle.
DRY-FLY: Willow Fly (Taff Price)**; Willow Fly (W. H. Lawrie)**.
Spent female: Eric Taverner****; G. E. M. Skues***.

**ORDER: MEGALOPTERA**

Alder *(Sialis lutaria, S. fuliginosa).*
No list of river patterns would be complete without mentioning the alder, a largish fly, very similar to the sedge fly. It has two pairs of large wings which, when at rest, lie roof-like over the abdomen and extend well past its tip. Unlike the sedge, the wings of the alder are heavily veined and lack the covering of fine hairs.

Recommended patterns:
SPECIES: Period May/June.
*Alder:* (Hook Size 12 and 10).
Larvae: Alder Larva (C. F. Walker)**; Alder Larva (Bob Carnill)**/****. Alder Larva (Stewart Canham)****.
WET-FLY: Oughton Alder (Richard Walker)**; Canon Eagles Alder***; Adult Alder (Charles Kingsley)**/***/****.
DRY-FLY: Adult Alder (Charles Kingsley)**; Herefordshire Alder ***; Oughton Alder (Richard Walker)**; Adult Alder (David Jacques)**/****; Wonderwing Alder (Bob Carnill).
(The latter dressing is not to be found in any reference book); briefly, it is as follows:-
Hook: 10 and 12 standard shank.
Silk: Black.
Body: Bronze peacock herl, dressed slim.
Wings: Two dark body feathers from a grouse, dressed 'wonderwing-style', tied-in roof-like and low over the back to extend beyond the bend of the hook.
Hackle: Black or very dark brown cock, wound in front of wings.
This is the only fly I now use when the alder is on the water. It has proved exceptionally effective on my home water (Derbyshire River Derwent) for trout and grayling.

**NOTE:** W/W prefix indicates 'winged-wet' as in wet-fly.
* *The Truth About Fluorescents* (Thomas Clegg).
** *The New Illustrated Dictionary of Trout Flies* (John Roberts).
*** *The Dictionary of Trout Flies* (A. Courtney Williams).
**** *Robson's Guide* (Kenneth Robson).

**A rainbow trout cruising in clear, shallow water takes remarkably little notice of the presence over its head of the photographer.**

## SEA TROUT

Like salmon, young sea trout migrate seawards as smolts from their native waters, and return one year later as herling, weighing up to 0.45 kg (1 lb), or two or more years later as sea trout, reaching 9 kg (20 lb) or even more. Unlike salmon, sea trout can be caught from a much wider range of aquatic habitats.

Salmon migrate far out into the ocean to feed, but sea trout hug the coastlines taking small fish and crustaceans. In some of the Irish loughs, Shetland voes and from some Hebridean storm beaches, they can be hooked on spinning gear or on the fly. Small Mepps, Devon Minnows or Toby spoons are very effective spinning lures. Even more exciting is a sand-eel imitation or Hugh Falkus's Sunk Lure, fished on a single-handed fly rod with a sinking line.

On their return to freshwater they pass through estuaries, in some of which they do not feed and are difficult to catch. In others, such as the Scottish Spey and Ythan, Cumbrian Leven or Irish Moy they do feed and are caught on natural sand-eel baits, or the same kinds of fly and spinner that are used in the sea.

## SEA TROUT TACTICS

For most anglers, sea trout fishing means night fishing on wild rivers, or drift fishing in a boat on Scottish or Irish waters. Through one summer's night on a sea trout river several tactics must be employed, though too many anglers arrive at the river at dusk with just one rod and line and a box of similar small trout wet flies. As the light fails, sea trout might be caught using small flies such as a Williams' Favourite or Teal and Silver. But when darkness falls much larger flies such as the Medicine and Stinchair Stoat's Tail, dressed on Sizes 2–6 salmon hooks, are more often successful.

Early in the night, when the river is running clear and low, a floating line or sink-tip might be used. If the river is running high and clearing after a spate – when often the fish will be running in good numbers – a sinking line might be more appropriate. Later, after about midnight, it is invariably best to fish these large flies, together with even bigger tandem-hooked lures, slowly in the deeper pools on a fast-sinking line.

In the blackest night some fish might take a wake-lure, for example Falkus's cork Surface Lure or Greenhalgh's Night Muddler. These are fished on a floating line so that they drag across the surface, creating a wake. They ought to be in the armoury of every night sea-trout angler, for on some nights they will succeed where all others fail. Finally, as dawn breaks, the small trout wet flies might take a final sea trout before the sun puts the fish down. So at least two sets of tackle are needed.

## GRAYLING

*Thymallus thymallus*

A sleek, beautifully coloured fish with a large dorsal fin, the grayling lives in clean rivers and streams that have a fairly fast-flowing current. It is a salmonid, but does not enjoy the brown trout's same protection in both seasonable and in reputation terms. Both species live together, the trout taking first place in the minds of anglers. But the grayling is not only a fighter, it makes good eating and brings an additional period of sport for the game fisherman after the trout is denied him. The grayling is not a large species, a fish of 1.8 kg (4 lb) is a good one. It spawns in the spring, about March to late April, so tends to be thought of as a coarse fish. The grayling puts up a good fight on artificial flies and is noted for the way in which it uses the large dorsal fin to cut across the stream in an effort to throw the hook.

**Bait:** Flies and trotted worms, grub baits as for coarse fish.

GRAYLING FLIES

Dry flies
*1* Sturdy's Fancy
*2* Grayling Witch
*3* Greenwell's Glory
*4* Kite's Imperial
*5* Green Insect

Standard wet flies
*6* Orange Partridge
*7* Yellow Partridge
*8* Snipe and Purple

Special wet flies
*9* Red Tag
*10* Treacle Parkin
*11* Bradshaw's Fancy

Weighted Bugs
*12* Hare's Ear Goldhead *(Greenhalgh)*
*13* Killer Bug *(Sawyer)*
*14* Bare-hook nymph *(Kite)*

*Grayling flies tied by Malcolm Greenhalgh*

## SMELT

*Osmerus eperlanus*

A small, sleek salmonid with a projecting, turned-up snout. It has a sharply forked tail and the lateral line is rudimentary. The fish has a cucumber-like odour, giving it a number of local names. The smelt lives most of its life in shallow coastal waters, entering brackish estuaries in April to spawn. Not an angler's species, it can be taken on tiny baits fished on fine float tackle.

### DAPPING

Many sea trout are caught from the lakes of Ireland and Scotland by two contrasting methods. The first is by dapping, where a 4.8 m (16 ft) rod is necessary. The line is made of light floss silk and known as dapping, or blow-line. At the end of the monofilament leader a large bushy dapping fly is attached. The art in dapping is to keep the rod held high so that only the fly touches the water, bouncing from wave to wave in front of the drifting boat. When the fly is taken the rod is slowly lifted to hook the fish. Using the wind, dapping can place flies in areas difficult to reach by other means and strangely the pattern does not seem particularly important. The strike is important – it must never be fast and snatchy.

### WET FLY

Although dapping can be successful, wet fly is far more popular. A wide range of two or three wet fly casts will work, including those that are commonly used for catching lake brown trout and salmon. However, where there are lots of sea trout and they are the sole intended quarry it is better to employ flies specially designed to catch them. As a point fly, few can rival the Goat's Toe. The bob fly must be heavily dressed so that it creates a wake as it is drawn through the water surface; the Grey Ghost, Blue Zulu or Claret Bumble are excellent in this respect. On some days only the point fly is taken, on others the bob fly.

Sea trout are exciting fish to catch, whether on maggot, worm, spinner or fly. But by far the best is at night, when a

*FIG 11* FISHING FOR GRAYLING AT THE CORRECT DEPTH

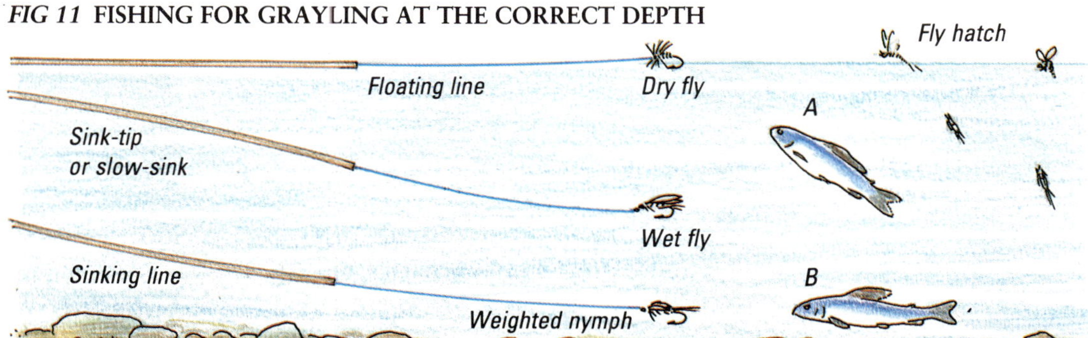


***Fig 11 (A)*** **When natural flies are rising to the surface to hatch, or resting on the surface, grayling will rise to take them and a range of dry flies fished on the surface and wet flies fished *below* the surface. *(B)* When there is no hatch then the grayling must be fished for *at their depth* with a suitably weighted fly.**

specimen takes the fly in the pitch dark, or on the vastness of a loch, when a leviathan reaches for the dap.

## GRAYLING

A curious species of fish the grayling, with that small, fleshy adipose fin behind the dorsal placing it in the salmon and trout family. But it spawns in spring, has the same close season as the coarse species and may be weighed-in during coarse-fish matches. Further, on many trout and salmon waters the grayling has long been considered vermin because it is said erroneously to compete with the trout. Happily, this attitude is changing as an increasing number of game anglers come to appreciate this superb fish that permits the trout angler to continue the sport of fly fishing when the trout are out of season.

## THE SEASON FOR GRAYLING

When the grayling season opens in mid-June the fish are usually still in poor condition following their spawning season. River trout fishing is still at its best then, so most serious grayling anglers do not seek them until late summer or early autumn, about mid-August. Then, right through to the opening of the next trout season in March the grayling provides exciting sport.

The grayling season can be divided into three periods. The first, which traditionally ends on November 5, is the period when there are large hatches of river insects and when dry-fly or traditional wet-fly fishing scores well. The second is through November and December when the water is cooling down and there are few hatches of fly at the water surface. Wet-fly or unleaded nymphs work well in this period.

The third period is from late December to the end of the season, when there is little insect activity in the water and the fish hug the riverbed and refuse to move even a short distance through the water to take a fly; then most anglers turn to trotting a maggot or tiny gilt-tail worm down the stream beneath a large float, but grayling can still be caught on fly on even the coldest of days provided the fly is weighted to get it to the depth that the fish are lying.

A

**A A typical winter grayling from the River Ribble. This fish's pear-shaped eyes, long and beautiful dorsal fin and underslung mouth are its distinctive features.**

## WHAT TO OFFER GRAYLING

Grayling are far less selective than trout when it comes to artificial flies. When they are feeding on a hatch of pale wateries, a Sturdy's Fancy or Grayling Witch is very successful, or during a hatch of blue-winged olives the artificial is Kite's Imperial or Greenwell's Glory, both on Size 14 or 16 hooks. Grayling are very partial to tiny midges and reed-smuts, which are often on the water in late summer. Then the same dry-fly patterns, or a Green Insect tied on very small hooks (down to Size 24) will take fish. Alternatively, wet flies might be tried, especially on the rivers of Northern England and Scotland; an excellent three-fly cast for grayling includes Orange Partridge (point fly), Yellow Partridge and Snipe and Purple (bob fly). In November and December fancy grayling wet flies are often more efficient than the insect-like patterns: flies such as the Red Tag, Treacle Parkin and Bradshaw's Fancy are particularly useful.

## FISHING METHODS

With no insects on the water surface and the grayling not rising, no matter what time of year, one must assume that the fish are taking food drifting underwater in front of them. In the clear chalkstreams of Southern England and the limestone rivers of Derbyshire one can see grayling darting about to take shrimps, hog-lice and nymphs close to the riverbed. Here, use a leaded fly that will fish at the correct depth (X), a leaded shrimp, or Sawyer's Killer Bug (once called the Grayling Bug), or a Gold Head or even Kite's Bare Hook Nymph – a hook with several turns of gold wire behind the eye.

On Northern streams, fancy grayling flies are often used such as the Red Tag or Priest, with several strips of lead wire tied under the body. One of these is attached to the leader-point and cast upstream of a shoal of fish so that when it has drifted downstream to them it is at their depth, just off the bottom. If you can see the fish it is easy. Watching the fish intercept the fly, all one does is hook, play and land it. When the shoal cannot be seen one must watch the tip of the floating fly line. As a grayling seizes the fly the tip of the line might twitch, jerk downwards or merely stop. The fish has the fly in its mouth, so tighten immediately, for if you wait a split-second later the fish will spit the fly out.

*FIG 12* FLY LINES

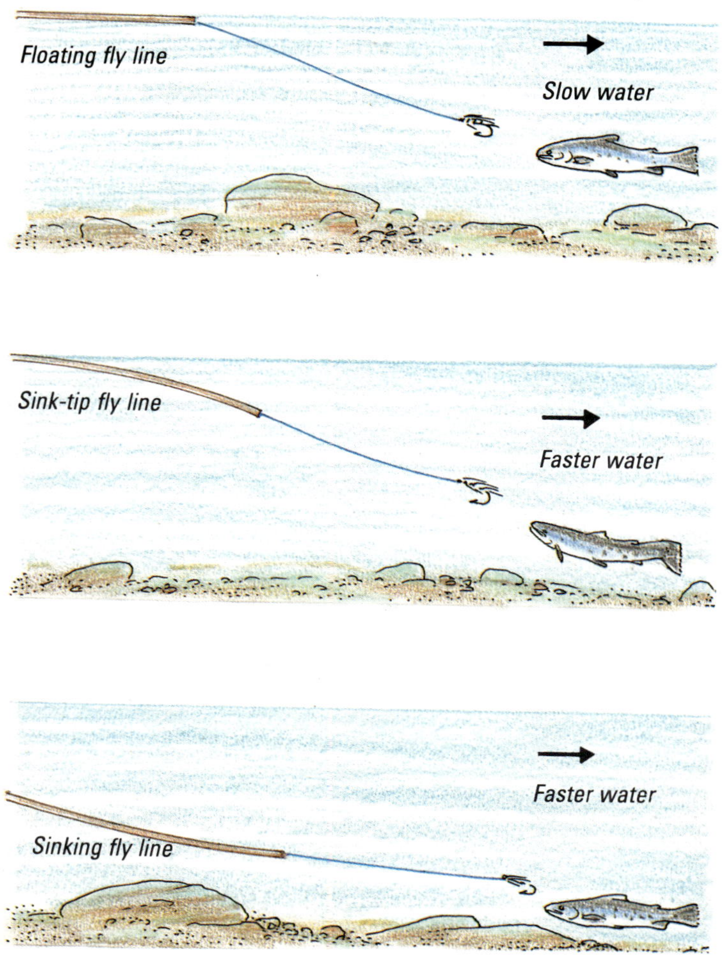


*Fig 12* For sea trout, select a line density that will fish the fly properly. Slow waters may accept a floating line; in faster water a line more dense will be needed. The faster the flow, the denser the flyline needs to fish a sub-surface line at the correct depth. In very heavy currents, a very high-density, fast-sinker might be needed.

B

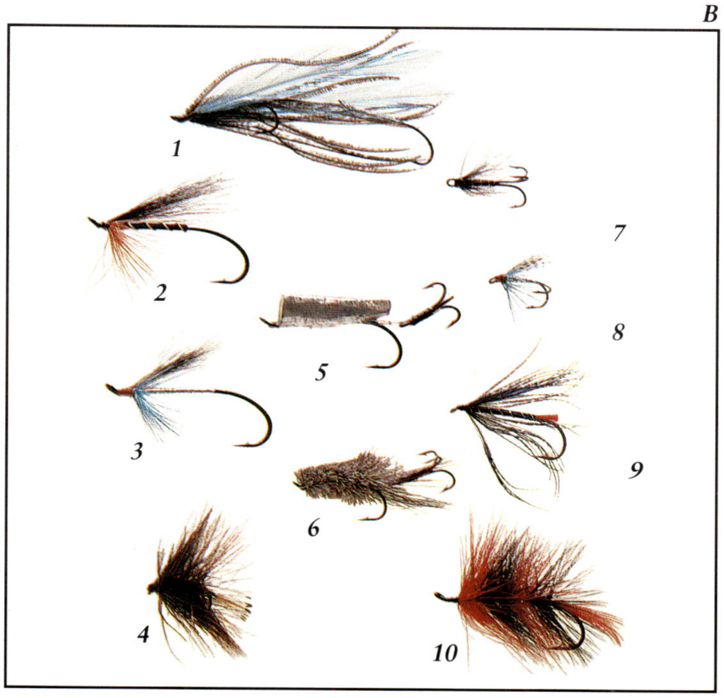


B SEATROUT FLIES

*1* Falkus Sunk Lure
*2* Stinchair Stoat's Tail
*3* Medicine
*4* Cock Robin *(dapping)*
*5* Falkus Surface Lure *(cork)*
*6* Greenhalgh Night Muddler
*7* William's Favourite
*8* Teal and Silver
*9* Goat's Toe
*10* Claret Bumble *(Rogan)*

*Seatrout flies tied by Malcolm Greenhalgh, except the Claret Bumble tied by Rita Rogan of Ballyshannon.*

C

*C* A late July evening as night falls over the River Spey at Grantown and another sea trout session is about to begin.

D

*D* Four fine trout from a lake on the River Fergus system in Co. Clare. The larger fish is a sea trout.

CRAWFORD LITTLE

# SALMON: AMAZING AND MARVELLOUS

The life history of the salmon is a wild tale of amazing nature. No one who has seen silver-flanked salmon fling themselves again and again at a sheet of falling water as they strive to pass a waterfall, until they reach the point of exhaustion, can fail to stand in awe of the instinct that drives the fish to behave in this way. Truly, they are marvellous fish.

All salmon found in British waters are of the Atlantic kind. A group of salmon species are found in the Pacific Ocean and its rivers but there is only one true native salmon of the North Atlantic, *Salmo salar*, although a stray 0.681 kg (1 lb 8 oz 1 dr) Coho salmon, *Oncorhynchus kisutch*, is listed in the British (Rod Caught) Record Fish list, being caught off a Guernsey, Channel Islands, beach in 1977. The main Atlantic-salmon producing countries are the British Isles, Norway, Iceland and the Maritime Provinces of Canada, but their distribution is far greater. They can be found from Portugal up to the Arctic coast of Russia in the east, and most major European rivers once had mighty runs of Atlantic salmon at one time but in most cases they were destroyed by pollution. In the west the salmon ranges from the Connecticut River, USA, to Ungava Bay, northern Quebec, Canada.

Salmon are hatched from the egg in freshwater, where they spend their early years, passing through the gradually maturing stages of alevin, fry and parr, by then looking very much like small brown trout. And it is then that these young fish are transformed, assuming bright silver coats, and becoming known as smolts. They fall downstream to

**Crawford Little on his home river, the Nith above Auldgirth. Many years ago this great Solway river was severely poached and had suffered neglect. Then riparian owners and anglers got to work and after much determination, a great deal of hard work and argument, the Nith was brought back to something like its past greatness. Will it ever yield a salmon the size of the fish Jock Wallace took in 1812, reputed to have weighed 30.6 kg (67 lb) on the bank in the Bargarg area?**

# SALMON

*Salmo salar*

From the moment the salmon is spawned in the redds to the time it grabs at the angler's fly it is under attack from the world's major predator – man. As a parr, it is taken by the tiny flies of the trout fisherman. But fed well, it becomes bright silver, is called a smolt, and begins the journey to the sea. There, it grows fast on shrimps and krill and then on small fish of the herring and other shoal species. Then comes sexual maturity and the desire to spawn. Nearly always, the salmon will return to its home river. Arriving in estuarine waters its body changes, allowing it to live in freshwater. On its oceanic feeding grounds the salmon was constantly harried by deepwater trawlers, but as it approaches inshore waters the danger becomes greater, for off-shore boats and estuary nets seek the returning fish. As the salmon ascends the river it has to pass netsmen and then rod-and-line anglers – and poachers. Its numbers have been so drastically reduced that man has to artificially breed salmon to maintain the stocks. Spawning takes place in the middle of winter and it will not feed, though the fish may have returned to the river in any month of the spawning year. Living on its accumulated fat, the fish changes its coloration to a nuptial dress before gathering on the gravels to produce the eggs and milt. Spawning is a rigorous occasion, and now as kelts few will succeed in returning to the sea.

**Bait:** Artificial flies, metal spinners, plugs, worms, prawns, trailed fish.

the estuary in shoals and then to the sea to disappear. The smolts have set off on an incredible journey to the Atlantic Ocean's rich feeding grounds close to Greenland.

They remain at sea, feeding and growing. Eventually, batches of salmon break away from those vast, maturing shoals, responding to the wild call of nature that draws them back to the river of their birth. It is on their return to the river to mate, spawn and give life to future generations that they may be caught on rod and line by the sportsman.

Salmon do not all return to the river at the same age. Some, called grilse, will have spent only one winter of feeding in the sea's rich larder. Because they have had limited time in which to grow they may only weigh 0.9 to 1.3 kg (2 to 3 lb) and will often be mistaken for sea trout. These fish may also be as heavy as 4 or 4.5 kg (9 or 10 lb), in which case they will be mistaken for the more mature salmon. The only certain way to tell the difference between a big grilse and a small salmon is by examining the scales under a microscope and counting the annual rings. Most anglers are just happy to have caught such a fine fighting fish and for the sake of convenience describe any salmon of less than 3.2 or 3.6 kg (7 or 8 lb) as a grilse.

A true salmon will have spent at least two winters at sea. Some will have spent three, four or more winters in salt water before returning. During this extended time of feeding they will have reached quite magnificent proportions, specimens of 9, 13.6 kg or more (20, 30 lb or more) – the stuff of the salmon fisherman's dreams and the angling press headlines.

## SALMON RUNS

Somewhere, salmon and grilse will be returning to a salmon river on virtually every day of the year. This is not the same as saying that all rivers enjoy steady and prolonged returns of fish. On the majority of individual rivers we associate the bulk of returning salmon with certain times of the year, when we expect the heaviest runs of salmon from the sea to enter the river, the runs being described by the season of the year in which they occur. Here, the point becomes a little stretched because there are spring runs and springers from the opening of the season right through to May, and there is nothing spring-like about a January day on a northern river. Spring runs are followed by summer runs which, in September, make away for autumn runs bringing the population of salmon in the river to its eventual peak. Because such a high proportion of their fish return in the autumn months, on

Parr

Smolt

Fresh-run fish

Spawning

Spawning

Kelt

Many river systems in Britain and Ireland are dominated by runs of small summer salmon known as grilse. This typical 2.7 kg (6 lb) fish is from Lough Conn on the River Moy system of Co. Mayo. Grilse have spent only one year feeding in the sea.

rivers such as the Tweed and the Nith the season is extended to the end of November.

All these are important points for the rod and line fisherman to recognise. If he is planning a trip to fish for salmon in the Solway rivers of South West Scotland he should be aware that they have only a trickle of fish in spring, a few more in summer and then in autumn the number of salmon returning soars, as do rod and line catches. On the other hand, on a river such as the Aberdeenshire Dee, the general pattern is for heavy runs in the spring, dwindling into summer and very few, if any salmon returning in the autumn.

So, it becomes obvious why the chances on the Solway are limited until autumn because earlier in the year there are very few salmon in its rivers. On the Aberdeenshire Dee, however, the salmon must still be there in the autumn, having entered the river in spring and summer. So why not fish the Dee later in the year? The answer lies in the nature of the salmon's river life and behaviour and the presence of fish does not necessarily mean that they will show an interest in the fisherman's lure, and, more significantly, it does not mean that they will even be worth the catching. The reason for this is that the salmon stops feeding on its return to freshwater.

## RIVER LIFE AND BEHAVIOUR

'Salmon do not feed in freshwater. They may go as far as to swallow worms, but they do not digest them. The scientists assure us that they do not even absorb the juices out of the worms. Nevertheless they do respond to the lures of the angler – artificial flies and spinning baits; metal spoons; and natural baits both fresh and preserved, including sprats and worms.'

Those are the words of the late Reg Righyni, writing in an earlier version of this encyclopedia. In those few well-chosen words that great and much-missed game fisherman summed up the magic, mystery and at times the frustration of salmon fishing.

Tens of thousands of words have been written in seeking an answer to why a salmon takes. It is one of the great mysteries of salmon fishing. It fills long hours with deep thoughts for armchair fishing theorists. But, at the end of the day, nobody can make anything more than broad and rather vague suggestions. And equally, for the practical fisherman theorising is not as important as discovering the when, where and what of the salmon's taking behaviour.

## WHEN A SALMON TAKES

From that moment in coastal waters when a salmon stops feeding and enters the river, the fish has started on a long, downhill slope of gradual decline. Its stores of energy are being used up and there is nothing to replace them. *The salmon does not feed in freshwater.* Clever old Nature at work again! Imagine what would happen if thousands of mature salmon returning to a river were to feed. In no time at all a vast amount of food would be taken and mature fish would have no alternative but to prey on the young of their own species and thus destroy the future generations.

How does this affect the salmon's behaviour? Salmon return to the river with all the vigour of well-fed sea fish. Their hard pink flesh is encased in a coat of silver flanks and blue-black ebony back. They have stopped actively feeding to be sure, but they are still active and alert. It is not surprising that it is among fresh fish newly entered the river that the fisherman is most likely to find one that is likely to respond to his lure. Here, then, is the first indication as to when a salmon is likely to take: when it is fresh off the tide.

Having entered the river the salmon's physical decline is started but it is a gradual process, for a salmon can survive on its own fat and flesh for up to a year in freshwater. It is only the final, violent exertions of mating and spawning that finally sap the last of the salmon's energy reserves. Only about 5 per cent of salmon survive spawning, after which they are known as kelts and return to the sea.

After the first few weeks of the salmon's return to the river, while the fish is still very strong and active, it must settle down into a fairly comatose existence if it is to survive to spawning time. The fish will seek out some quiet, safe temporary lie in which to stay and seems to spend most of its time in a near-trance state. Unless there is some external factor to disturb the salmon and put it on the alert, its natural behaviour will be totally to ignore every offering that the angler might make to it. In spite of its inactivity, the salmon is slowly but steadily losing condition.

By the autumn, those fish that entered the river in spring and summer will be transformed. The silver and ebony sheen of their coat will have faded to a motley mixture of reds, purples and browns. The lower jaw of the cock fish will have developed an ugly, hook-shaped kype. Scottish ghillies will describe such a fish as an 'auld kipper in his tartan breeks'. The bellies of dark hen fish are heavy and distended with thousands of growing eggs, ripe for spawning. The sportsman does not wish for such a fish and the cook will see it as unfit for the table. If one is caught, it is far better to return it alive to the river with great care, for such fish hold future salmon generations and sport in their bellies.

But before their deterioration salmon are worth catching and keeping for months after their return. So what about this class of fish? As we have seen, after leaving the sea the fish will adopt a quiet existence and will generally ignore the fisherman's offering unless something happens to disturb it and put it on the alert. This disturbance must be of a positive nature. For example, rocks thrown into a pool full of salmon will certainly disturb them and, occasionally, it might cause one to take. But it is far more likely to put an end to any chances the fisherman might have had of catching one. This is a negative kind of disturbance. Another is where, perhaps due to low water, a large number of salmon are concentrated into one short section of water, and there is competition for resting places; the fisherman sees disturbed fish lunging on the surface, jumping in an aimless way and again the salmon are not likely to take. These negative disturbances do little if anything to improve one's chances of taking a fish. What, then, is a positive disturbance?

We know that positive disturbance occurs through natural means and at those times when salmon are likely to run up-river. The nature of the salmon's progression from river-mouth to spawning redd must be understood, for it does not follow the steady progress of a well-planned cruise. The salmon's journey is one of stops and starts, with trots, sprints and rests, rather than a steady swim upstream.

Salmon enter a river and run up it on a rise in water level. Dark clouds gather over the hills, rain falls, filling the burns and streams that feed the main river. Salmon that are already in the river will respond to the start of the rise in water, alert and feeling the urge to be on the move. For a brief time, perhaps the first hour and small rise in water-level, the salmon are likely to respond to the angler's offering. But then the river is rising quickly; the force of the current becomes such that the fish are forced to find shelter out of the main streams. Then the spate passes, the water begins to clear and to fall.

At the height of the spate, water flowing off peat moorland will be black and carry a creamy-coloured froth. Rivers in spate flowing through richer, agricultural land can turn the colour of potter's clay. The froth clears on highland rivers and the colour of clay fades to strong

**Playing a good salmon on Scotland's River Dee. Estimated to weigh 13.6 kg (30 lb), the fish was lost after a struggle of 45 minutes. The famed Dee, Britain's greatest salmon river, flows 145 km (90 miles) down to Braemar and has produced a fish of 25.5 kg (56 lb), taken from Ardoe Pool in 1886. The Dee's great attraction is its gin-clear, shallow runs.**

tea in the lowlands. The full force of the flood is abated and soon salmon will be on the move. Peak running time occurs when the water has cleared and fallen to about a third of its full height. In other words, following a 1.8 m (6 ft) spate the fisherman's chances of catching salmon will be at their best when the water is showing 0.6 m (2 ft) on the gauge.

When the salmon are rushing through rapid water and leaping falls is a time of intense excitement on the river. It is in such conditions that they are most likely to be caught. Salmon show in purposeful, porpoise-like rolls as they swim up from the rough, broken water and into the pool tails. The angler sees them leap once more into the body of the pool, then up in the throat, alongside the mainstream, before they move on to the next pool and the next.

## WHERE A SALMON TAKES

When salmon are running upstream following a full spate they are likely to be covering ground at a rate which may be as slow as 1.6 km (1 mile) in three hours. On other rivers they may be faster. So considering the far greater speed at which a fish the size of a salmon can travel, it is obvious that they are not continually on the move. They must be pausing and resting for about three-quarters of the time during which they are running upstream. It therefore is not difficult for the fisherman to predict where he should be fishing his lure. Consider the nature of a typical salmon river: deep pools alternate with shallower rapids of fast, broken water. Having shouldered its way up through these rapids, the salmon is likely to pause in the tail, the downstream end of the pool, to regain its strength. No wonder, therefore, that the tail of a pool is a favourite place to fish when salmon are on the move, for there the salmon may pause for a few brief moments, perhaps minutes. Swim an attractive lure in front of it and it is on!

Where else should the angler try for a pausing fish? It enjoys a fairly easy passage up through the body of the pool and then begins to feel the push of the streams that enter into the neck of the pool. It senses the rough water upstream and pauses to summon up its energy for the race ahead. Here are likely takers, these salmon that are pausing on the cheeks of the streams fanning out into the body of the pool.

## WATER HEIGHT

At this stage the novice salmon-fisherman may ask when and where he should try for a salmon when there has not been a recent spate to bring in fresh fish off the tide and set those on the move which are already in the river. It might be suggested that having travelled a huge distance and spent hundreds of pounds on tackle, fishing rents and accommodation, the hopeful angler will just have to grin and bear it, but of course that is not the case. For the persevering angler, so long as there are salmon in the river there is always the chance of taking one. But it must be emphasised that water height and running and pausing fish are what is needed to create good fishing prospects where salmon fishing is concerned.

*A*

There is no point in pretending that salmon fishing is easy for the holiday visitor. But then, one year, he arrives when the conditions are just right. Locals will be taking up their rods and laying aside their gardening tools and paint-brushes. The spate has cleared and the water is falling. The rich salmon harvest is about to be taken and having once encountered it there is no turning back.

Take the example of a river such as the Spey. In the early season the height of this river is dependent upon snow melt and, with fairly warm weather conditions on the Cairngorms after deep snow in winter, it will maintain water heights and fishing prospects throughout the spring. Then, once the snow is but a memory the height of the Spey and level of sport that it can produce become dependent on rainfall.

A long period of drought on any salmon river means that there will be few if any salmon entering the river off the tide. Those salmon that are already in the river will have settled in long-term lies rather than temporary resting places. The chances of finding a taking fish grow ever slimmer until rain and freshwater arrive to transform the river and fishing scene.

## TIME OF DAY

As well as water height, the hour of the day affects the chances of an angler finding a taking fish. Even in a good

*A* A fine hen 'springer' of 11 kg (24 lb) from the River Tweed.

*B* A late summer evening on the River Spey near Abernethy Forest. Spey casting is essential to effectively cover such a wide and powerful river.

height of water there are times when salmon are most likely to take. This reflects their tendency to run at particular times. In the cold water and weather conditions encountered during the opening and closing months of the season, peak salmon activity occurs at about midday, so the angler fortunate enough to find himself fishing the Helmsdale in February or the Tweed in November should not waste time over a lengthy lunch. The last hour of light can also be productive.

Conversely, from May until the end of November, peak salmon activity occurs at dusk and dawn, so late to bed or early to rise become the maxims for summer salmon fishermen. Even when the water is low during a summer drought, fish will respond to the urge to be on the move by cruising up to the head of the pool to tarry for a while before returning to their resting places. This behaviour creates the best opportunity for catching summer salmon and grilse. In the summer it would be wise to swap the last or first few hours of the day for all the rest.

## OUR OFFERING TO THE SALMON

It has already been stated that the salmon stops feeding on its return to freshwater. This might seem to create major problems. We know that there are salmon in the stretch that we intend to fish, the water height is at a nice 0.6 m (2 ft) after a 1.8 m (6 ft) spate, the time of day is best to improve our chances and we have established in which part of the pool we are most likely to find a taking fish. But if the salmon is not feeding what manner of lure should we offer for its inspection? Well, as has also been stated, the experience of generations of anglers shows that salmon will respond to artificial flies and spinning baits, metal spoons and natural baits such as prawns and worms.

Salmon fishing, however, is undertaken within what is usually a clearly defined set of rules. Besides the law of the land, any proprietor of salmon fishings may introduce whatever rules he chooses. Associations have rules as to what lures or baits may be used, when and where. Often, this will mean that the spinning rod is acceptable only when the water is above a certain height, the worm may be used in a spate, and the prawn is banned entirely. It will be noted that there is little if any restriction on fishing the fly. Indeed, many rivers, particularly those in North East Scotland, have introduced a fly-only rule.

To some, this might be seen as little more than arrogant snobbery. Certainly on some rivers the fly-only rule would be a piece of nonsense. Generally, however, on most rivers the fisherman who concentrates on fishing the fly throughout the season will find that his catches do not suffer and he gains great pleasure from fly casting with ever-increasing effectiveness as his experience grows.

## SALMON FLIES

We call them salmon flies but they bear little resemblance to any natural insect other than perhaps those gaudy butterflies found in the Amazon jungle. What we are

**_A_ Salmon tube flies tied by Crawford Little. _B_ Salmon flies tied on double hooks by Simon Ashworth of Sowerby Bridge, Yorkshire.**

***Fig 1*** **An outstandingly strong hook, the traditional salmon irons. With a reasonably long, very sharp point. For all styles of the heavier type salmon flies. Used in deep or fast-flowing water. Very popular in the past but now superseded by trebles and doubles for the modern styles of dressing.**

fishing at the ends of our fly lines are, in their larger sizes, representations of small fish and in their smaller sizes they could be said to imitate even smaller fish or crustaceans such as shrimp. We do not know what the salmon mistake them for, we can only assume that our salmon flies act as a stimulus, provoking a memory of their ocean-feeding days, that produces an instinctive, predatory response from the salmon.

What we do know, because experience has shown it to be so, is that in cold water salmon are most likely to respond to a larger fly fished deep; in warmer water they will respond best to a smaller fly fished quite close to the surface. We accept that their shift of interest occurs when the water temperature passes the figure of 10°C (50°F). While the water temperature remains below 10°C (50°F) we fish with flies that are 50 mm (2 in) or more in length and use sinking lines. When the water temperature is above 10°C (50°F) we fish with flies of 25.4 mm (1 in) or less and use a floating fly line. These are the broad, general rules of salmon fly fishing.

## COLD-WATER FLIES

The salmon season opens at a time which, frankly, is midwinter. The angler should not be fooled by any talk of 'spring' fishing and 'spring-run' salmon. Often, January and February are the hardest months of the year, even the early season river may be frozen over. The vastness of the sea is less readily affected than rivers by plunging air temperatures and salmon are not inclined to leave salt water if its temperature is higher than that of the river.

When these early-season fish arrive it will be found that they are fairly lethargic and prefer slow, deep-water lies out of the main push of the current. They do not seem prepared to move far in order to take the fly and experience shows that what flies they do take will normally be long ones.

It is only during the past quarter-century that the modern, articulated style of fly has been used on a wide scale. Prior to that time, big salmon flies for use in cold water were tied on single hooks in sizes best known to big-game fishermen. Now, single hooks are very much a thing of the past for salmon fishing. The commonest of the modern articulated patterns are tube flies. We describe them as 'articulated' because the hook is separate from the shank on which the pattern is tied, the same principle as an articulated lorry. The great advantage of this system is that once the fish takes and is hooked on the relatively small hook, leverage on the hold is minimised. In the case of the tube fly armed with a treble, the tube is free to slide up the leader in very much the same way as a Devon Minnow. In the days when big, single hooks were the only option for use in cold water an angler would think that he was doing exceptionally well if he eventually landed one out of every four or five salmon that came to his fly. Today, with tubes and trebles, we land far more salmon than we lose.

Thankfully, the choice of size of these long flies creates few problems. If a cold-water salmon is likely to take anything at all, it will probably take a 50 mm (2 in) tube armed with a Size 6 treble. Where variety can and should be introduced is in the material from which the tube is made. Brass, copper, aluminium and plastic tubes offer

*FIG 1* TRADITIONAL PARTRIDGE SINGLE SALMON HOOKS

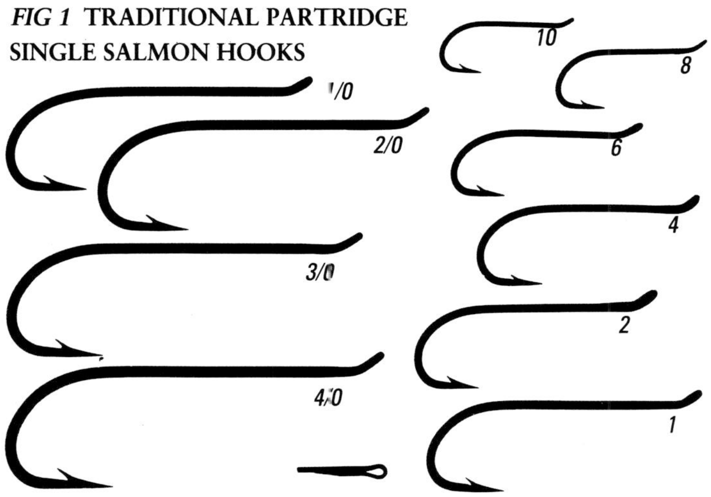


the full permutation of heavy, medium and light cold-water flies. (Fig. 1)

Why bother to carry tube flies in different weights? The reader will remember that cold-water salmon prefer deep-water lies and are not prepared to move far in order to accept the angler's offering. A light fly is fairly buoyant and while it will work well in quite gentle flows, it cannot produce the same action in deeper or streamier water where the line and fly must cut down through the water to swim close to the resting salmon.

What pattern of cold-water fly should be tried? If there is just one pattern that stands head and shoulders above the rest in tempting salmon during the opening and closing months of the season it is the Willie Gunn. This is an absolutely deadly fly and yet it is a very straightforward creation. Dress a black floss body on the tube, rib it with gold tinsel, tie on a wing of mixed black, orange and yellow bucktail or goat hair and there it is. Simple, but quite deadly to salmon.

The Willie Gunn is particularly well suited to fishing a falling and almost cleared water – conditions that have been described as almost ideal for fishing a taking salmon. For this period it is very good but there are alternatives for fishing in different conditions. While the water is still high and coloured, a bright fly with a gold or gold-ribbed black body and a mixed-hair wing of orange and yellow can prove very useful. The Garry Dog is another fly that works well in coloured water and toward the end of the season when autumn fish are entering the river. In its tube fly form, the Garry has a silver ribbed black body with a few strands of red in an otherwise yellow hair wing.

At the other end of the scale in terms of water conditions, the early season river may be flowing clear and it is then that an all-black fly with its funereal garb of black wing and body relieved only by a silver tinsel rib can work to the best advantage.

## WARM-WATER FLIES

When the water temperature of the river exceeds 10°C (50°F), experience shows that salmon are more active. They are now to be found in faster, streamier water and they are as a general rule most likely to show an interest in a fly of about 25.4 mm (1 in) or less in length.

Most authorities on salmon fishing have committed themselves to the belief that from mid-May until September in a normal season the size of salmon fly that we use in warm-water conditions is vitally important. It certainly seems that some salmon ignore, say, a fly tied on a Size 6 hook, but take one tied on a Size 8. The salmon's choice seems to depend on a number of factors: water temperature, its colour and height as well as the strength of the flow. From all that, it might seem that a riverside computer will be required to work out all the possible permutations, but thankfully this is not so. The river is likely to be cooler, higher and flowing powerfully all at the same time. In exactly the same way it will be warmer, lower and more gentle at the same time in summer drought conditions.

Bearing that in mind, we can discuss the size of flies used for warm-water salmon fishing. These generally range from Size 4 down to 10 tied on double or long-shanked treble salmon hooks. Make a start with a Size 4 when the water temperature is above 10°C (50°F) and the river is running high and with a touch of colour. Use the same fly also when the water has cleared but the river is running high in powerful flows such as the Spey. On smaller, more gentle rivers use a Size 6 at such times. As the water falls still further and is running clear a Size 6 would be a first choice on a big, powerful river while a Size 8 might be first choice on the gentler stream. Size 10 would be kept for those times when water levels fall under a summer sky. The application of a little common sense goes a long way in choosing the appropriate size of warm-water fly. The warmer, lower, clearer and more gentle the river that we are fishing the smaller our fly should be.

What patterns of flies should be carried? There are hundreds from which to choose. Nowadays, hair wings are favoured rather than feather. In the larger sizes, 4 and 6, the Munro Killer has gained the same reputation as being irresistible to salmon as the Willie Gunn has as a cold-water fly. Indeed, in terms of colour, black, orange, yellow and gold, the two patterns are very similar. In smaller sizes, 8, 10 and perhaps 12 for when a small river is really low and clear as well as warm, there are few patterns to beat the Stoat Tail and its Silver cousin. The Stoat has a silver-ribbed black body and a black hackle and wing. The Silver Stoat is identical except that its body is flat silver tinsel. Here, then, are three patterns, so let us keep things simple and suggest just three more: Blue Charm, Hairy Mary and a Shrimp Fly.

These six patterns in a range of sizes from 4 down to 10 can be regarded as a useful, basic set for warm-water use. Of course, there are many others and most rivers have a particular local favourite. It is always worth while visiting the local tackle shop to ask what fly, if any, has been doing well for other anglers, or what the proprietor would advise. Such shops can be a mine of information as to which fly to try, where and when and the cost of a few flies is a small price to pay for such an obviously short cut to success on an unfamiliar water.

Soon, the novice angler's fly box will be bulging. He will learn of the always-successful Such-and-Such and, very wisely, add a few to his collection and another and another. But, as with cold-water flies, he should start with a basic selection and concentrate on fishing them well rather than wasting too much time worrying whether a this or that fly might not prove that bit better. It is the fly in the water, not the one in your thoughts, that catches salmon – so long as it is fished well.

## OTHER TACKLE

It might seem odd to have started with a discussion about salmon flies before mentioning other tackle, but there is logic in this. Our chances of success in tempting a salmon, or any fish come to that, depend heavily if not entirely on what we have on our hook. It is those few pence-worth of hook, floss, tinsel and fur that is the most important part of our tackle and we should work back from it in order to achieve a balanced outfit.

## LEADERS

Leaders are a length of nylon monofilament which act as a link between the fly and the thick, heavy fly line. Normally we make them about 1.8 m (6 ft) long when fishing long flies in cold water and 3 m (10 ft) when fishing smaller flies in warm water.

Besides varying the length of the leader we should alter its thickness and weight to suit the fly that we are using. A large and heavy fly could crack-off when casting if light nylon is used. Tied to heavy nylon, on the other hand, a small fly will not fish well because its swimming action is destroyed. And so for those long, cold-water flies we use 6.8 to 9 kg (15 to 20 lb) nylon depending on whether we are using a plastic, aluminium or brass tube. The 6.8 kg (15 lb) nylon would also be suitable for a Size 4 warm-water fly, 5.5 kg (12 lb) for a No. 6, 4.5 kg (10 lb) for an 8, and 3.6 kg (8 lb) for a Size 10.

## FLY LINES

There is very little weight in a salmon fly, even a relatively heavy brass tube fly is only a fraction of the weight of a metal spinner or ledger weight. But we need weight in order to work the fly-rod and be able to cast. In the case of fly fishing that weight is to be found in the fly line itself. Modern fly lines can be considered as a plastic coating over a braided core with the weight of the line incorporated into the plastic.

Any line-manufacturer's catalogue will show that they have taken this concept of line much further. For a given weight of line, the angler is able to choose from a whole range including floaters, floaters with sinking tips, intermediates, slow sinkers, medium, fast, very fast, ultra-fast, express and even lead-cored lines. All that is very impressive but except in fairly exceptional circumstances the salmon fly-fisher is fully served by just two of these options. He will have a floater for fishing Size 4 down to Size 10 flies close to the surface in warm water, and a fast sinker for fishing his long flies deep in cold water conditions, the best known of this class being the Wetcel 2.

Other options to be considered are the line profile. Nowadays it is rare to find a level fly line. The weight-forward line tapers out from a relatively thin point into a section of heavy line that is about 9 m (10 yards) long behind which is thin running line. The idea is rather like casting with a lead weight. The line is drawn in until the heavy section is just outside the rod tip. The cast is made and the heavy front section flies out, carrying the thin running line with it. The double taper, by comparison, is a much simpler affair with tapers from fine points at either end leading into a long and thicker central section. This might seem a disadvantage. There is certainly not the same potential for shooting line in the cast. And yet most experienced modern salmon fishermen choose the double taper. This is because they rely heavily on the Spey rather than the overhead cast with a fly rod. Casting techniques will be dealt with later in this section of the book. For now, it has to be accepted that the double taper line will be the correct choice.

We have looked at the weight of the line but have not yet said what it should be. Line weights are defined by the AFTM system. This gives a number for a given line weight; the higher the number the heavier the line. Those lines that are normally available range between AFTM 3 and 12. What weight of line should the angler choose?

A big salmon fly is a bulky, wind-resistant object to cast and therefore we need a heavy line in order to be able to cast it effectively. Lines in the range of AFTM 10 to 12 prove ideal for presenting cold-water flies. Smaller, warm-water flies are less of a problem and can be cast with ease on line of AFTM 8–10.

But the matter cannot be left there because, as is about to be demonstrated, rods are matched by their power to a certain weight of line. Thus, a powerful rod would be best suited to an AFTM 12 line and a far gentler, softer model to an AFTM 8. If we wish to fish with perfectly balanced tackle regardless of fly size, then we have to invest in perhaps three rods: AFTM 8, 10, and 12. With the cost of modern salmon rods, that represents a very serious capital investment. One rod is quite expensive enough for most of us, and therefore we should seek a compromise. This will be found in a rod and line rated at AFTM 10. There may be times when we would prefer just that little bit more power when fishing with long brass tube flies, or a shade

*A*

*B*

**A A well-matched graphite rod, reel and line from an economy range, offering the salmon angler an inexpensive start to outfitting himself for the challenges he will face in this exciting sport.**

**B A contented young angler with a fresh-run fish from Lough Currane, Co. Kerry. Salmon have only 1.6 k (1 mile) to travel before reaching the lough as it is connected to the sea by a very short river, including the famous Butler's Pool.**

more delicacy when a size 10 double in low, clear water, but the AFTM is as near to being the ideal solution as can be found for the one-rod salmon fly fisherman, and thus he will choose AFTM 10 in floating and sinking lines.

## THE FLY ROD

Much of what has aready been said in the context of lines applies equally to the choice of rod. We have already seen that it should be a model rated at AFTM 10. That only leaves questions as to length and material.

Dealing first with the question of material, virtually all modern salmon fly rods are made of carbon fibre. You can save a bit of money by searching out a fibre-glass model, but it will not perform as well. Also, carbon fibre is by far the lightest rod-building material; at the present time, if you wish to achieve true potential in salmon fly-fishing, there is no alternative to the carbon rod.

That leaves us with the question of length. There is a strong tradition on British rivers toward double-handed rods. Some traditions should be put out with the rubbish, but not this one. Longer, double-handed rods make casting a long line far easier and improve our control of the line and thus how the fly is fishing. Looking at the two extremes, gentle rods of 3.9 and 4.2 m (13 and 14 ft) loaded with AFTM 8 lines are ideal for presenting the smaller class of flies, while big and powerful 4.8 and 5.1 m (16 and 17 ft) rods are unmatched for presenting the largest flies in heavy conditions. But unless we wish to give family and bank manager a hard time, we will again be looking for a compromise. This we find in a 4.6 m (15 ft) model – the general-purpose weapon that meets virtually all our needs for most of the time.

## THE REEL

Very little need be said about the salmon reel. It should be a single-action centre-pin with a diameter of about 10 cm (4 in) in order to accommodate the fly line and about 91 m (100 yards) of backing. This backing may be monofilament nylon of 11.4–13.6 kg (25–30 lb) b.s., attached to the fly line with a needle knot. We all dream about catching a big, powerful salmon that runs us down to our last piece of backing before finally giving us the fight! An exposed rim and variable check are great advantages in playing a fish. Anything else should be viewed with a suspicion and perhaps as nothing more than gimmickry.

## WADERS AND ACCESSORIES

Waders are a necessity on all but the smallest of rivers in order to cover the water effectively. Thigh waders may be suitable at times but anything they can do is more easily achieved by chest waders, and on large rivers these can make all the difference between success and failure. When you are wading a river with a powerful current or one with which you are not familiar a wading stick is invaluable, acting as a third leg and perhaps saving you from a ducking. Take an ordinary staff, weight it at the bottom with about 0.45 kg (1 lb) of lead and attach a lanyard at the top. An unweighted staff will float and catch in your line but when it is weighted only the top sticks out of the water, instantly to hand if you lose your footing. Any angler who is a poor swimmer should also purchase one of the buoyancy suits specifically designed for fishermen.

Blunt-nosed or folding scissors are very useful for cutting leaders and trimming knots. Polarised glasses reduce glare on the bright days and help avoid headaches. They also protect the eyes from a wayward hook should a bad or mistimed cast be made. A spool of insulating tape is vital for taping joints of carbon-fibre rods, something that must be done if you intend to use the Spey cast. Otherwise the joints become twisted, work loose, the tip section flies off and may well break in the process.

## CASTING

Having purchased a 4.6 m (15 ft) fly rod rated AFTM 10 and both floating and sinking lines to match, plus all the other paraphernalia of the sport, all that remains is to learn how to use it in something approaching its and the angler's potential. It is impossible to learn casting and fishing with a fly rod in a few hours, and it would be silly to pretend that casting can be learned by studying diagrams and descriptions in a book or on video. The actual motions of the various casts are fairly simple and straightforward but it is the timing of the casting that baffles most people and this can be learnt only on the riverbank in company with a competent instructor.

Most anglers come to salmon fishing after previous experience with trout. For salmon, they may need to do little more than change the pattern and size of the flies they are using, sticking with conventional downstream wet-fly fishing and overhead casting. Such anglers will certainly catch salmon and particularly in summer when neither the size of fly, nature of the river, nor size of fish are likely to be too powerful or heavy. However, over a season or more they will have problems if they stick to trout tackle and technique.

Spey casting and long rods are best for the majority of experienced salmon anglers. Once the single and double Spey casts have been learned there is no looking back. Like riding a bicycle, after some initial help it all starts to come naturally. Casting 27.4 m (30 yards) of fly line and any size of fly for maximum effect using the minimum of effort with a 4.6 m (15 ft) rod is just one of the advantages and pleasure of the Spey casts: they make the overhead cast virtually redundant.

The only other cast besides the Spey that needs to be learnt is the roll cast and this is required only when fishing a sinking line. The roll is the most simple of all casts, simply raise the rod to the vertical, then punch it down, rolling up a loop of line and lifting the sunk portion on to the surface from where the Spey cast can be started. To try to Spey cast or overhead come to that, when the line is deeply sunk is to overload the rod and court disaster. You must start off with that initial roll cast.

*A*

*B*

## FISHING A POOL

Experience shows that most salmon are tempted by a fly that swims over them quite slowly. Salmon flies do not generally need to be fished fast. The slowest moving fly of all is one that is hanging at the end of a straight line directly below the angler. We describe a fly thus as being 'on the dangle'. It is not moving laterally across the stream but because it is relatively light it will respond to the vagaries of the current, hovering, rising and falling as its hair-wing works in a lifelike fashion.

In order to cover all those fish that are lying out farther from the bank than be covered by the dangling fly, the fly must be cast out at an angle to the stream and fished across. Cast the fly too square and the river's central current catches the line and swims the fly across too quickly. Cast straight down the stream and although the fly will swim attractively on the dangle the water is not being covered properly. In these circumstances the usual solution is to cast downstream at an angle of about 45 deg to the flow. (Fig. 2)

Line and fly swim slowly across the river like a pendulum. A salmon may have followed the fly across without taking. When the fly comes on to the dangle, draw in a few yards of line. This causes the fly to accelerate forward in the water, and the previously uncommitted salmon may grab the fly as it speeds away. That arc of water has now been covered. Take one or two paces downstream and cast again. By casting at the same angle with the same

C

D

*A, B* Crawford Little, Spey casting on the River Nith.
*C* Line is retrieved as the fly swings 'on the dangle'.
*D* The rod is bent, the line tight and the gillie waits with sunk net. Salmon fishing on Ireland's Burrishoole Fishery.

*FIG 2* COVERING THE WATER AND 'MENDING' THE CAST

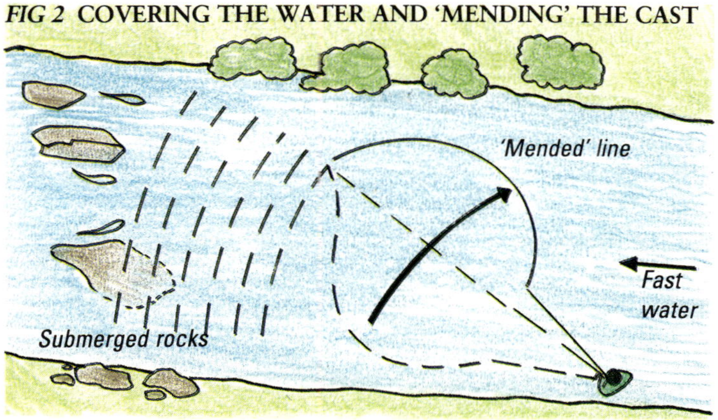


*Fig 2* Never make a hopeful cast to where a salmon might be. Plan your approach.

*Fig 3* Hold your salmon by this grip. Any other and the fish will slip from your grasp.

*FIG 3* TAILING BY HAND

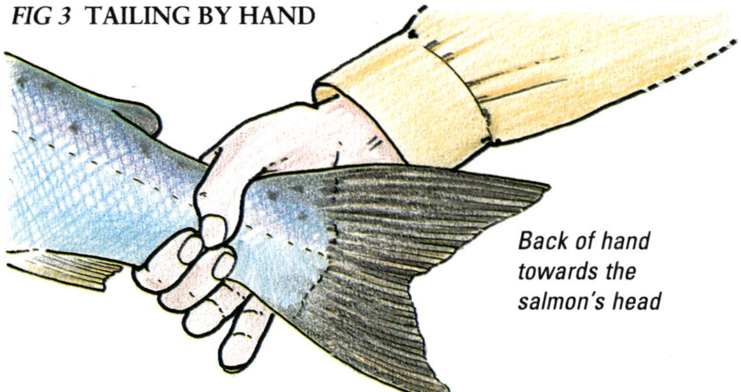


length of line, the water is covered systematically by taking a good pace between casts.

You may be asking which parts of the river should be covered. You will understand that salmon rivers are generally divided into pools and runs. The runs are shallow, streamier sections of water between the pools. It is the pools themselves which yield the majority of salmon. Now, we said earlier that the tails and necks of the pools are particularly good following a spate when fish are running. Equally, there are some pools that fish well in high water but others that only fish well when the river is low.

Without local advice the angler does best to fish each pool from top to tail, taking a pace or two between casts and persevering just so long as there is sufficient current to swim the fly. Some gentle handlining to aid the fly across slower sections can be a great help when required to maintain life in the fly.

This, then, is the basis of salmon fishing with the fly. It does not matter whether we are fishing a long fly on a sinking line in cold water or a much smaller fly close to the surface of warm water with a floating line. Start up at the top of the pool. Repeat the casts with a yard or two more line each time until you have got as long a length of line as you can comfortably handle, making your casts at an angle of 45 deg. When the fly has swum around on to the dangle, draw in a few yards of line by hand, then take one or two paces downstream and cast again. Over and over, down the pool, a pace with each cast until that wonderful moment arrives when you feel your line pulling tight and then realise that you are attached to one of the gamest fighting fish in river or sea.

## GRASSING THE SALMON

It is one of those little niceties of salmon fishing that the fish is 'grassed' rather than landed whether the fish is brought ashore on to shingle, rock or anything else.

There are a number of ways of getting a salmon ashore. First, there are what might be described as the mechanical methods involving a gaff, tailer or a net. Nowadays it is rare to see a gaff in action because nearly all salmon anglers believe that sticking a metal hook into a salmon's side is a singularly cruel and ignoble end for a noble fish. Mechanical tailers have also fallen out of fashion. These consist of the noose to be drawn up round the wrist of the fish, just above the tail. Last of the mechanical means of grassing a salmon is a net. It must be big, more than 0.5 m (20 in) in diameter.

If we decide against the mechanics what are we left with? It has been said that the Almighty in His wisdom gave us two hands, one to hold the rod and the other to wind the reel-handle or to pick up an exhausted fish from the water. Experience brings confidence in this matter, but it really is a simple task to wade in quietly alongside the fish, reach down and close the hand tight around the wrist of the tail, then carry it ashore.

Another very useful alternative is to beach the fish, but this does require a fairly gentle, shelving shore. A pebble or sandy bay is ideal. With the played-out fish on a fairly short line, hold the line to the rod handle and walk the fish ashore like a dog on a lead. When the salmon's head comes out of the water it will give a few last, feeble kicks. Walking backwards steadily, the angler uses these kicks to get the fish father out of the water. With the salmon now stranded, the angler walks down to it, picks it up and carries it away from the water's edge.

### THE FINAL SCENE

Just before you administer the *coup de grace* take a quick look at the fish you have just grassed. It is to be hoped that it is a fresh, shining bar of silver, blue and ebony, but it might not be and there are some fish that should be returned to the river.

In the opening months of the salmon season, fish that have spawned in the previous season will still be in the river. They are known as kelts. It is illegal to kill them and they must be returned. A well-mended kelt may fool the novice into thinking that it is a fresh fish, but things to look for are a thin body with the back and belly almost parallel, an apparently over-sized head in relation to its body size, a 'tinny' sort of silver sheen and the presence of freshwater maggots in the gills. If in doubt, you are advised to return any suspect fish.

Another class of fish that should be returned, this time in the closing months of the season, is the salmon close to spawning. These are instantly recognisable, their silver coats have turned to the rusty colours of the rainbow, their bellies are a greyish, yellowy white rather than pearl and heavily distended with ripe spawn or milt. Now, the law does not say that you should return such fish but we should be sportsmen rather than slaughterers and I for one see no excuse for killing the heavily pregnant female of any animal species. Besides that, the flesh of a gravid fish is, like that of the kelt, not worth the eating. Far better to take a little pride and satisfaction in returning coloured salmon with the knowledge that you have done something to ensure more salmon for the future.

Take some care when returning live salmon to the water. Cause the minimum of injury when removing the hook and waste no time in getting the fish back into the water. In fact, far better not to remove the salmon from the water at all, but carry out the operation in shallow water with one hand grasping the wrist of its tail. Lay your rod down and get to work. With the hook free, do not let the fish go, but hold it with its head facing into the current and hold on to the fish until it regains strength and swims away to freedom. (Fig. 3, p. 111 )

Now let us put all that to one side and assume that we have caught a real beauty of a fresh-run fish. We do not know whether fish suffer on being taken out of water but lest they do the fish should be struck firmly on the back on the head as soon as possible. And this is where you may find that sticks and stones of suitable proportions are like policemen, never there when wanted. This is why you should carry a priest, so named because it administers the

A

*A* Crawford Little fishing downstream and across on the River Nith, a prolific and rewarding salmon river. Following conservation measures the Nith is recovering much of its former glories.

B

C

*B* Fishing for salmon on the Cumbrian Eden. *C* A fine cockfish taken from the Dee while spinning. *D* Action and vibration are vital in a lure, then come colour combinations and flash patterns to trigger attack response. New generation Kilty lures designed by Finbarr McSweeney fulfil the criteria *l to r*: the 'Sonic' has a slow wobbling action; 'J3' takes almost any predator; '15' a lure for distance casting, and the Flying 'C', an upstream casting lure for salmon.

D

last rites. Your priest can be an old chair-leg, my priest is a length of brass rod inside an alkathene pipe and about 25 cm (10 in) long. I do not buy those expensive ones from tackle shops because I lose them.

Weigh and photograph your salmon, then gut it and throw the entrails back into the river. This is not an ancient, bloodthirsty ritual, it aids the flesh to remain as fresh as possible. If you want a nice, whole fish to lay out on a silver platter back at the hotel, at least remove the gills, which are the first part of a fish to deteriorate. Place the fish in a cool spot. If you are fishing a private beat there may be a stone or a marble slab in the fishing hut. And use some common sense, do not place the fish in the closed boot of your car on a hot summer's day.

## SPINNING FOR SALMON – WHEN TO SPIN

Once experienced anglers realise that there is more to fishing than catching fish, many find little enjoyment or satisfaction in any method other than fly. But at times spinning becomes a logical alternative.

First, safety. Handling a large, heavy tube fly on a fast-sinking line is a challenge. In a gale it can become dangerous unless the fisherman has mastered the technique of roll and Spey casting.

Secondly, depth of water. The fly is ideally suited to searching out water down to a depth of about 1.8 m (6 ft), or slightly more, but salmon can be found in deeper water. Here, one must fish really deep to be in with a chance on some stretches. The spinner achieves this most effectively.

Thirdly, casting range. On a big river, a hefty proportion of the salmon in a pool may be lying beyond the range of a normal fly cast, or even a long one. A spinning rod will double that range.

Fourthly, overgrown bushes and trees, with fishing reduced to a few casts here and there. In cold water a large lure can be used and in summer a tiny spinner can be usefully employed. To attempt to use a fly rod in such circumstances could become time-wasting and frustrating.

Finally, the spinner may be used only where and when it is allowed. Entire rivers or stretches of them are subject to a fly-only rule. On others, the spinner is allowable only when the water is above a certain height.

## SPINNING RODS, REELS AND LINES

Glass and carbon-fibres have produced long but light spinning rods. A sensitive 2.4 m (8 ft) model may be right for flicking out a tiny summer lure, and one of 2.7 m (9 ft) will suffice on a medium-sized river. My longest and most powerful rod is 3.6 m (12 ft) of carbon-fibre. It will hurl a lure out, control the spinner with ease and play a big salmon to the shore with the maximum efficiency.

The choice of reel comes down to a fixed-spool or a multiplier, the former the easiest to master and generally cheaper. However, once the multiplier has been mastered it will be recognised as an excellent casting, fishing and salmon-fighting reel. Fixed-spools are at their best when fishing fairly light lines, while the multiplier proves its worth with heavier lines.

So, the fisherman equipped with a 2.4 m (8 ft) rod, medium-sized fixed-spool reel and 4–4.5 kg (9–10 lb) b.s. line, plus 3 or 3.33 m (10 or 11 ft) rod fitted with a multiplier and 6.8–8 kg (15–18 lb) b.s. nylon, may consider himself ready for any British salmon, and perhaps for some of the considerably larger fish to be found in Norway or Alaska.

## SPINNING RIGS

As in most fresh and saltwater situations, the best advice on rigs is 'Keep it simple'. Attach a swivel to the end of the line, then tie about 0.6 m (2 ft) of nylon to the opposite eye of the swivel to make a leader. Ball-bearing swivels are expensive but extremely efficient and avoid line twist.

Two lures have emerged as the outstanding salmon catchers: the Devon Minnow and the Toby spoon. My preference is to fish the Toby in streamier, fairly fast water and reserve the Devon for gentler flows. Devons are available in basic types separated by weight. Wooden and plastic Devons are generally lightweights. Plastic models with heavy, metal inserts are heavyweights along with the metal ones. The lightweights will need some weight to be added to the trace in order to cast effectively. Now that lead substitutes are available in many forms, the best alternative is an anti-kink style weight, attached to but above the swivel.

In cold waters, stay with Devons ranging in size from 50–76 mm (2–3 in). The colour range is enormous and one should heed the advice of the local tackle shop, but thousands of salmon have fallen to brown and gold! In warm water, where and when spinning is allowed, try a small, sombre Devon or a Mepps spoon.

## SPINNING

On the river, spin in the same way as you fished the fly. Cast the spinner out at about 45 degrees downstream. Do not turn the reel handle until the spinner is on the dangle. A few turns to tempt a following fish, then reel up quickly; take a pace downstream and make another cast, searching the water systematically. If the lure is scraping and catching the bottom, exchange it for a lighter one.

You will have set the slipping clutch on your reel so that a fish can take line. To recover line when a fish is being played requires a pumping action. Playing a fish has been summed up this way: 'When it pulls, let it go; when it stops, then you pull!' This may sound fairly basic, but, how it works!

There is perhaps some temptation to hurl a spinner out as far as possible but being able to cast a Devon Minnow a huge distance does not automatically confer on the angler the badge of the expert. Distance and catching salmon are not the same thing, for spinning demands the same understanding of the fish as that required by the angler who prefers the artificial fly.

In some circles, spinning for salmon was considered not the done thing, not respectable. There are anglers who still feel this way, but in all fishing there is but one simple objective, that of inducing a fish to take a bait, fly or lure fished on the end of the line. To this end, spinning is but one of the choices open to the person on the bank.

**Spinning in the autumn in Scotland. The River Nith has a late closing date, because of its autumn-running fish. There is hardly any spring run.**

# Glossary

# Topography of Lakes

# British and Irish Record Fish Tables

# Useful Addresses

# Index

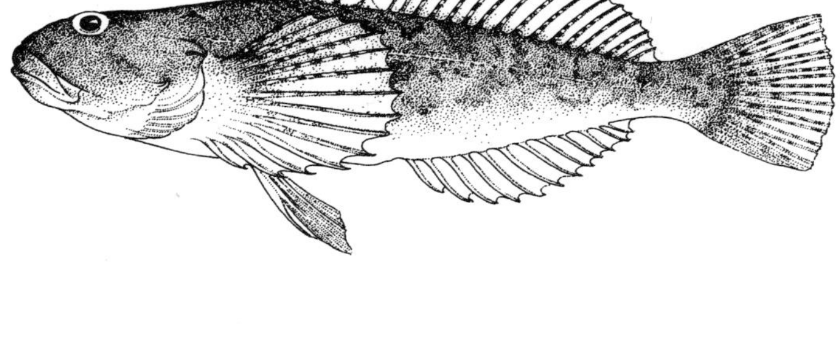

# Knots for the Fisherman

Many knots are used in fishing, but these are the basic ones which will preserve the breaking strain of nylon and Terylene materials. All these knots are simple and have proved to be effective.

BLOOD LOOP
Used to form a snood or dropper for hook attachment. The loop may be any length and is cut close to the hook to make the hook link.

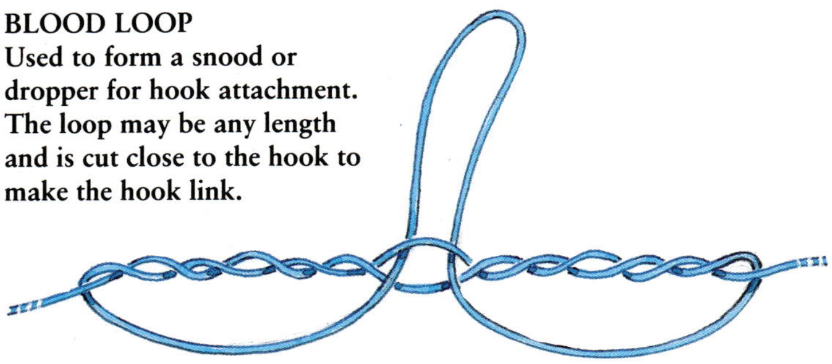

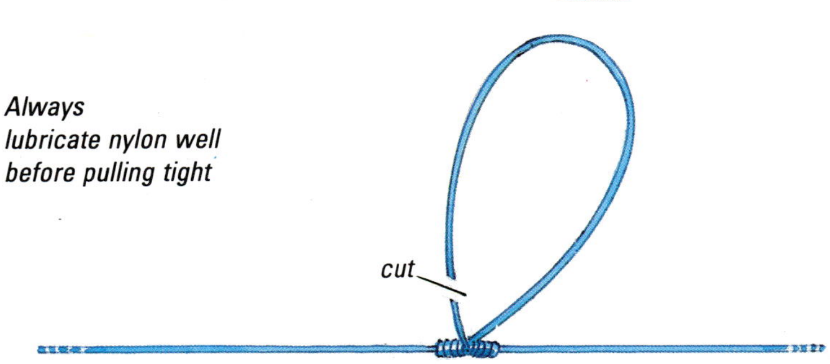


TUCKED HALF-BLOOD KNOT
For attaching booms, hooks, lures or swivels to nylon monofilament line.

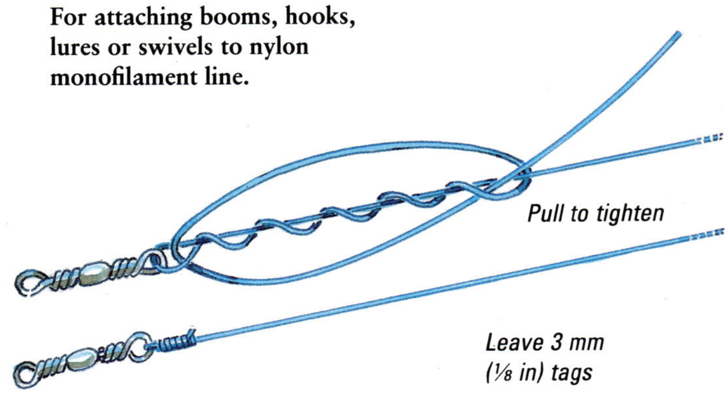


BLOOD KNOT
For tying two pieces of nylon together. The lines must be of similar diameter. If not, use a connecting link or swivel.

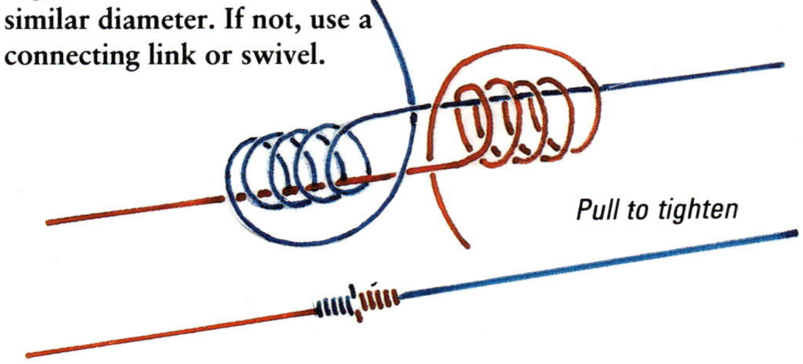


# Glossary of Fishing Terms

## A

**ABSTRACTION** Every riparian owner of a watercourse has the right to abstract from it water for his own domestic use including watering livestock. Water can be abstracted for other purposes *providing it does not injure the rights of other riparian owners.* It is alleged that severe abuses of certain rights has led to the deterioration of many rivers.

**ADIPOSE FIN** A fleshy appendage between dorsal and caudal fin on members of the salmon family.

**AFTM** Association of Fishing Tackle Makers.

**ALASTICUM** Single-strand, stiffish wire used to form short traces. Withstands the cutting action of sharp teeth and resists rust.

**ANGLERS' COOPERATIVE ASSOCIATION** By far the most active body representing anglers and their fight against pollution. Founded in 1947, the ACA has a long history of success against public bodies responsible for allowing a deterioration of water quality.

**ANTENNA** A float that has most of the body supporting weight and bait below the surface of the water. The fine tip is relatively unaffected by strong breezes.

**ANTI-INERTIA** A stiffening-up of the bale arm release mechanism to prevent the bale closing in mid-cast.

**ANTI-KINK** A lead or plastic vane used in spinning. It is designed with a keel to prevent line twist while retrieving and sometimes adds weight.

## B

**BACKING** Braided or monofilament line attached to a fly line to extend the amount of line that a strong fish can pull off the reel spool.

**BAG** The number of fish forming an angler's catch.

**BALE ARM** A hinged metal arm that picks up the reel line on the retrieve and distributes it round the spool of a fixed-spool reel (which see).

**BARBULE** A fleshy appendage found on the head or round the jaws of fishes, often in pairs or fours, and used as sensory organs.

**BEAT** A length of water and bankside allocated to one or more game anglers.

**BELLY** A curve in a fly or other fishing line caused by a current moving the line downstream faster than the fly or bait, resulting in drag.

**BITE** Indication from a fish, either visual or tactile, that a bait or lure has or is being taken by a fish.

**BLANCHED MAGGOTS** Maggots which have been put into heated water. This stretches them so that they cannot wriggle down into the mud and silt and makes them ideal for loose feed.

**BLANK** A hollow-glass, carbon or kevlar fibre tube from which a finished angling rod can be made.

**BLOODWORMS** Not true worms but the larvae of midges found in the mud and detritus of small ponds.

**BLOW** A fly 'blows' a suitable food-source for its maggots when it deposits its eggs there.

**BLOW-LINE** A light fly line by which a natural or artificial fly is dapped (see DAPPING) on the water's surface to catch feeding fish. The technique relies on a breeze to carry line and lure out.

**BOB FLY** In a team of artificial flies, that nearest to fly line. The bob fly is intended to 'bob' or dance attractively on the surface.

**BREAD FLAKE** Bread bait pinched out from the soft inside texture of a new loaf.

**BREAD PUNCH** A cutting tube used to form small pellets of bread of equal shape and size.

**BREAKING STRAIN (BS)** The pull in kilos or pounds at which a fishing line will break in the dry state.

**BUNG** A thick-bodied, onion-shaped float, usually used for pike fishing or to support a heavy bait.

**BUTT INDICATOR** A form of bite indicator located near the butt section of a fishing rod. Used in ledgering (which see).

**BUZZER** Angler's name for any *Chironomid* fly, midge and gnat that hovers close to the surface of the water.

## C

**CARBON-FIBRE** Introduced from the US and originally used in the manufacture of light spinning rods, carbon-fibre is now used for all kinds of equipment including rodblanks and reel casings.

**CASTER** The chrysalis stage of the maggot, and a useful hookbait and addition to groundbaits.

**CASTING** The act of propelling the hooked bait or fly out to where the fish are assumed to be. Propulsion is gained from the power inherent in the flexibility of the rod.

**CENTRE-PIN REEL** A revolving-drum reel having a fixed spindle with a 1:1 gear ratio. The handle is fixed to the side of the drum.

**CHECKING THE FLOAT** Halting the passage of a float down-stream to ensure that the baited hook-link precedes the float.

**CLOUD-BAIT** Particles of fine ground-bait intended to slowly sink down through the water, producing a cloud of edible, attractive, but not filling items to bring fish into the swim.

**CLUTCH** A mechanism whereby the reel drum can be put in or taken out of gear to revolve freely. Also a slipping system of washers which

OVERHAND KNOT
Forms a loop in a hook snood, dropper or fly cast.

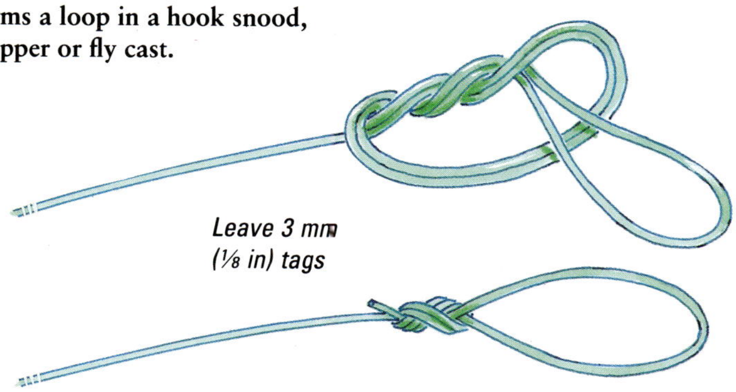


WHIPPING KNOT
For tying spade-and or eyed hooks to nylon links or droppers.

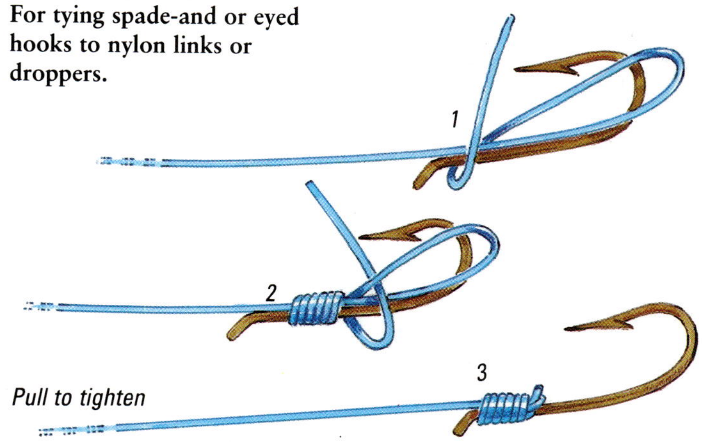


STOP KNOT
Allows a carerful correction of float-fishing depth as it slides freely along reel line.

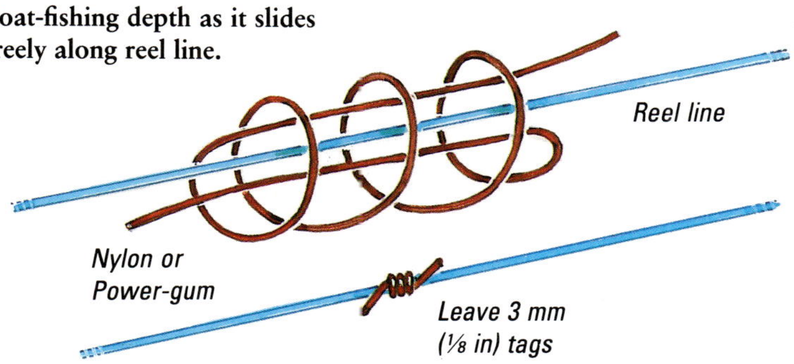


HITCH KNOT
This simple hitch resists the loose, slipping tendency of other, more complex knots.

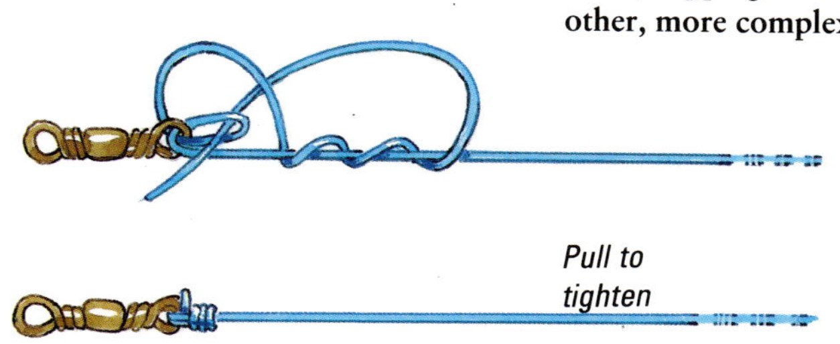


allows powerful fish to pull line off the reel before the breaking strain of the line is reached.

**COCKTAIL** A mixture of two or more different baits on the same hook.

**CONSERVATION** The consideration shown by all sections of the sport for the well-being and preservation of fish stocks, the maintenance and proper upkeep of fisheries and the future of the sport.

**CONTROLLER** A form of float used to provide sufficient weight to cast an ultra-light bait without resort to additional weights.

## D

**DAPPING** The art of presenting a natural or artificial lure by skilfully presenting the bait through bank-side obstacles. Also using a BLOW-LINE (which see) to float a natural or artificial fly out on the breeze.

**DEAD BAITING** Using a dead fish as bait for a scavenging or predatory species.

**DEVON** A wooden or metal spinning lure that revolves round a wire mount carrying a treble hook. Plastic vanes are fitted to impart spin.

**DINGHY** A small boat of wood or glass-fibre, used for inshore or enclosed-water fishing.

**DORSAL** Strictly 'top-side', but used to identify fins sited on the top of a fish's body.

**DOUBLE TAPER** A fly line which has a swollen middle section, tapering at each end.

**DOUGH BOBBIN** A simple method of bite detection made by squeezing a piece of bread-paste on to the line. Its weight registers the pull of a biting fish.

**DRAG** Unnatural movement of a fishing line caused by the line and lure travelling at different speeds. Also the slipping clutch found on most multipliers and fixed-spool reels.

**DRAINS** Man-made canal-like waterways which drain huge areas of agricultural land, mostly in the Fens and East Anglia.

**DRESSINGS** Combinations of different materials – fur, feather, silk, tinsel and so on – that are used in fly-tying.

**DROPPER** A hook-link of nylon or wire attached to the reel line. Also the nearest artificial to the rod of a string of wet flies.

**DRUM** On a fishing reel, usually a fixed-spool (which see), the spool round which line is wound.

**DRY FLY** An artificial fly so tied that it floats on the surface of the water.

**DT4F** This describes a Double Taper Size 4 Floating line.

**DUN** The emergent fly after it leaves its nymphal case.

## E

**ELASTICATED THREAD** Used by dressmakers to gather pleats and so on, but in fishing it is perfect for tying a soft bait to a hook so that it can be presented correctly.

## F

**FALSE CASTING** In fly-fishing, a method of casting a fishing line back and forth several times to remove water from the artificial and line so that they float.

**FIXED-SPOOL REEL** A fishing reel on which a rotating bale arm (which see) wraps the line round a spool set at right-angles to the axis of the rod. The spool itself does not turn to recover line, although it can be allowed to revolve to provide a slipping-drag facility.

**FLASHERS** Spoon blades or metal strips used to attract predatory fish species by their movement and flash in the water. Usually used in conjunction with natural baits.

**FLOATANTS** Once grease but now usually silicone-based aerosol sprays applied to fly-lines and artificial flies to ensure that they float on the surface of the water.

**FLOAT FISHING** A fishing style which employs a float of buoyant material to suspend bait and weight at the required depth. The float also registers the bite of a taking fish.

**FLY** A loose term describing most lures presented on a fly line and rod. These artificials may simulate flies, fish or invertebrates.

**FLY LINE** A line which has weight so that it sinks, or has buoyant materials coated on the line so that it floats.

**FLY SPOON** A tiny metal lure that can be cast using a fly rod and fly line.

**FODDER-FISH** Species of small shoaling fish which form much of the food of the predatory species.

**FORWARD TAPER** A fly line that tapers in one direction only, toward the fly.

**FREELINING** A fishing style that dispenses with any form of float or weight to carry the bait out to the fish.

**FRY** Very young, immature fish of most species.

## G

**GAFF** A metal hook fixed to a shaft and used to impale a fish and lift it from the water. A barbarous fishing accessory that is rapidly going out of use in these conservation-minded times.

**GEAR RATIO** This is the difference between one turn of the reel handle and the number of turns produced on the reel spool or drum. It is given in figures such as 1:35.

**GORGE FISHING** Once common but now illegal, gorge fishing uses a method of allowing a fish to take the baited hook down into its stomach, ensuring the fish's death.

**GOZZER** A maggot produced by a fly *Calliphora eryphrocephala* and a favourite for home-breeding. The fly blows (see BLOW) in the dark, producing a large, white, succulent grub ideal as a warm-weather bait.

**GRILSE** A small salmon, generally thought to have spent only a single year feeding at sea.

## TUCKED TURLE KNOT

The best knot for attaching a trout or salmon fly to the nylon leader.

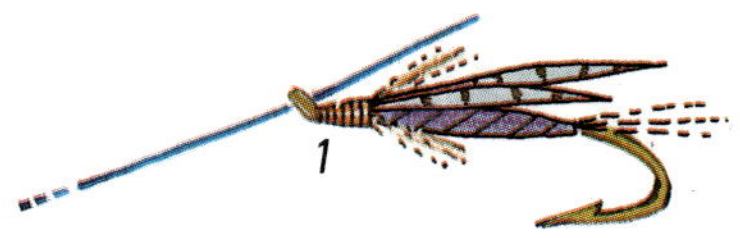


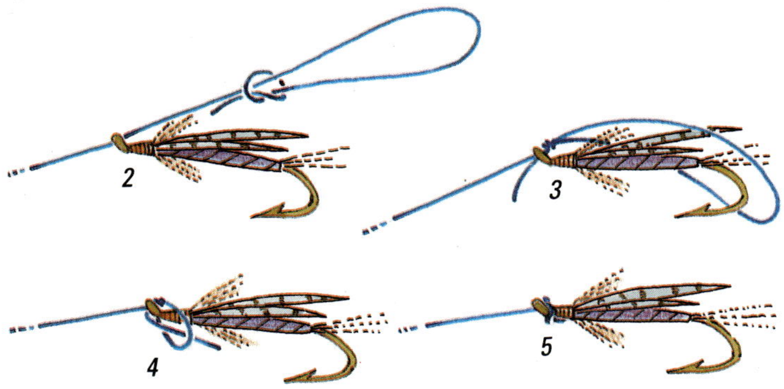


## NEEDLE KNOT

Provides a smooth join between a fly line and the nylon leader. Push a needle 3 mm (1/8 in) into centre of flyline. Heat the needle slightly and remove. Insert butt or leader. Hold small tube along line and wrap nylon round both four times. Thread nylon through tube and withdraw tube. Pull both ends of nylon tight.

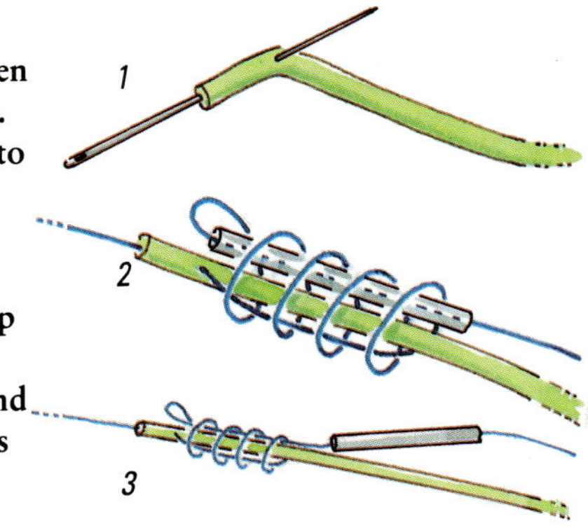


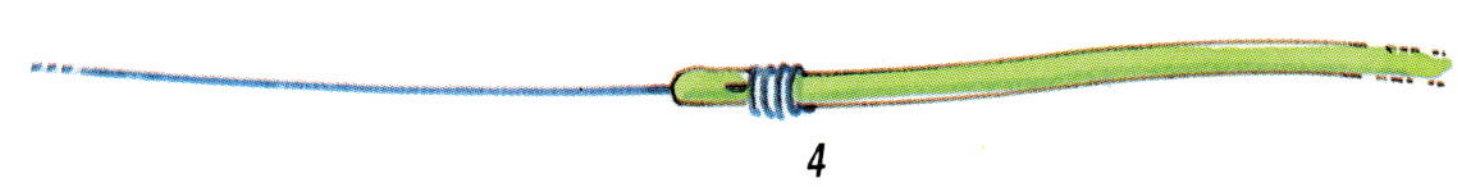


## WATER KNOT

For tying a made-up leader to provide one or more links or droppers.

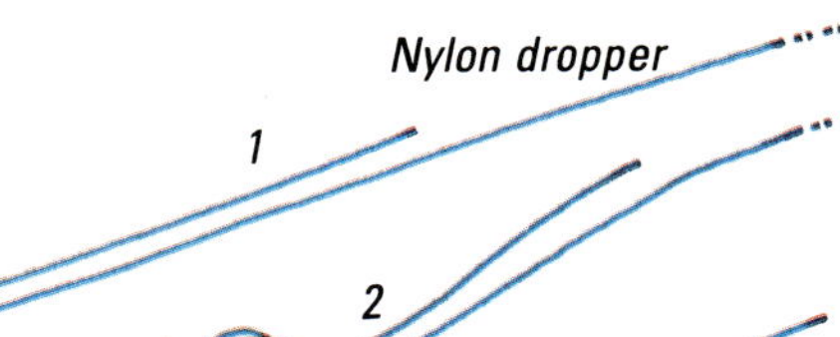


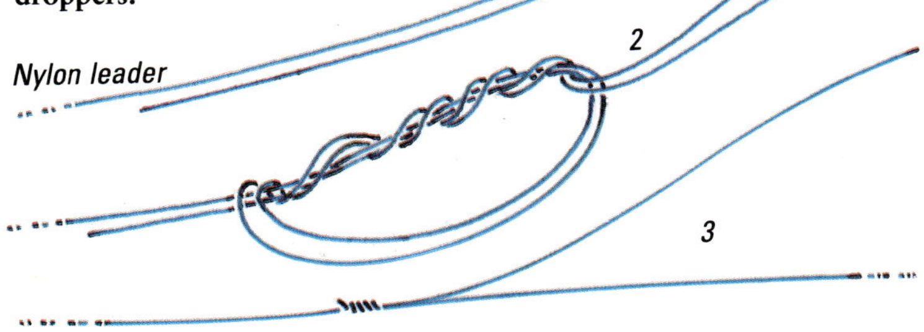


## BACKING SPLICE

Attaches braided backing line to fly line. Strip away 1 cm (3/8 in) outer plastic and harden core with Super glue. Push braided line on to the point of the core. Work braid on to fly line for 2 cm (1/4 in). Tack with Super glue. Trim and 'varnish' joint with Super glue.

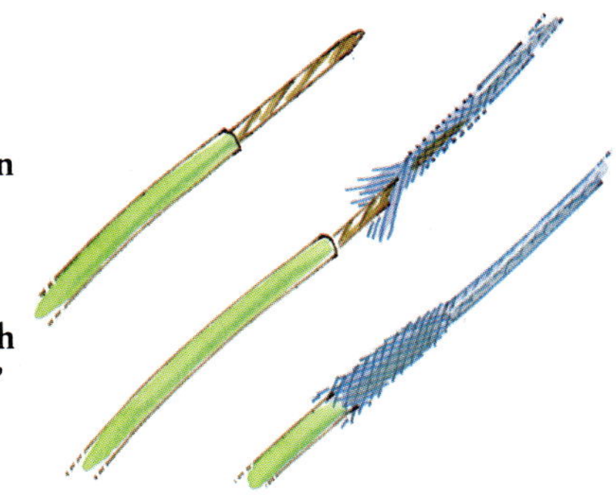

**GROUND BAITING** Feeding a predetermined area of water with cereal or hookbait to attract and hold fish near to the angler's baited hook.

## H

**HACKLE POINTS** Two stiff hackles from a cockerel cape, used to represent wings.

**HATCH** The time when the nymphal form of some water-living fly rises to the surface and hatches to emerge as a fully-winged insect. At such times it produces a frantic feeding frenzy among the trout.

**HOLT** The place where a pike lies up after feeding. A resting place.

**HOOK LENGTH** The length of nylon to which hooks are whipped. The hooks are whipped commercially to various lengths which are looped for quick attachment to the reel line.

**HOT SPOT** One kind of hot spot is that place where two or more fish patrol paths cross. Here, at regular times, fish are present and the thinking angler will watch and note these times for future reference.

## I

**IGFA** International Game Fish Association, based at Fort Lauderdale, Florida, USA. The IGFA publishes lists of world record fish, at least those notified to it.

## J

**JARDINE TACKLE** See SNAP-TACKLE.

## K

**KELT** A salmon in its weakened state after spawning. Many kelts die in their attempt to return to the sea. It is illegal to take fish in this condition.

**KNOTLESS TAPERED LEADERS** A one-piece nylon cast in which there is a continuous taper from butt to point.

**KYPE** At spawning time the males of salmonids develop a hooked protuberance of the lower jaw, large enough for it at times to prevent closure of the jaws.

## L

**LARVA** A grub that has hatched from the eggs of an insect and which is mobile. This is the stage before the pupa, or chrysalis.

**LATERAL LINE** The line of connected cells running along the flanks of fish which sense vibration, water-borne sounds and pressure changes. It is part of the fish's nervous system.

**LAYBACK STYLE** A method of shore casting devised by the late Leslie Moncrieff.

**LAYING ON** A float-fishing technique where the bait is fished hard on the bottom. Some weight is also lying on the bottom, with the float virtually tight-lined.

**LEADER** A length of nylon line preceding the main line. It can be of lesser or greater breaking strain.

**LEADS** Various forms of weight used to assist casting or to sink baits and floats. (See LEAD SHOT REGULATION)

**LEAD SHOT REGULATION** From 1 January 1987 the import, sale and use in angling of lead shot between No. 8 shot (0.06 g) and 28.35 g (1 oz) was banned by HM Government. The legislation was to reduce the alleged deaths of mute swans through ingestion of anglers' lead shot. Lead used in swim-feeders (which see), self-cocking floats, lead-core lines and weighted lines was not affected.

**LEAD SUBSTITUTES** Substances devised by the manufacturing industry which act as substitutes for the lead shot which is now illegal between certain weight limits (see LEAD SHOT REGULATION).

**LEDGERING** Fishing with the bait held on the bottom by a weight and usually a float. Ledgering with a float is called float ledgering.

**LIE** A known resting place of fish.

**LINE-BITE** A false indication of a bite brought about by the body of a fish striking or rubbing against the line or some part of the terminal tackle.

**LINK** An accessory used to join various items of tackle together or to lines.

**LINK SWIVEL** A useful swivel for quick attachment of traces and casts.

**LOADED (WEIGHTED) FLOAT** A float carrying an in-built weight to assist casting. It also overcomes some of the float's natural buoyancy.

**LOCK SHOT** Split-shot placed either side of the float to fix its position relative to the depth of fishing. See also LEAD SHOT REGULATION.

**LURE** Any artificial bait, spinner, pl pirk or fly.

## M

**MAGGOT** The larval form of the fly any Diptera species.

**MAGGOT-DROPPER** A case that is filled with maggots, dropped into the swim and capable of being opened by the angler to release tl offering accurately into position to entice fish near the hook-bait.

**MENDING THE LINE** A means of avoiding drag and sinking an artificial fly down in the water. It is accomplished by throwing a loo in line upstream.

## N

**NYMPH** A larva of the *Ephemeridae* group of flies or an angler's artificial representation of the same.

## O

**OPERCULAR BONES** The group of several bones that form the gill-case or cover which protect the delicate gill filaments of fish.

**OVER-RUN** A bunch of intertwined nylon on the drum of a centre-pin reel caused by inefficient casting and/or poor line control.

## P

**PASTE** Hookbait made by soaking bread, squeezing out the water and kneading it into a stiff dough.

**PATERNOSTER** A form of terminal tackle having the weight at the bottom and fished with a tight line to the rod. Booms are used to suspend hook links and baits.
**PATTERN** A fixed, often traditional design of materials and positioning of parts that form an artificial fly.
**PECTORALS** Paired fins behind the gill-case (see OPERCULAR BONES).
**PEG** A numbered position drawn by a match-fisherman which allots him a limited stretch of bank of a contest venue.
**PELAGIC** Life that inhabits the surface and upper layers of water.
**PELVICS** Paired fins situated low down on the fish's body, usually behind the pectoral fins (which see) and sometimes called the ventrals.
**PENNELL TACKLE** A two-hook rig with the hooks placed in tandem.
**PICK-UP** The bale arm (which see) of a fixed-spool reel.
**PINKIE** The maggot, or grub, of the greenbottle fly, of the Dipteran flies.
**PITCH** A place from which an angler fishes, in front of which is the swim (which see).
**PLANKTON (ZOO- AND PHYTO-)** Minute animal and vegetable life, free-floating and moving, found in freshwater and saltwater.
**PLUGS** Artificial lures, usually of wood or plastic, intended to simulate the movements of fish and other aquatic creatures.
**PLUMB-BOB, PLUMBING** By use of a weighted plumb-bob the depth of water anywhere in front of the angler can be assessed. The weight is attached to the hook and lowered down, the float's position on the line can then be adjusted so that the bait is suspended at the required depth.
**POINT** The finely tapered end section of a fly cast, or the fly at the tip of the team. Also sharp end of the hook.
**POLLUTION** The greatest threat to angling and must be fought at all levels.
**PRICKED** When the point of the hook is pulled lightly into a fish so that the contact is felt but momentarily, the fish avoiding being properly hooked. The fish has been 'pricked'.
**PUT-AND-TAKE WATER** A fishery where trout are placed into the water for anglers to catch, the fish having been reared to a certain size elsewhere.

## Q

**QUILL MINNOW** An old-timer's light artificial bait for use when spinning for trout in fast, streamy water.
**QUIVERTIP** A sensitive rod-tip bite indicator that visibly trembles when a fish takes the baited hook.

## R

**RATCHET** A checking device that prevents line running too freely off the reel and gives an audible warning of a pull on the bait.
**RIM CONTROL** An exposed rim on a fly-reel drum which allows an angler to control line running out to a hooked fish by applying light finger-pressure.
**RINGS** Circular guides, whipped or sleeved on to a rod blank that spread the stress of playing a fish along the entire length of the rod, and which also allow free passage of line on and off the reel while casting or playing a fish.
**RISE** The surface indication of the presence of a fish, usually indicated by a series of widening rings or the dimpling of the surface.
**ROACH POLE** A multi-sectioned, very long fishing rod to the end of which is fixed a short length of line and baited hook. A reel is not used, and a fish retrieved and unhooked by unshipping pole-sections until the hook length is to hand.
**ROD REST** Usually made of metal, rod rests support fishing rods at angles suited to the style of fishing being practised, such as ledgering.
**ROLL CAST** A method of fly-casting in places where there is no room for a back-cast.

## S

**SEDGES** Waterside plants; insects belonging to the Order Trichoptera.
**SHOCK LEADER** Nylon that is stronger than the reel line, and is intended to absorb the shock of casting.
**SHOT LEAD** The amount of weight that a float will carry before sinking below the surface.
**SINKING LINE** A fly line with built-in weight that sinks below the surface.
**SKIMMER (BREAM)** Small freshwater fish which when hooked come skimming back across the surface on their flat-sided bodies.
**SLIDER FLOAT** A float that allows an angler to fish at a greater depth than the length of the rod. The float is held by a stop knot (which see) that can be any distance from the hook, yet will pass easily through the rod rings when line is being retrieved.
**SMUTTING** Surface-feeding trout that are taking minute flies, midges and other small insects.
**SNAP-TACKLE** Two treble hooks joined by a wire trace on which a live or dead fish is mounted when fishing for pike.
**SPECIMEN** A good-sized fish when compared with the average size of the species found in the water.
**SPIGOT** A modern method of joining two sections of hollow-glass blank, replacing the ferrules of the cane and split-cane rods.
**SPINNERS** A general term for metal artificial lures although the description should apply only to those that spin round the axis of the lure rather than wobble through the water.
**SPLIT CANE** Top quality rods were once produced by glueing together usually six lengths of best bamboo to form a hexagon. Strength and the traditional 'sweet' action were the hallmark of these fine rods.
**SPOONS** Metal fishing lures that wobble or move erratically but do not spin (see SPINNERS).
**SQUATT** The maggot or grub of the common housefly *(Diptera)*.
**STOP BEAD** A bead placed between a slider float (which see) and stop knot (which see), or between a running boom and swivel (which see) to prevent jamming of the knots.
**STOP KNOT** A knot used to stop or fix the depth of a slider float (which see).
**STREAMER FLIES** Large artificial flies tied generally to represent small fish.
**STRET PEGGING** Float-fishing down-stream in stages. The bait is allowed to settle and fish for a short period. If bites do not come the float is lifted and the bait allowed to move farther down-river in a series of static fishing movements until the float is too far away for a strike to be made.
**STRIKE** The sharp movement of the rod-tip that sets the hook firmly in the fish's jaw.
**STRIPPING LINE** A term that describes two operations: (1) pulling a fly line off the reel by hand, and (2) playing in a fish by pulling line back through the rod-rings by hand rather than retrieving it by reeling in.
**SWIM** An area in a coarse-fishing situation known to hold fish.
**SWIM-BLADDER** Found in most bony fishes. More correctly the gas-bladder, it is filled with air to allow the fish to adjust its buoyancy at different depths to compensate for varying pressures.
**SWIM-FEEDER** A container attached to the terminal tackle from which maggots or other forms of feed can trickle in close proximity to the hookbait.
**SWINGTIP** A swinging, hanging arm, through which the line runs, that is lifted by the pull of a biting fish. It is screwed into the rod-tip.
**SWIVEL** A metal device for joining lines and preventing line twist from being transmitted back along the line by the actions of a spinning lure.

## T

**TACKLE** An embracing term that describes all of an angler's fishing gear; also just the hook end of the terminal tackle.
**TAKES** Bites from fish, either successful or missed. Usually applied to game fishing.
**TAKING SHORT** A bite from a fish where the bait or lure is only nipped at the extreme end, missing the hook.
**TAPER** The amount of decrease in diameter of a rod from butt to tip.
**TARES** A species of pea used to feed pigeons, but also used as a hook- and groundbait by coarse anglers.
**TEAM OF FLIES** Three wet flies fished on a game-fisherman's cast.
**TEASER** A bait presented to predatory fish in a lifelike way to induce them to strike at a hookbait.
**TERMINAL TACKLE** The trace, rig or combination of parts that form the business end of the angler's gear. The hook, swivels, and so on nearest the hook.
**TEST CURVE** The amount of pull on a line that will put a curve into a rod so that the tip and butt section are at right-angles. Often used as a way of expressing the line strength (in kilos or pounds) that a rod can accommodate.
**TINSEL** Thin-strand metal foil wound round the body of an artificial fly to give flash or to break up its outline.
**TRACE** A length of nylon or wire used to form any rig or terminal tackle.
**TRAIL** The hook length between the ledger weight and hook-bait.
**TREBLE HOOK** Three hooks joined together on to a common eye, mostly used on spinning lures and tube flies.
**TROLLED BAIT** A bait, or lure, that is towed behind a boat at a speed slow enough to attract predatory fish.
**TROTTED** A lure or bait that is allowed to run downstream at the speed of the current.
**TUBE FLIES** Salmon and trout flies where the dressing is applied to a tube made of plastic, aluminium or brass, depending on the weight of lure needed. The line or cast runs through the tube to a treble hook.

## W

**WET FLY** An artificial fly intended to fish below the surface in the manner of a small fish. The hackles are tied to sweep backwards.
**WINGS** The slip of joined fibres, taken from the wing feather of various birds to form the wing of an artificial fly; also the 'wings' of skates and rays.
**WRIST** The section of a fish's body just before the tail (or caudal) fin.

## Z

**ZOOMER** An antenna-type float with an in-built weight to give long and accurate casting.

# Topography of Lakes

MOUNTAIN LAKE

Very deep, vegetation poor with marginal water clear. Cold, except in layer near the surface.

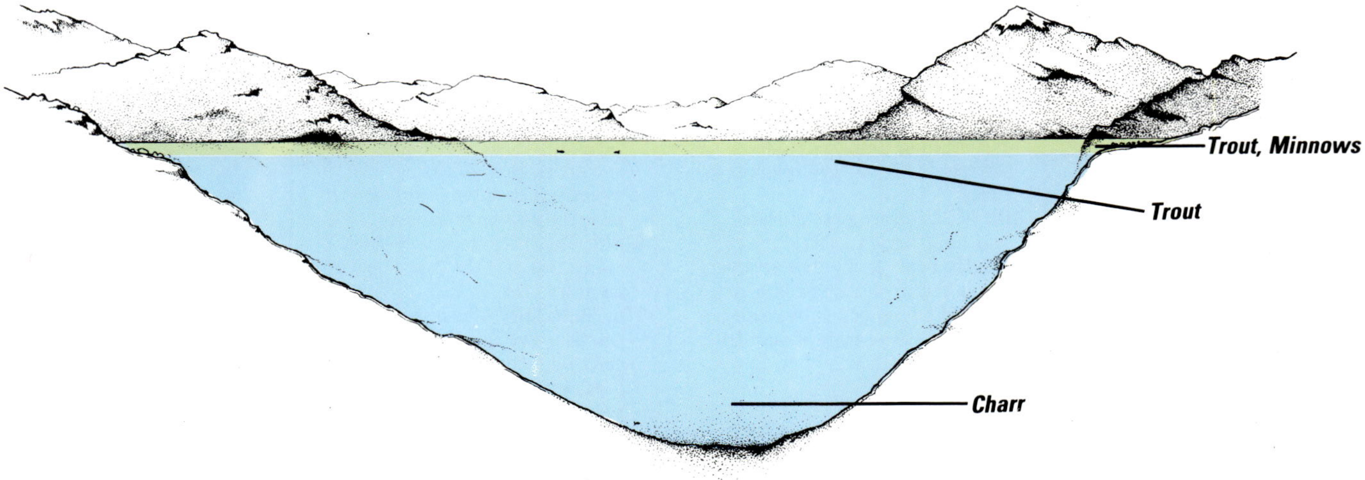


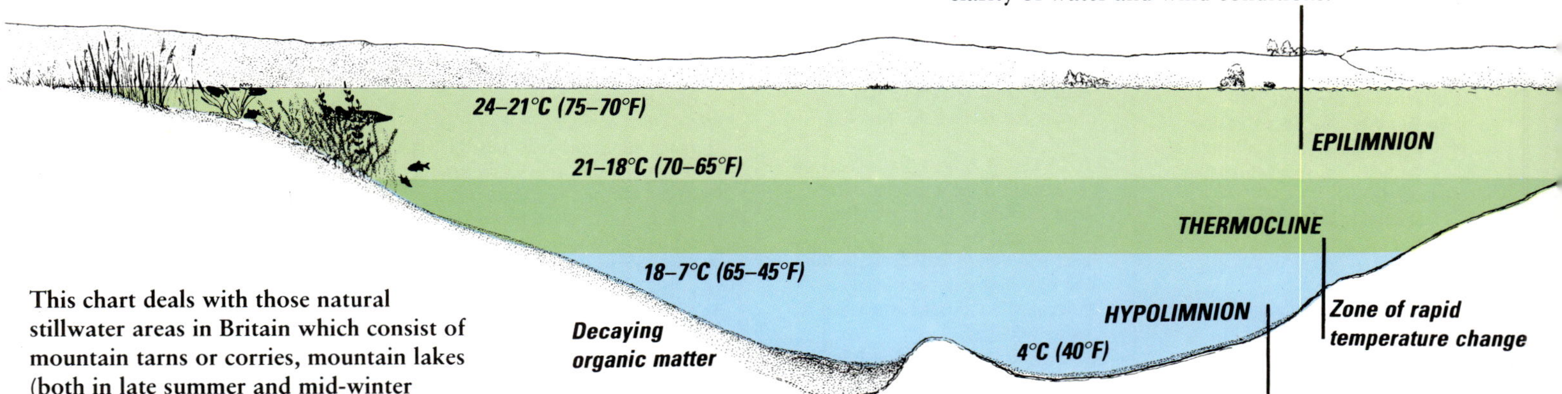


This chart deals with those natural stillwater areas in Britain which consist of mountain tarns or corries, mountain lakes (both in late summer and mid-winter conditions) and lowland ponds. Where the bands on the pools and lakes shown are of the same colour, the same temperatures apply. For example, the area of warm water in mountain lakes, lowland lakes in late summer and lowland ponds in late summer are coloured the same. Of course, the warm water depth varies considerably. In the high mountain tarns there is no warm water level. By reading the chart in this fashion the reader will obtain a quick idea of the life and ecology of these waters.

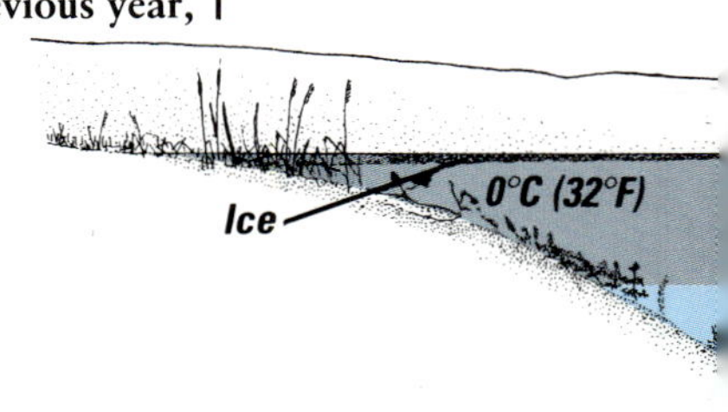


LOWLAND POND

Shallow water in late summer when there may be an oxygen deficiency throughout. The water is turbid.

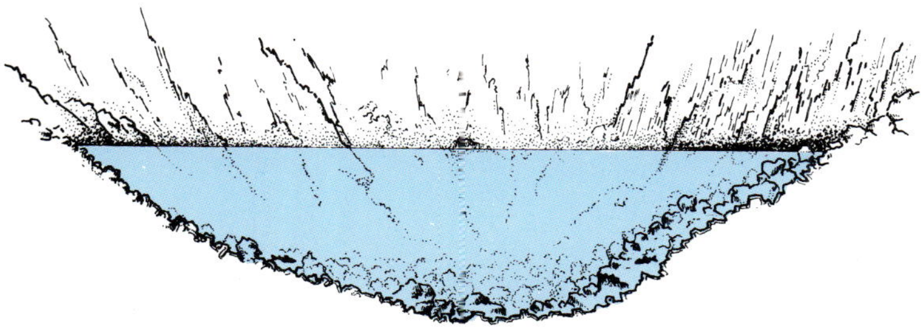

MOUNTAIN TARN OR CORRIE LAKE

Always cold, vegetation and animal life is very poor. Small trout and charr may be present if the water is deep enough to withstand freezing to base.

*A*

*B*

*C*

Some of the aquatic creatures that form part of the fishes' food chain.

*A* The water louse, *Asellus aquaticus*, related to marine crustaceans. It is found in most slow-running and stillwaters. Feeds on decaying matter on the bottom of streams and ponds. *B* A water-beetle larva, one of the many species of carnivorous beetles found during the warmer months in freshwater. *C* Snails and their eggs are a source of food for many species of fish. The great pond snail, *Limnaea* (or *Lymnaea*) *stagnalis*, and ramshorn snail, *Planorbis planorbis*, with their spawn.

LOWLAND LAKE

Vegetation marginal and rich.

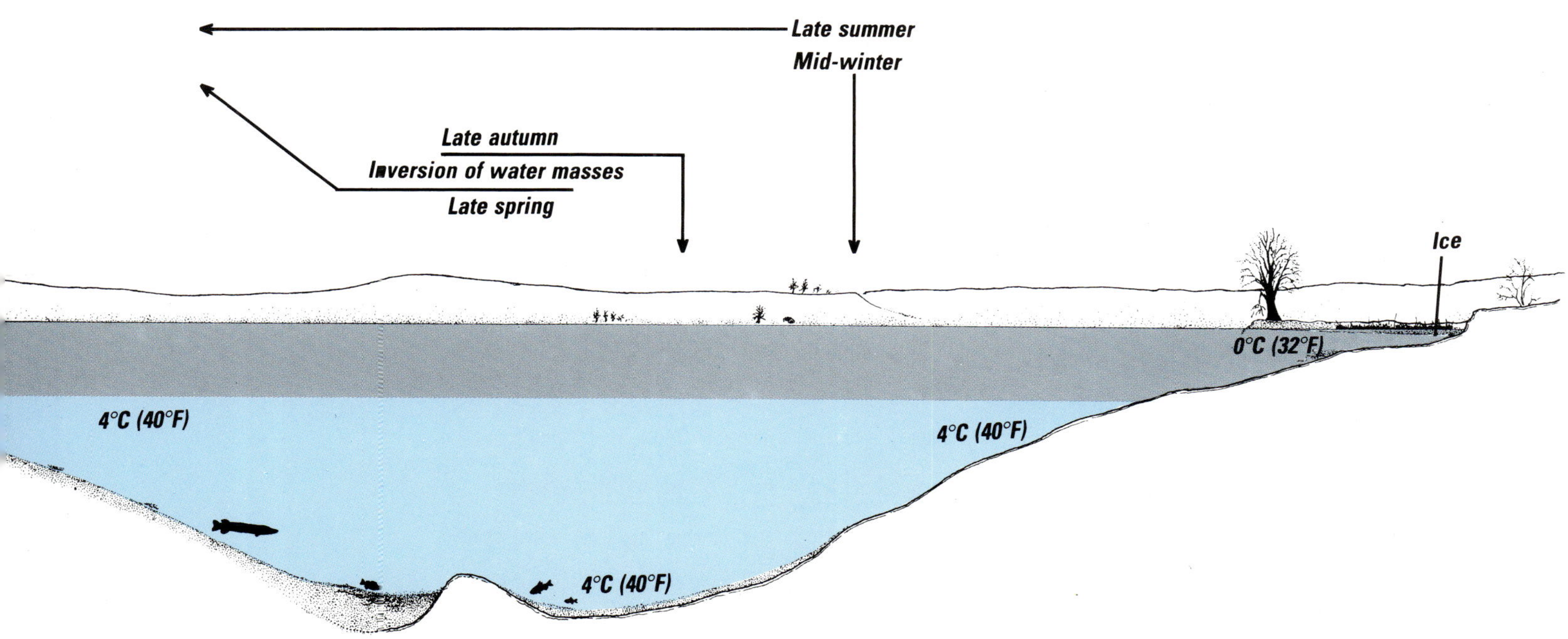

# British and Irish Record Fish Tables

## THE BRITISH RECORD (ROD-CAUGHT) FISH COMMITTEE
## BRITISH RECORD FRESHWATER FISH LIST

| Species<br>Scientific Name | Weight<br>lbs | ozs | dms | kilos | gms | Date | Captor and Location |
|---|---|---|---|---|---|---|---|
| Barbel<br>*Barbus barbus* | 14 | 6 | – | 6 | 520 | 1934 | The Hon. Aylmer D. Tryon, Royalty Fishery, Hampshire |
| Bleak<br>*Albumus albumus* | – | 4 | 4 | – | 120 | 1982 | B. Derrington, River Monnow, Wye Mouth, Monmouthshire |
| Bream (Common, Bronze)<br>*Abramis brama* | 16 | 6 | – | 7 | 427 | 1986 | A. Bromley, Private Fishery, Staffordshire |
| Bream, Silver<br>*Abramis bjoerkna* | – | 15 | – | – | 425 | 1988 | D. E. Flack, Grime Spring, Lakenheath, Suffolk |
| Bullhead (Miller's Thumb)<br>*Cottus gobio* | – | 1 | – | – | 028 | 1983 | R. Johnson, Bramley & Shamley Green River, Nr. Guildford, Surrey |
| Carp<br>*Cyprinus carpio* | 51 | 8 | – | 23 | 358 | 1980 | C. Yates, Redmire Pool, Hereford & Worcs. |
| Carp, Crucian<br>*Carassius carassius* | 5 | 10 | 8 | 2 | 565 | 1976 | G. Halls, at lakes Nr. King's Lynn, Norfolk |
| Carp, Grass<br>*Ctenopharyngodon idella* | 16 | 1 | – | 7 | 285 | 1990 | John P. Buckley, Horton Fishery, Berks. |
| Catfish (Wels)<br>*Silurus glanis* | 43 | 8 | – | 19 | 730 | 1970 | R. J. Bray, Wilstone Reservoir, Tring, Herts. |
| Charr, Arctic<br>*Salvelinus alpinus* | 7 | 7 | – | 3 | 373 | 1990 | J. MacDonald, Loch Arkaig, Fort William, Inverness-shire |
| Chub<br>*Leuciscus cephalus* | 8 | 4 | – | 3 | 743 | 1913 | G. F. Smith, Avon at Christchurch |
| Dace<br>*Leuciscus leuciscus* | 1 | 4 | 4 | – | 574 | 1960 | J. L. Gasson, Little Ouse, Thetford, Norfolk |
| Eel<br>*Anguilla anguilla* | 11 | 2 | – | 5 | 046 | 1978 | S. Terry, Kingfisher Lake, Nr. Ringwood, Hants |
| Grayling<br>*Thymallus thymallus* | 4 | 3 | – | 1 | 899 | 1989 | Sean R. Lanigan, River Frome, Dorset |
| Gudgeon<br>*Gobio gobio* | – | 5 | – | – | 141 | 1990 | David H. Hull, River Nadder, Salisbury, Wilts. |
| Minnow<br>*Phoxinus phoxinus* | – | – | 13 | – | 023 | 1981 | R. Merrifield, River Calder, Nelson, Lancs. |
| Orfe, Golden<br>*Leuciscus idus* | 5 | 15 | – | 2 | 693 | 1990 | Gary Sherwin, Lymm Vale, Cheshire |
| Perch<br>*Perca fluviatilis* | 5 | 9 | – | 2 | 523 | 1985 | J. Shayler, from Private Lake, Kent |
| Pike<br>*Esox lucius* | 45 | 6 | – | 20 | 581 | 1990 | G. O. Edwards, Llandegfedd Reservoir, Pontypool, Gwent |
| Walleye (Pikeperch)<br>*Stizostedion vitreum* | 11 | 12 | – | 5 | 329 | 1934 | F. Adams, The Delph, Welney, Norfolk |
| Zander (Pikeperch)<br>*Stizostedion lucioperca* | 18 | 8 | – | 8 | 390 | 1988 | R. N. Meadows, Cambridge Stillwater |
| Pumpkinseed<br>*Lepomis gibbosus* | – | 4 | 9 | – | 129 | 1987 | D. L. Wallis, Whessoe Pond, Darlington, Co. Durham |
| Roach<br>*Rutilus rutilus* | 4 | 3 | – | 1 | 899 | 1990 | Ramon N. Clarke, River Stour, Dorset |
| Rudd<br>*Rutilus erythrophthalmus* | 4 | 8 | – | 2 | 041 | 1933 | Rev. E. C. Alston, Thetford, Norfolk |
| Ruffe<br>*Gymnocephalus cernuus* | – | 5 | 4 | – | 148 | 1980 | R. J. Jenkins, West View Farm, Cumbria |
| Salmon<br>*Salmo Salar* | 64 | – | – | 29 | 029 | 1922 | Miss G. W. Ballantine, River Tay, Scotland |
| *Schelly (Skelly)<br>*Coregonus clupeoides* | 2 | 1 | 9 | – | 950 | 1986 | S. M. Barrie, Haweswater Reservoir, Cumbria |

*Note: Schelly (Skelly) – as this fish is now protected no further claims can be considered.

## THE BRITISH RECORD (ROD-CAUGHT) FISH COMMITTEE
## BRITISH RECORD FRESHWATER FISH LIST continued

| Species<br>Scientific Name | Weight<br>lbs | ozs | dms | kilos | gms | Date | Captor and Location |
|---|---|---|---|---|---|---|---|
| Tench<br>*Tinca tinca* | 14 | 3 | – | 6 | 435 | 1987 | P. A. Gooriah, Wraysbury One, Middlesex |
| Trout, American Brook<br>(Brook Char)<br>*Salvelinus fontinalis* | 5 | 13 | 8 | 2 | 650 | 1981 | A. Pearson, Avington Fishery, Hants. |
| Trout, Brown<br>*Salmo trutta* | 19 | 9 | 4 | 8 | 880 | 1978 | J. A. F. Jackson, Loch Quoich, Inverness, Scotland |
| Trout, Rainbow<br>*Oncorhynchus mykiss* | 24 | 2 | 13 | 10 | 965 | 1989 | J. Moore, Pennine Trout Fishery, Littleborough, Lancashire |
| Trout, Sea<br>*Salmo trutta* | 22 | 8 | – | 10 | 205 | 1989 | S. Burgoyne, River Leven, Scotland |

*Information supplied by the British Record (rod-caught) Fish Committee of the National Anglers' Council*

## IRISH RECORD FISH

| Species | Weight<br>lbs | ozs | Date of Capture | Place of Capture | Captor |
|---|---|---|---|---|---|
| Salmon | 57 | – | 1874 | River Suir | M. Maher |
| Sea Trout | 16 | 6 | 29.10.1983 | Shimna River, Co. Down | Thomas McManus |
| Brown Trout (River) | 20 | – | 22.2.1957 | River Shannon, Corbally | Major Hugh Place |
| Brown Trout (Lake) | 26 | 2 | 15.7.1894 | Lough Ennell | Wm Mears |
| Bream | 11 | 12 | 1882 | River Blackwater (Monaghan) | A. Pike |
| Carp | 26 | 2 | 28.5.1989 | The Lough, Cork | Kieron V. Bend |
| Dace | 1 | 2 | 8.8.1966 | River Blackwater, Cappoquin | John T. Henry |
| Perch | 5 | 8 | 1946 | Lough Erne | S. Drom |
| Pike (River) | 42 | – | 22.3.1964 | River Barrow | M. Watkins |
| Pike (Lake) | 38 | 2 | 25.2.1973 | Lough Corrib | Brendan Hardiman |
| Roach | 2 | 13.5 | 11.8.1970 | River Blackwater, Cappoquin | Lawrie Robinson |
| Rudd | 3 | 1 | 27.6.1959 | Kilglass Lake | A. F. Biddlecombe |
| Rudd/Bream Hybrid | 6 | 4 | 5.3.1990 | Monalty Lake | Peter Walsh |
| Roach/Bream Hybrid | 4 | 8.5 | 2.7.1989 | Drunucask L. | Philip Arthur |
| Tench | 7 | 13.25 | 25.5.1971 | River Shannon, Lanesboro. | Raymond Webb |
| River Eel | 6 | 15 | 12.6.1979 | L. Droumenisa, Bantry | J. Murnane |

*Information supplied by the Irish Specimen Fish Committee, Balnagowan House, Mobhi Boreen, Glasnevin, Dublin 9, Eire.*
*Record claims for fish caught in Ireland should be made to the Irish Specimen Fish Committee at the above address.*

# Useful Addresses

**River pollution**
To report river pollution in England, contact: National Rivers Authority, Rivers House, Albert Embankment, London SE1 7TL; (071) 820 0101

**Fishing licences and information**
The ten water authorities of England and Wales will provide information on licences for fishing within their area and may be able to provide details of where to fish. The addresses and telephone numbers are as follows:

Anglian Water Plc, Ambury Road, Huntingdon, PE18 6NZ; (0480) 433055

Northumbrian Water Group Plc, P.O. Box 4, Regent Centre, Gosforth, Newcastle upon Tyne NE3 3PX; (091) 284 3151

North West Water Ltd, Dawson House, Great Sankey, Warrington WA5 3LW; (0925) 234000

Severn Trent Plc, 2297 Coventry Road, Sheldon, Birmingham B26 3PU; (021) 722 4000

Southern Water Plc, Southern House, Yeoman Road, Worthing, West Sussex BN13 3NX; (0903) 64444

South West Water, Peninsula House, Rydon Lane, Exeter; (0392) 219666

Thames Water, Nugent House, Vastern Road, Reading RG1 8DB; (0734) 593333

Wessex Water Plc, Wessex House, Passage Street, Bristol BS2 0JQ; (0272) 290611

Yorkshire Water Plc, West Riding House, 67 Albion Street, Leeds LS1 5AA; (0532) 448201

Welsh Water Plc, Plas y Ffynnon, Cambrian Way, Brecon, Powys; (0874) 3181

In Scotland, contact your local Regional Council, Islands Council or the Central Scotland Water Development Board. The addresses and telephone numbers are as follows:

**Borders**
Water and Drainage Service, West Grove, Waverley Road, Melrose, Roxburghshire TD6 9SJ; (089682) 2056

**Central**
Woodlands, St Ninians Road, Stirling FK8 2HB; (0786) 64213/62811

**Dumfries and Galloway**
Department of Water and Sewerage, Marchmont House, Dumfries DG1 1PW; (0387) 61234

**Fife**
Craig Mitchell House, Flemington Road, Glenrothes, Fife KY7 5QH; (0592) 754411

**Grampian**
Woodhill House, Westburn Road, Aberdeen AB9 2LU; (0224) 682222

**Highland**
Regional Buildings, Glenurquhart Road, Inverness IV3 5NX; (0463) 234121

**Lothian**
Water and Drainage Department, 6 Cockburn St, Edinburgh EH1 1NZ; (031) 229 9292

**Strathclyde**
419 Balmore Road, Glasgow G22 6NU; (041) 336 5333

**Tayside**
Water Services Department, Bullion House, Invergowrie, Dundee DD2 5BB; (0382) 562581

**Orkney Islands**
Council Offices, Kirkwall KW15 1NY; (0856) 3535

**Shetland Islands**
Town Hall, Lerwick, Shetland ZE1 0HB; (0595) 3535

**Western Isles**
Council Offices, Sandwick Road, Stornoway PA87 2BW; (0851) 3773

Central Scotland Water Development Board, Balmore, Torrance, Glasgow G64 4AJ; (0360) 20511

**In Northern Ireland, contact:**
Department of the Environment for Northern Ireland, Water Service, 3 Frederick Street, Belfast BT1 2NS; (0232) 244711

**In the Republic of Ireland, contact:**
Central Fisheries Board, Balnagowan House, Mobhi Boreen, Glasnevin, Dublin 9, Eire; (0001) 379206

The Irish Tourist Board's Angling Consultant in the UK will supply information on fishing in Ireland: Paul Harris, 47 The Crescent, Nr Rugby, Warwickshire; (0788) 833203

# Index

Italic = illustration